Sounding THUNDER

Critical Studies in Native History
(continues Manitoba Studies in Native History)

JARVIS BROWNLIE, SERIES EDITOR

19 *Sounding Thunder: The Stories of Francis Pegahmagabow*, by Brian D. McInnes

18 *Two-Spirit Journey: The Autobiography of a Lesbian Ojibwa-Cree Elder*, by Ma-Nee Chacaby, with Mary Louisa Plummer

17 *Elder Brother and the Law of the People: Contemporary Kinship and Cowessess First Nation*, by Robert Alexander Innes

16 *Indigenous Women, Work, and History: 1940–1980*, by Mary Jane Logan McCallum

15 *Life Stages and Native Women: Memory, Teachings, and Story Medicine*, by Kim Anderson

GERALD FRIESEN, SERIES EDITOR

14 *"A Very Remarkable Sickness": Epidemics in the Petit Nord, 1670–1846*, by Paul Hackett

13 *Preserving the Sacred: Historical Perspectives on the Ojibwa Midewiwin*, by Michael Angel

12 *Muskekowuck Athinuwick: Original People of the Great Swampy Land*, by Victor P. Lytwyn

11 *"A National Crime": The Canadian Government and the Residential School System, 1879 to 1986*, by John S. Milloy

10 *Night Spirits: The Story of the Relocation of the Sayisi Dene*, by Ila Bussidor and Üstün Bilgen-Reinart

9 *Women of the First Nations: Power, Wisdom, and Strength*, edited by Christine Miller and Patricia Chuchryk, with Marie Smallface Marule, Brenda Manyfingers, and Cheryl Deering

8 *The Ojibwa of Western Canada, 1780 to 1870*, by Laura Peers

7 *Severing the Ties that Bind: Government Repression of Indigenous Religious Ceremonies on the Prairies*, by Katherine Pettipas

6 *Aboriginal Resource Use in Canada: Historical and Legal Aspects*, edited by Kerry Abel and Jean Friesen

5 *The Dakota of the Canadian Northwest: Lessons for Survival*, by Peter Douglas Elias

4 *The Plains Cree: Trade, Diplomacy and War, 1790 to 1870*, by John S. Milloy

3 *"The Orders of the Dreamed": George Nelson on Cree and Northern Ojibwa Religion and Myth, 1823*, by Jennifer S.H. Brown and Robert Brightman

2 *Indian-European Trade Relations in the Lower Saskatchewan River Region to 1840*, by Paul Thistle

1 *The New Peoples: Being and Becoming Metis in North America*, edited by Jacqueline Peterson and Jennifer S.H. Brown

Sounding THUNDER

The Stories of Francis Pegahmagabow

Brian D. McInnes

Foreword by Waubgeshig Rice

UMP

University of Manitoba Press

22 21 20 19 18 3 4 5 6 7

University of Manitoba Press
Winnipeg, Manitoba, Canada
Treaty 1 Territory
uofmpress.ca

Cataloguing data available from Library and Archives Canada
Critical Studies in Native History, ISSN 1925-5888 ; 19
ISBN 978-0-88755-824-5 (PAPER)
ISBN 978-0-88755-524-4 (PDF)
ISBN 978-0-88755-522-0 (EPUB)

Cover design by Kirk Warren
Interior design by Karen Armstrong
Cover image: Francis Pegahmagabow, Ottawa, 1945. Canadian Museum of History, 95292. Digital restoration by Dana Keller.

Printed in Canada

This book has been published with the help of a grant from the Federation for the Humanities and Social Sciences, through the Awards to Scholarly Publications Program, using funds provided by the Social Sciences and Humanities Research Council of Canada.

The University of Manitoba Press acknowledges the financial support for its publication program provided by the Government of Canada through the Canada Book Fund, the Canada Council for the Arts, the Manitoba Department of Sport, Culture, and Heritage, the Manitoba Arts Council, and the Manitoba Book Publishing Tax Credit.

Funded by the Government of Canada | Canada

CONTENTS

LIST OF ILLUSTRATIONS

LIST OF TABLES

FOREWORD

by Waubgeshig Rice

For all of my life, Francis Pegahmagabow has personified legend. His picture, placed high on the wall in our only classroom at Ryerson Indian Day School, gazed back at us Nishnaabe children with a proud, hardened fortitude. The renowned black-and-white image of the war hero shows him sitting in his military uniform, his almond-shaped eyes peering into the lens from under a tight cap, while the medals on his chest glisten even in the rudimentary photography of the early twentieth century. This was the only visual reference we had for the legends that would echo through our school and homes about the war hero, community leader, activist, respected elder, and above all proud Nishnaabe.

Pegahmagabow was, and continues to be, the most prominent figure from our community of Wasauksing First Nation. Growing up in the 1980s, decades after he died, my cousins, friends, peers, and I heard story after story about his triumphs and troubles fighting for Canada in the First World War. How he used the traditional medicines for strength and guidance through ferocious battle. How he spent days on end in the foreign terrain, patiently waiting to snipe the enemy. How he returned home to find a community and world around him moving away from his beloved Nishnaabe way of life, while the country he served was outright destroying the traditions he held so dear.

Pegahmagabow is the most decorated Indigenous soldier for bravery in Canadian history. This fact was echoed to our generation, and to the ones that followed, to instill pride in us as we grew into adults. He became a scarce role model at a time when there were so few of our own people reflected as such in history books and mainstream Canadian society. Many of us looked fondly at his photo with an unwavering sense of honour and accomplishment, and, whenever an outsider would question or recognize our community as the home of the great war hero, we would keenly affirm it.

But that picture, those tales of survival, and his extraordinary success were all we had as children. I remember rarely learning anything new about Pegahmagabow in school and the wider community. For a long time, his image never changed in my mind. The stories stayed the same. They always intrigued me, but they remained in a cerebral time capsule, static reference points to a bygone era and the type of man I was led to believe I would never see again in my lifetime. The impressions were that soldiers like him fought so we would never see wars like that again and that our old Nishnaabe ways would stay in the past too.

Eventually, that changed. There was a cultural renaissance of sorts in Wasauksing. Dedicated people started to bring back ceremonies like the sweat lodge and celebrations like the powwow. I might have been too young to understand why or pinpoint how all that happened, but looking back I believe it was because of a reconnection with the land and water around us and a desire to understand and foster that bond. That is what being Nishnaabe is about, and many people embraced that spirit and the traditional teachings at the foundation of that beautiful and powerful way of life. Ryerson Indian Day School was renamed Wasauksing Kinomaugewgamik.

With that revival came stories many of us had never heard. They explained our ceremonies and how life as we know it came to be. Some stories taught us about the songs we sang and the Ojibwe language we learned, and others showed us how our people came to our place on Georgian Bay. With that revitalized passion for culture, there were stories about Pegahmagabow that had not been spoken to me before.

I remember hearing about how he struggled to keep the language alive. I also heard about how he led a delegation to Ottawa to advocate for Indigenous rights. Someone even told me once about how Pegahmagabow was one of the last people from our community to cut his long hair in the face of colonial assimilation. Other stories were not as surprising, such as how he was an expert hunter and trapper. These additional tales helped to clear some of the mystique around him while simultaneously painting a picture of a profoundly complex man fighting for a way of life that was fading away.

Although these formerly unknown stories and details made Pegahmagabow less of an enigma, they created more of a legend that had yet to be substantiated by anyone outside our community or the wider Nishnaabeg nation, as far as I could see. To me, he was the war hero who continued to fight a greater battle for his culture decades after he left the battlefields of Europe, dedicated to a way of life the Canadian authorities were attempting to strip from him and his loved ones. I perceived that as the greater mission of his life, and it became clearer to me why our culture was able to grow strong once again thanks to his efforts.

A fuller, richer icon emerged, thanks to a stronger return to fundamental oral traditions. It was as if that old black-and-white picture on the wall at our school had been restored in colour. But there was still something missing: Pegahmagabow's own voice in the narrative of his remarkable life. There was nothing we could hear or watch; in his time, such recordings were not as prevalent or accessible as they are now, especially on the reserve. More remarkably, though, there was nothing we could read. His own words eluded us. His vast knowledge and experiences were not widely documented on the page, immortalized for his own community and the rest of the land to read and learn from for generations.

But now one of his descendants has changed that. His great-grandson Dr. Brian McInnes, Waabishkimakwa, has created a quintessential account of Pegahmagabow's life, spanning his childhood in Shawanaga to his elderly years back in the Wasauksing community following his military career. In the spirit of Nishnaabe storytelling, Waabishkimakwa recounts the tales he heard from his great-uncle Duncan and great-aunt Marie, Francis's children. That perspective is heartfelt, compelling, and crucial. As such, we get the hero's life story in as close to his own words as possible. In our tradition, his voice has strongly echoed through his lineage, and we readers are extremely fortunate to have that immortalized for us in the written word.

In the vein of that vital oral custom, Waabishkimakwa has magnificently made Nishnaabemowin, our Ojibwe language, a cornerstone of this great literary effort. To the reader's benefit, and to honour the stories of his great-grandfather and his family, along with the traditional teachings themselves, he has included the voice and language of our people throughout this book. As an expert speaker himself, he has not only honoured his family, our community, and our nation but also made a powerful contribution to the survival of Nishnaabemowin by making it a fundamental storytelling element of this project.

This book will be a vital resource for generations to come. It will bolster pride in Nishnaabeg, young and old alike. It is a crucial document of the history of Wasauksing and the wider Nishnaabeg nation. It is a powerful reflection of the resilient spirit of our people and the frustrating struggle many of our leaders had to overcome. Pegahmagabow's experiences reflected here will teach non-Indigenous Canadians about the unfair challenges Indigenous soldiers faced upon return from war and about the beautiful way of life that has endured as a country evolved around it.

I am proud of Francis Pegahmagabow. I am proud to be Nishnaabe, from the same community. I understand now why his efforts to keep our culture strong have inspired me to become a storyteller today. And I am very grateful that this book now exists. Chi-miigwech, Waabishkimakwa.

A NOTE ON THE TEXT

Orthography

This version of the double-vowel Roman orthography was standardized by Richard Rhodes in 1993 for Eastern Ojibwe dialects. The double-vowel system is now widely used by language teachers, students, and linguists in both Canada and the United States. This particular orthography is inclusive of the vowel-syncopating nature of Wasauksing Ojibwe. A number of features of this orthography, including relevant vowel and consonant sounds, are found below.

Short, Long, and Nasalized Vowel Sounds

Short Vowels	English Example	Ojibwe Example	Gloss
a	c**u**p	d**a**sh	and, but
i	p**i**t	k**i**do	s/he says
o	**o**f	nagam**o**	s/he sings

Long Vowels	English Example	Ojibwe Example	Gloss
aa	s**aw**	m**aa**ng	loon
ii	s**ee**	nak**ii**	s/he works
oo	s**oa**p	b**oo**zh**oo**	hello
e	m**ay**	nishnaab**e**	Native person

Long Vowels	Nasalized Vowels	Ojibwe Example	Gloss
aa	**aanh** **aans**	memengw**aanh** memengw**aans**	butterfly small butterfly
ii	**iinh** **iins**	binooj**iinh** binooj**iins**	child baby
oo	**oonh** **oons**	bood**oonh** bood**oons**	tadpole small tadpole
e	**enh** **ens**	mshiik**enh** mshiik**ens**	turtle small turtle

Consonant Sounds

Consonants	English Example	Ojibwe Example	Gloss
b	**b**ut	**b**ine	partridge
ch	**ch**in	miigwe**ch**	thank you
d	**d**og	en**d**aa**d**	his/her home
g	**g**oat	**g**oodaas	dress
h	**h**ow	**h**aaw	okay
j	**j**oke	**j**ina	a little while
k	stic**k**	baa**k**aa**k**wenh	chicken
m	**m**e	**m**iinwaa	and, again
n	**n**ot	**n**aa**n**a**n**	five
p	**p**ot	**p**waagan	pipe
s	**s**ee	wiiyaa**s**	meat
sh	**sh**e	bngi**sh**in	s/he falls
t	**t**alk	giizhii**t**aa	s/he finishes
w	**w**alk	**w**aasa	far
y	**y**ak	bineshiin**y**ag	birds
z	**z**oo	biin**z**i	s/he is clean
zh	plea**s**ure	**zh**iiwtaagan	salt

Glottal Stops

A glottal stop, written here as **h**, is equivalent to the sound of the break in the English expression **uh-uh**. This "catch in the throat" sound is found in the following Ojibwe words.

nsaw**h**igan	teepee, lodge
mzin**h**igan	paper, book
aabji**h**aad	s/he uses or employs someone
gshki**h**ewzid	s/he has power, ability

Presentation

Francis Pegahmagabow's stories are presented using a parallel line-by-line format. Ojibwe-language text is presented in italic font with an English translation running directly beneath in regular font. All of the stories featured in this book emerge from the oral storytelling tradition of the Ojibwe people and were told in the Native language. All instances in which only an English sentence appears mean that this portion of the text was delivered in English.

Other Grammatical Notes

The punctuation used in the Ojibwe texts is generally consistent with the English-language conventions. This primarily refers to quotation marks, parentheses, periods, question marks, colons, semicolons, and explanation marks. Commas are used to mark phonological and grammatical pauses, and dashes are used to extend a sentence when necessary.

Sounding THUNDER

INTRODUCTION

Gnimaa-sh go naa ji-ni-aanke-aajmoyin.
Perhaps now you can pass on these stories.

—Duncan Pegahmagabow

This book began on the shores of Georgian Bay almost 100 years to the day my great-grandfather Francis "Peggy" Pegahmagabow enlisted for the Great War. It would involve the coming together of many things, including the discovery of tapes I had originally made in the mid-1990s of my great-uncle Duncan Pegahmagabow and great-aunt Marie (Pegahmagabow) Anderson telling me about the traditional history of our family and community. Somehow these tapes survived over a decade of being lost in a shed that endured the temperature extremes of the Georgian Bay climate. Their quality was remarkable and enduring—very much like the messages and stories they contained.

A common thread in many of Duncan and Marie's stories was the life of their much-loved father, Francis Pegahmagabow. I had always found pride in being a direct descendant of this distinguished military and political hero, and to have the opportunity to learn more about his life was a privilege. Over the many years I visited with these wonderful storytellers, I listened avidly—enraptured in age-old stories and philosophies of my people. Their beautiful Ojibwe language filled the air countless nights as it likewise fed my spirit with the wisdom and lessons learned by generations of our ancestors.

Whenever I asked a question about their father, Duncan and Marie enthusiastically responded. Chief Francis Pegahmagabow had many roles, after all. He is generally known as the most decorated Canadian Aboriginal soldier for bravery, and the most accomplished North American military sniper of all time. His accomplishments as a political activist and Indigenous rights champion, although lesser known, proved equally impressive and important as his efforts on the battlefields of World War I. Francis was a proud member of the Ojibwe nation, a Great Lakes tribe with broad historic influence in both Canada and the United States. He remained a tireless advocate for a better path forward in the relationship between Indigenous and non-Native peoples.

Born on the Shawanaga Indian reserve, Francis was orphaned at a young age. He overcame a childhood beset with loss and illness to become one of the most accomplished military and political leaders of his time. After answering the call to service with the advent of the First World War, Francis distinguished himself through his legendary exploits as a scout and sniper. His charismatic and strategic disposition won the respect of his fellow officers in an age when equal treatment was rarely afforded to Native people. Following his military service, Francis established a homestead in the Wasauksing community where he was elected chief and raised his family. He later made invaluable foundational contributions to national Indian political efforts, notably serving as Supreme Chief of the National Indian Government.

He was also an exceptionally kind father who loved history, languages, religions, and stories. The poor treatment of Aboriginal veterans and communities would profoundly frustrate Francis, but he remained a stalwart individual who cared about his family and community. On the vast majority of occasions that I visited with his children, I lacked a tape recorder, but somehow their stories became imprinted deeply within me.

Francis Pegahmagabow was my *aanikobijigan* and I his. It is an old Ojibwe word shared between great-grandparents and their great-grandchildren: in the beliefs of the Nishnaabe people, we are tied together on an unbroken string of lives that goes back to the beginning. It must have been the same connection Francis felt with his great-grandfather Chief James Pegahmagabow Sr. (Beskinekwam), whose legacy he upheld and strengthened. So now, over a century since the beginning of the Great War itself, I too feel a need to contribute to the legacy of my *aanikobijigan* so that he is remembered with dignity and respect, and the critical work he dedicated his life to continues. Duncan and Marie always wanted me to help correct some of the misconceptions about their father that had emerged in written discourse. I felt compelled to do something with the stories they wanted me to share.

In my earliest imaginings of what this book would become, I envisioned calling it *The Story of Francis Pegahmagabow.* I quickly realized this was a far more comprehensive endeavour than what was possible in the present. For this reason, I have chosen to share some of the *stories* of Pegahmagabow, indexing several key events, places, and people in his life. There was a need above all else to tell these stories honestly and authentically—gently correcting any historical inaccuracies or cultural misinterpretations in the record. I had to decide on which stories to tell as well, making sure they were told for the right reasons and would not be injurious to anyone. Many stories of this era were tragic and intimate. They were part of Francis's larger story but are not included in this collection. Private details are better left in the past or within the blood memories of his descendants.

The concept of blood memory remains important to Ojibwe people. It is what connects us to our inherent spiritual legacy when the circumstances of our lives deny us such continuity. It is what inspires us when we hear the drum, smell our plant medicines, or listen to the gentle cadence of our language. Even if these are things we don't understand well, something about the attraction remains overwhelmingly real and poignant. In such moments, we inescapably feel the knowledge and hope of our ancestors running through our veins. Blood memory is the inspiration and instinct unique to a people: the genetic memory, if you will. Stories too, it seems, are part of this unique remembrance. It is what guided me to discover truths about my great-grandfather obscured by historical violence or omission and somehow made so many of his stories seem familiar even when I had never heard them before.

Within these pages, the terms "Aboriginal," "First Nations," "Indigenous," "Native," and even "Indian" are all used somewhat interchangeably. Although the last term might be somewhat politically incorrect in the present, many Indigenous communities continue to identify with it—at least among each other. It is also a term that the people knew themselves by in the English language. All Indigenous nations have their own names for themselves. The terms "Ojibwe" and "Nishnaabe" are perhaps most fittingly used in this book, since this was how Francis best knew his own people ("Nishnaabeg" in the plural).

His stories, told with brilliant recollection by his children Duncan and Marie, are featured first in the Native language. The rhythmic Eastern Ojibwe dialect, much like the distinct and unforgettable sound of water lapping on the rocks of Georgian Bay, was the language with which Francis first knew the world. Many of the English-language translations provided here were made with either Duncan or Marie many years ago. No claim is made here that the English-language renditions do justice to the descriptive or emotive power of the original Ojibwe-language narratives.

The near disappearance of Ojibwe from community life today is something that Francis could not have imagined: no one can anticipate that his or her ancestral legacy of thought and language would be lost among descendants two or three generations later—at least not in one's own homeland. It is also why I have chosen to ground the stories of his life in the place names, cultural perspective, and language most familiar to him. A hope is that language and stories nearly lost in the present will have some renewal in the future. Relearning one's land, history, and ancestral language is an important task for all peoples, Indigenous North American or otherwise. It is what connects us to our respective pasts such that we might honour the people and places from which we come. Such relearning is what connects us to the stories in our blood.

The stories featured in this book describe many facets of Francis Pegahmagabow's life. It is a unique collection with many elements of classic Ojibwe narrative. Traditional legends that describe the formation of the land, such as "Thirty Thousand Islands" and "*Gchi-Ngig*—The Giant Otter," illuminate the unique intersection of human and spiritual worlds common in that era of North American history. Other stories, such as "*Nimkiik*—The Thunders" and "*Gchi-Mishoomisaatig*—Grandfather Tree," provide rich insight into the sense of reverence and respect the Wasauksing people maintain for the natural world. The perennial struggle for survival has remained a source of humility, resilience, and strength for the Ojibwe. The stories "*Enawendiying*—We Are All Related" and "*Enendaagwak Bmaadziwin*—What Is Expected of Life" help us to better understand the intricacies, interrelationships, and responsibilities that characterize Nishnaabe society and existence.

Sergeant Pegahmagabow's distinction as a soldier necessitated the inclusion of at least one story featured here. "*Tkwaans*—The Dead Branch" is an intriguing narrative that credits Francis's strong Ojibwe beliefs with ensuring his survival—and perhaps the survival of the many Native soldiers who sought his counsel before travelling overseas. Francis was proud to be a First Nations man and believed that the Native language and culture would keep the people true to themselves no matter what changes occurred. The story "*Nishnaabemwin*—Language of the People and the Land" poignantly articulates such credence. Although he will undoubtedly be most remembered for his military and political accomplishments, many of the stories found throughout this book attest to his special love for and belief in family and community. Both Duncan's initial and his final narrative contributions to this work, "*Ngii-zaagidimin*—We So Loved Each Other" and "*Ndedem*

Gaa-Giiwed—When My Father Went Home," provide insight into Francis's everyday experience of and belief in family, community, culture, and leadership. Each story—in and of itself—could stand alone from the book. There is a greater story, however, that emerges from their unique arrangement, and the interceding chapters offer further and perhaps necessary explanation and contextualization of the life and world of Francis Pegahmagabow.

The first four chapters of the book describe his life experience as an Ojibwe man of Georgian Bay. This foundational understanding of the importance of Nishnaabe history, landscape, place names, stories, and traditional culture frames the latter half of the book, in which the more intimate and direct stories of his life appear. They include family, community, war, and leadership. Chapter 5 is a valuable transition piece in that it directly brings together the stories and the scholarly narrative of the chapters into one. Importantly, the first half of the book also teaches us to comprehend and respect more fully the world and life of Francis Pegahmagabow through stories. Although for some there might be an inclination to bypass these chapters, there is much to be gained by reading them; an appreciation of the socio-cultural world within which he lived is helpful in understanding the unique choices and circumstances that shaped his experience in ways we might otherwise struggle with in the present. By the last few chapters, the stories, historical information, and family anecdotes seamlessly merge into a cohesive narrative.

There is a strange connection between the stories of this text and the enduring sadness in so many Aboriginal communities. The mournful and melodic sounds of the old Indian-language hymns sung during community funerals when I was a boy echoed throughout my thoughts at the most unexpected times. At other moments, I could almost smell both sweetgrass and birch bark—staple stores in Wasauksing homes for many generations—while deeply engaged in writing. Reminders of past and continuing injustices across Indian country in other instances incited anger such that I had to leave this manuscript for a time. But as I look at this now—writing this introduction as my final contribution to the book—I feel a much stronger sense of hope. So much seemed to lie on the sadness-hope continuum during Francis's life and perhaps still today in Native communities. I am optimistic that this book will provide an enlightening and honest read that will pique interest both in the facets of life that Francis himself most loved and in his long-overdue recognition as a national hero. No matter how sad the story might seem at moments, may his indefatigable belief in the goodness of the world inspire us all to do a little better.

Ngii-zaagidimin—We So Loved Each Other

Duncan Pegahmagabow is the primary narrator of this collection of stories. As the youngest son of Francis Pegahmagabow, Duncan often had the pleasure of his father's undivided attention. He shared Francis's interest in stories, history, and both traditional and contemporary ways of life. Duncan was an exceptionally gifted storyteller—renowned throughout many parts of Ojibwe country for his ability to tell a wide variety of stories, including legends, humorous anecdotes, philosophical accounts, and historical reports. His remarkable memory allowed him to readily recall details of conversations that had taken place many years prior. He was the ideal person to recount the stories and philosophical world view of his father.

This short narrative provides some insight into the relationship between Duncan and Francis. Many qualities of Nishnaabe parenting are revealed, as is the mutual respect engendered between father and son. Their dedication to each other is undeniable and built on a foundation of kindness and love. It is a delightful story that reveals much about the kind of man Francis Pegahmagabow was at his core and why his family and community continue to remember him so fondly.

Mii-sh go naa genii ezhi-mnjimendmaan.
This is what I myself remember about this.

Mii go naa gii-bi-gwiiwizhenzhishwiyaan mii go pane baa-noopnanag niin mii go naa gaa-zhichgeyaan.
When I was just a silly little boy, I would always follow around my father—this is what I would do.

Mii go pane gaa-bi-zhi-noopnanag ndedem pii dibi go ezhaagwen mii go maa gii-baa-noopnanag dbishkoo go naa yahaa nimoons!
I would always follow my father around wherever he went just like a little puppy would!

Dibi go ezhaagwen mii go maa shkweyaang gii-bimi-yaayaan ngii-baa-noopnanaa.
Wherever he went, I was right there behind him, following him along.

Mii-sh kwa gaa-zhiwebak.

This is how it happened back then.

Aazhgo bmi-daapnang iihow ayhii waagaakwad miinwaa iw ayhii giishkboojgan miinwaa niw doo-daabaanan—mii iw wedi gaa-mnenmag geget daabaan mii maa baa-bgwaashkwaniyaan maa indaa-bmi-daabaanig dash.

He would get an axe, a saw, and his sled—I so loved the sled that I would be jumping around as I rode along.

Mii gaa-nji-wiijiiwag awi-mnised wii-bmi-daabaangoyaan ngaashiiniy maa go naa kaa ndaa-gii-gshkitoosiin anooj ji-yaamaan iw ayhii waagaakwad.

I would go with him as he went to cut wood, but I just rode on the sled, for I was too small to handle anything like an axe.

Gnimaa go naa ge gegoo ndaa-gii-naapanandiz ngaashiiniy maa naa gaawiin ngii-nenmigsii ji-baamendmaan iihow waagaakwad zaam maa naa ndagaashiiniy.

I would likely just have hurt myself on something as I was so little—but I was never really expected to help with an axe or anything because I was too small.

Mii-sh maa baa-dzhiikeyaan maa gnawaabmag aw epiichi-mnised; gii-shkwaa-mnised mii aazhgo booztaasod maa doo-daabaaning.

And so I would just play around there, watching him as he gathered wood; when he was finished cutting, he would then load that wood onto his sled.

Mii-sh odi gwajiing miinwaa aazhgo nimaajiidaabaanig wodi gjiyiing nmadbiyaan iihow ayhii msan maa kosing maa daabaaning.

He would pull me along there outside, and I would sit in the sled on top of the woodpile in that sled.

Dbishkoo-sh go naa yahaa mdaabiichke nbezhgoogzhiim ndaa-bmi-dzhiike!

He would pull like he was my horse, and I would just play along!

1. Old Parry Island wagon road. Photo by Brian McInnes.

Mii-sh iw gii-o-daabaadang niw ayhii msan.
He would then haul that firewood home.

Ngoji go odi gaa-zhaad gii-mnised wodi gii-baatiinwaad gow dino wenzhishid yahaag mtigoog.
There were always so many beautiful different kinds of trees where he would go to cut wood.

Mii odi gaa-zhaad miikan gii-yaamgad gii-izhitoon shko naa.
He would go over to where he had made a road back there.

Mii-sh go gaa-nji-mnsed mii-sh go pane gaa-zhaayaang odi pane ngii-wiijiiwaa dbi go gaa-zhaagwen.
This is how he would go about cutting wood, and I would always go with him wherever he went.

Miinwaa ge baa-giigoonked mii go genii odi genii shkweyaang dbiiyidag ko gaa-zhaagwen mii shkweyaang gii-bmi-noopnanag.
And if he went around fishing, well, I would make sure I was there behind him, for wherever he went I was there following along.

Gii-zhaad ingii-zhaa ge ko odi ayhiing maa halling giigidowaad mii go maa gii-bi-wiijiiwag maa dbiyish go gaa-zhaagwen ngii-noopnanaa.
Even when he went over to the community hall for a meeting, I went as well, for I followed him wherever he travelled to.

Mii-sh go naa pii go naa nmanj go naa gaa-ni-mndidiyaan mii aazhgo gii-gshkitooyaan iihow wii-naadmawag enokiid mnised aazhgo go gii-mndidiyaan go naa gii-naadmawag gii-giishkwahaad niw mtigoon.
There came a time, though, when I was big enough to actually help him with work like cutting wood; now that I was bigger, I was actually able to help him cut down those trees.

Naangodnong ge go ngii-o-giishkboojige miinwaa ge gwa aazhgo ge go ngii-booztoon iihow msan maajiidaabiid

2. Duncan Pegahmagabow as a boy. Courtesy of Parry Sound *North Star.*

ngii-bmi-gaanjwebnaa ow daabaan gaawiin geyaabi maa ngii-bmi-boozsii maa ngii-bmi-gaanjwebnaa naadmawag. Sometimes I would go and saw the trees, load the wood, or even push the sled—I no longer rode on top but would instead help him by pushing it along from behind.

Wiiba-sh ko maabam mii go nii naa gaa-zhi-kenmaan wiiba go naa gii-baa-wiijiiwag pane maabam ndedem baandawenjged gegoo ngii-wiijiiwaa baa-wniiged ge gwa ngii-gnawaabmaa.

Soon I came to know all of this work, in no time at all, for I was always travelling around with my father whenever he went hunting, or I would be there watching him on his trapline.

Gaawiin ngii-kinoomaagsii mii eta gwa gii-naanaagdawaabmag iihow ezhchiged.

He never directly taught me what to do, but I instead just carefully observed whatever it was he was doing.

Mii-sh go genii pii go nmanj go naa gaa-ni-mndidiyaan go naa mii go genii gaa-zhichgeyaan.

For there came to be a time—I don't know exactly how big I was—when I was able to do all of these things myself.

Gaa-sh geyaabi ngii-bmi-wiijiiwigosii.

He no longer went with me.

Niin dash go ngii-ni-zhichge.

I had to do this myself.

Niin ngii-o-mnise gaa gegoo ngii-nendziin iihow mniseyaan.

I would go and harvest the wood, but I didn't have to think too much about how I would manage to do this.

Mii maa naa ndedem gaa-zhi-kinoomawid ji-zhichged iihow wii-gzhideg iihow wiigwaam dbikak.

I had learned from my father about what he did to keep the house warm at night.

Aabdeg go njekaakwam naadiiyaan niw msan.

I would even go into the forest to get firewood.

Mii-sh go gaa-zhichgeyaan mii-sh go naa eshkiniigiyaan.
This is what I had to do now that I was a young man.

Wiin dayaanan niw meshkwiskaakin niw msan.
He always had good hardwood there.

Niin dash ngii-yaanan niw ayhii tkwaansan mii niin gaa-nakiiyaan iw ngii-tkwaanske.
I would get plenty of small dry branches, too, for it had always been my job to prepare the kindling.

Mii-sh iw aabdeg go teg maa tkwaansan niw wewiib wiiba ji-maajiikneg iw shkode.
Those branches had to be ready to get the fire started right away.

Kina-sh go maanda gaa-zhichged gaawiin ngii-kinoomaagsii, ngii-naadmawaa shko naa mii-sh go eta go gaa-ni-zhi-kendmaan ezhchiged.
He never directly taught me about any of the things he did, but I would always help him, and that is how I learned to do what he did.

Gegpii dash go niin gii-ni-nakiiyaan iihow gaa-ni-gchi-yahaawiyaan go naa.
When I was finally old enough, I was already able to work.

Gaawiin go gegoo ngii-nendziin enakiiyaan mii maa naa nake gaa-bi-naadziiyaang iihow.
I didn't really think of this as work, though, but I guess that was just the way we were back then.

Gaa go gegoo ngii-nendziin jekaakomaan o-mniseyaan naadmawag.
I didn't think anything of going into the forest to help him get wood.

Ngii-gchi-nendam gii-naadmawag.
He was so happy whenever I helped him.

Ngii-mina-doodaag kaa go gegoo ngii-nshkaaji-gnoongosii.
He always treated me well and never said anything to make me angry.

Weweni go ngii-gnoonig gegoo ndawendang ngii-zhichgesh gwehow gaa-zhi-gwejmid.
He always spoke to me kindly, even when there was something he wanted me to do, he would ask me in a good way.

Kaa go gegoo ge-nji-nshkaadenmagoban baatiinad maa naa ekinoomawid mii maa go naa gegoo gegoo menpogwak mii debnang ndashamig gwehow.
He never did anything to make me angry—there was so much he taught me in this alone—and he would always make sure he had something good for me to eat out there.

Kina shko go naa maa ngii-zhi-mino-doodaag.
He always treated me so well in every way.

Kaa go wiikaa gegoo ngii-mji-doodaagsii.
He never treated me badly.

Zhimaagnish ge gii-aawi zhimaagnishii-gimaa gii-aawi ow.
He had been a soldier, a sergeant even.

Miinwaa weweni enenmagiban iw ji-bmaadzid ji-naanoondaagzid giigdad.
I always thought well of the way he lived his life, even when he was speaking aloud during military drills.

Mii-sh go naa enaabminaagziwaad giw nishnaabeg yahaag zhimaagnishiiwi-gimaag.
There were some Indians who would try to act like the non-Native sergeants.

Gaa gii-zhihaasii gtaamgwaadkamig gaa-izhi-mino-yaad.
But he would never treat or speak to others badly, he was always a good person.

Weweni ngii-zaagaa ow ndedem.
I truly loved my father.

Ngii-kenmaa shko genii ngii-zaagig go genii.
And I know that he really did love me as well.

Daadaapshkoo ngii-zaagidimin.
We really did love each other.

Stories as a Means of Understanding Life

Ga-dibaajmotaagoo gaa-nji-bmaadzid ow ndedeminaan.
We will tell you the story of how our father lived.

Aapji go gii-minwaadzi kina gegoo ezhichged.
He was a good person in everything he did.

Nshke ow gaa-naadzid mii go gegii waa-ni-naadziyin.
You see, the way he was in life is the way that you yourself should aspire to be.

—Duncan Pegahmagabow and Marie Anderson

Stories and the Ojibwe People

Stories have always had deep and enduring meaning for the original peoples of North America. They are an invaluable source of wisdom, inspiration, humour, and help. Stories help us to understand everything from birth to death and, perhaps as importantly for Indigenous cultures, everything that comes before life and after it. We seek stories like a plant seeks sunlight. They are vital to our growth and well-being in the world.

Stories continue to have special significance to my Ojibwe Nishnaabe people of the Great Lakes region. A map to both the structure of the universe and our lives, stories provide direction and hope during even the most challenging times. The many narratives in Ojibwe country are unique in their respective focus and recitation style. From legends to sacred teachings, humorous tales to war remembrances, general news accounts to historical epics, each genre of story has a distinct modality and protocol of delivery.

The stories of Francis Pegahmagabow featured here invoke elements from each of these broader genres. His life is the stuff of legend and ballad, victory and defeat, love and loss, and oppression and liberation. One cannot know his experience without an appreciation of the places he came from, the complex spiritual reality of the Ojibwe, the extremities of the Great War itself, and the dynamic oscillation of subjugation and liberation that has characterized settler-Indian relations since the beginning of contact. For the old Ojibwe, boundaries between physical and spiritual worlds were more fluid—no matter what one's religious orientation. To understand such a world requires being open to what the stories tell us. This might involve considering, if only for a short time, that the truth of another people is equal to that of one's own. This was a philosophical prerequisite in pre-contact Indigenous North America, where understandings of the world so often exceeded empirical limitations and varied from tribe to tribe. It is this willingness to accept reality different from one's own understanding that makes the stories of Francis Pegahmagabow comprehensible on their own terms.

There is much to learn from these stories if we remain open to their possibilities. Our homes and institutions of learning are replete with the tales of many cultures from other places. But perennially absent are the authentic stories of Native North America itself. I therefore hope that the narratives of Francis Pegahmagabow will have special meaning to all who now make their homes in Indian territories. Perhaps his are the kinds of stories that everyone should have to know as a means of understanding the original and continued history of Indigenous peoples.

Of Heroes and Men

Just as veneration of elders and ancestors is a deeply ingrained tradition of many North American Native nations, so too is the honouring of warriors and veterans a continuous part of North American Indian ceremony and community life. A single yearly moment of remembrance could never be enough to commemorate the freedoms and continued protection their sacrifices brought. It is within this tradition of respect that the life and memory of Francis Pegahmagabow finds expression and continuity. Over 100 years since he first set foot on foreign soil during the Great War, hundreds of military missions have filled North American history pages and movie screens. What makes his story worth our collective interest and attention?

Francis Pegahmagabow was a member of one of the original waves of recruits to voluntarily enlist in the Great War. Unlike in previous wars, in which Aboriginal peoples were recruited to fight in one European nation's conquest over another, enlistment meant being part of a unified effort to protect a shared North America. The Great War would bring everyone together.

Brave men and women from many backgrounds united across their historical differences in support of a greater human good. And though they were not full citizens under the law, young Aboriginal people enlisted in numbers disproportionate to their population. Whether it was to honour ancient warrior traditions or treaties signed with the Crown, or the opportunity to find transient equality on the battlefield, participation in the war seemed to herald something different in Indian-settler relations.

A good war story, it seems, often ends in victory. Evil is vanquished, the names of the fallen are venerated, and those who return bask in the glory and adulation of the community the rest of their days. Wounds heal, losses are forgotten, and memories of blood and death fade like the rays of the setting sun into oblivion—no longer visible in the new light of the next day. At least this is how we want to believe it turns out. But this is not the story told here. Notwithstanding the many varied chapters of his life, it does seem that the tale of Francis Pegahmagabow was a true war story from beginning to end: improbable, drudgerous, violent, redemptive, blessed, and forgotten.

There have been many written accounts of his life and achievements. From the cultural and social narratives collected by Diamond Jenness, the detailed historical accounts of Adrian Hayes, the inspirational storyline created by Joseph Boyden, to the innumerable short tributes of many others, the varied sides of Francis Pegahmagabow reveal a historical figure as fascinating as any other: brave recruit, powerful Indian medicine man, deadly sniper, dejected veteran, celebrated hero, dedicated lay clergyman, talented musician, fierce politician, and peaceful family man. Few of these identities coalesce in a logical way. But perhaps such was the nature of life with the interlude of war and the intense transformations happening throughout Native North America. This book is not meant to retell the stories others have shared; rather, it explores the hidden spaces between the lines of each. It is also intended to clarify some of the inevitable contradictions that have arisen in the many years since his passing.

All of the stories of Francis Pegahmagabow affirm him as a man of many talents, but he always saw himself as an ordinary man who often happened to find himself on the cusp of extraordinary circumstances. My hope is that the choices he made will be regarded equally with the exceptional abilities to which he was predisposed.

The Legend and the Man

I have heard the name Francis Pegahmagabow since I was a young boy. I vividly remember the day my great-uncle Duncan Pegahmagabow showed

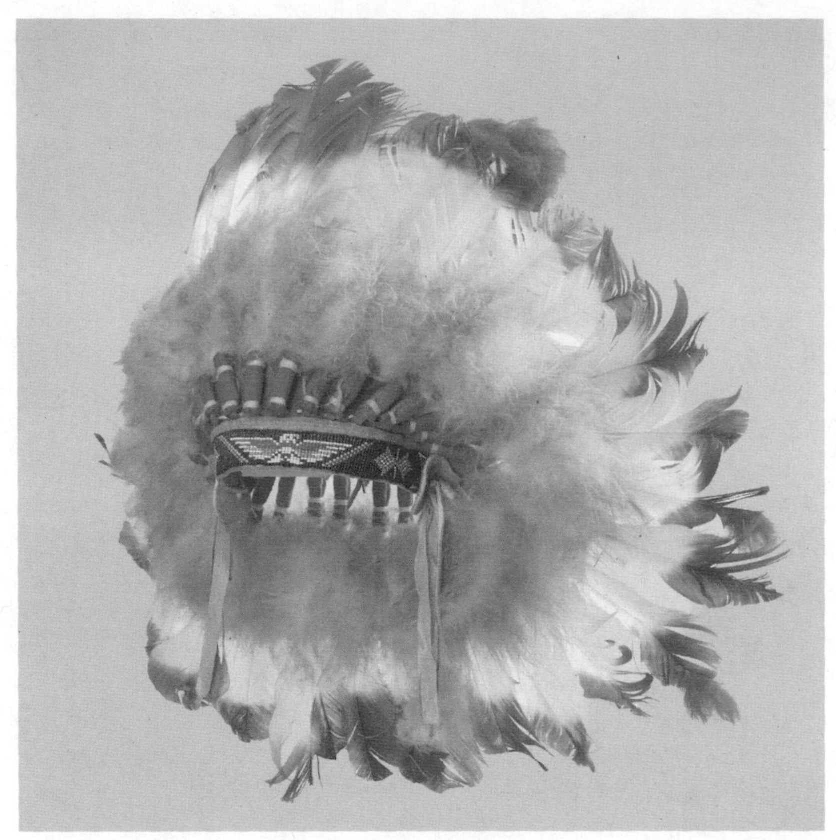

3. Chief Francis Pegahmagabow's headdress. Canadian War Museum, George Metcalf Archival Collection, CWM 20040035-002.

me his father's ceremonial chieftainship headdress and war medals. They made me very proud to be connected to this legendary man, however long ago his passing had been. A national newspaper headline tribute to Francis a few years later again spotlighted my interest. How many seven-year-olds get to take a cover story to school celebrating a family member who was a First Nations hero in the truest sense of the word? Although he seemed to be unknown to the vast majority of Canadians, this was not the case throughout Indian country. The mere utterance of his name inevitably drew recognition if not reverence in many Native communites.

As I grew older and became more interested in the history of my great-grandfather, I was fortunate to find so many family and community members willing to share stories about him. Simple inquiries turned into detailed recountings of his life and relationships. No matter how long ago events had

4. Francis Pegahmagabow photographed shortly after the war by William Boyd. Mathers Museum of World Cultures, Indiana University, 1962-08-7679. Photo by William Boyd.

taken place, the enthusiasm of elders for the old stories made them vivid and almost tangible. And no matter how difficult the circumstances, life seemed to be happy at the community level. People worked hard and treated each other well. While aspects of economy and culture were rapidly shifting, community and family life remained distinctly Nishnaabe in the sense of shared values, traditions, and dedication to a greater collective good.

What I appreciated from the experience of listening to these stories was the affirmation and explanation of what it meant to live in a well-rounded and happy community definitively Nishnaabe in character. I had expected mostly to hear stories of battle and the glory of postwar life, but there were relatively few such tales. People were mostly interested in talking about their personal experiences with Francis, and none of those still alive had spent any time with him in the trenches. So I came to understand his life and character based primarily on his experience as a community member and family man rather than as a soldier. The pictures of him on the wall—mostly posed photographs from military service or political function—were elegant yet austere. Only one seemed to betray the stoic and striking features of the Wasauksing band Indian-turned-soldier. A single half smile seemed to capture the essence of his being: brave, kind, and unfaltering to the end.

Facts about Aboriginal history and historical figures are vital parts of the greater story of North American experience. The continued exclusion of such details from mainstream life, celebration, and curriculum is unnecessary and even disrespectful. From writings in churches, pictures taken by curious tourists, to lists maintained by Indian Affairs, there is a surprising amount of information that can be uncovered. The research traditions of North American Indian scholarship have provided an equally vast collection of facts and descriptions of early Indigenous life. All of them have value. However, decontextualized from the perspectives and metanarratives of the people themselves, such historical writings are limited in what they present. I remain grateful for every detail that emerged from the written record. Most sources provided valuable leads in uncovering hidden and essential details of Francis's experience. Deep and integrated investigation of life, language, and landscape is perhaps what has been missing. This book is my attempt to make sense of many disconnected facts and bring together the different elements of Francis's life in a common narrative.

Summaries of the brave and unrelenting sniper and politician discerned from secondary sources became subsidiary to family stories of the dedicated community member, caring father, Indigenous philosopher, and man of faith. These narratives provided scaffolding for the linear timelines of facts

5. Francis Pegahmagabow photographed in Ottawa in 1945. Canadian Museum of History, 95293.

and figures I had assembled from the written record. Stories, after all, are dedicated to understanding the intricacies of life; they have the capacity not only to teach us but also to involve and include us. Stories help us to build connections to what we are living or studying and, in the most unexpected ways, sometimes make us part of the narrative. Stories must always be a core component of Aboriginal teaching and learning traditions.

Indigenous Ways of Knowing

My primary understanding of Francis Pegahmagabow's life comes from the Indigenous storytelling tradition. For nearly twenty years, I visited with various community members from Shawanaga and Wasauksing, the places where Francis spent most of his life. I am especially grateful for the many years I spent with his children Duncan Pegahmagabow and Marie Anderson, who shared their father's penchant for history and tradition. I heard many varied stories during these years. War stories and experiences were part of those conversations, but more pronounced were the stories of Francis's life in Shawanaga, Wasauksing, and the surrounding area. So much was shared about the woods and waters of Georgian Bay that to this day I am unable to separate his person from those places.

Over two decades of listening to and documenting stories, I became familiar with many details of Francis's life. The colours were faded in the old photographs; there were no smells or tastes, no matter how visually revealing. Yet the stories transcended two-dimensional experience and required my full participation. Perhaps it was the lived quality of sharing in laughter, surprise, and tears, but detached objectivity was not an option. I am grateful for the chance to have sat with such master storytellers. They not only shared so many details of Francis's life but also helped me to experience many key elements of his world. We ate the foods Francis loved, travelled to his former homesteads, prayed at the sacred places he knew, and honoured his spirit with both food and ceremonial tobacco. Duncan and Marie unconditionally demonstrated the kindness described in their stories and forever transferred to me their love of both story and language.

Stories of everyday life, *dibaajmowinan,* were the dominant kind of narrative that emerged during our visits over the years. They were often humorous, revealing, tragic, poignant, or profound and sometimes all of these things in the same story. Such narratives indexed childhood experiences, memories of war and family life, and accounts of political struggle, sickness, and even death. These stories were often complemented with direct teachings, *kinoomaagewinan,* about rituals of life or death, the earth, or the spirit realm. Special favourites, told only in the winter, were the traditional legends that seemed to be cornerstones of understanding Francis's world. These stories, known as *aadsookaanan,* brought together the spiritual and physical realms in tales of the origin of the world, epic journeys, morality, and human interrelationships with the rest of creation. Particularly memorable was that so many of these stories had been told by Francis himself, recounted to me with impeccable detail by his children.

The many hours of recorded Ojibwe-language narratives that remain from these visits are among our greatest treasures. I would not have guessed that such a beautiful language would virtually disappear throughout these years, but it did, right before our eyes and ears. It does not seem right that the beloved language of Francis Pegahmagabow now faces extinction. If there is anything we can now do in recognition of his sacrifices—and of the contributions of all Aboriginal soldiers and warriors—it is to work together to ensure that the next decade does not see the end of the Native language in Georgian Bay—or anywhere, for that matter. Without the language, the stories also seem to lose meaning and fade.

All of the community members I visited while bringing this book together were very capable speakers of English. They all thought unequivocally that these stories would lose their vital life and spirit if told in English. Francis's own children were insistent about this. Although they were determined that I heard and remembered their father's stories in Ojibwe, they were always very supportive and helpful with the English-language translations I subsequently made. I can never thank them enough for letting me share in this celebration of language in a time when English was insidiously and surreptitiously subsuming virtually every aspect of Aboriginal life and discourse. If I wanted to truly understand Francis's life, then I had to experience as much of his world as I could; this included knowing how Francis thought about and gave voice to it.

Cultural Change and Revitalization

One of the greatest legacies of Francis Pegahmagabow's life is the renewal of many of his people's ways. Francis learned the old Nishnaabe traditions and ceremonial customs of his adopted relatives. He attained all of the survival skills vital for life in Georgian Bay, including marksmanship skills with a bow and arrow, slingshot, and later rifle. He distinguished himself early with his abilities in finding medicinal plants, tracking animals, and never wasting a shot. As Francis later remarked, these skills were as much about observation as patience, and he had an aptitude for both. All of these talents would help him later in life as a soldier, father, and political leader.

It was dedication to the old ways of his people that gave Francis the strength and perseverance for which he was legendary. He lived in a time of marked change in the traditional culture of the Ojibwe. His ancestors had lived independent lives with relatively little contact with settler cultures. This was not the era in which Francis was born. Treaty misinterpretation and Indian Affairs regulation had placed a stranglehold on Nishnaabe people to freely access historical hunting or fishing grounds, practise ceremonial traditions, or enjoy the basic human freedoms we take for granted in contemporary North American life. The battle against hegemonic and paternalistic structures was the ultimate battle Francis would face and would rival any conflict he had endured in the trenches of the Great War.

The loss of traditional ceremony and social structures caused him great concern. All of the great societies of the Ojibwe were driven underground with the arrival of the missionaries and the implementation of the Indian

Act that controlled virtually every aspect of Indigenous life. The Waabanowin and Midewiwin were two such societies that had broad historical presence throughout pre-European-contact Georgian Bay, and Wasauksing itself was once renowned for the ceremonies of the latter. The virtual disappearance of the ceremonial lodges had significant consequences for the social and religious lives of the people. Many like Francis embraced the introduced Christian faith ways but never lost connections to their Nishnaabe beliefs. He maintained that traditional rites and practices had to be held in balance with any adopted practices.

Although the revival of traditional ceremonial societies seemed to be impossible in that age of restriction and outlaw, Francis remained committed to the education of his family and community about Nishnaabe lifeways. He was known by his friends and family to travel many days to participate in a ceremony or to visit with a learned elder. Perhaps it was his early life experience as a crewman aboard Great Lakes ships that instilled his interest in the vast ceremonial knowledge of his people. He shared with anthropologist Diamond Jenness that he had documented his learning from various Ojibwe communities at each of the stops he made but had lost the notebook of this record.[1] He credited the ceremonial and traditional knowledge he had attained for his success as a soldier and politician.

An unusual ability to escape from situations of certain death earned Francis great repute with fellow soldiers and historians. He was somehow able to pass unseen through enemy lines and report back with valuable tactical information. After almost four years on the front lines, and with a reported 378 kills and 300 captures, Francis seemed the beneficiary of spiritual blessing. He shared with Jenness about receiving protective medicine from an old Ojibwe man he visited with near Thunder Bay, the likely informant of the "Thirty Thousand Islands" legend told in this book.

His reputation for escaping death aside, Francis was equally known for his respect of life. This quality made him the most highly decorated Aboriginal soldier for bravery and helped distinguish him as a community leader and later chief of a national Aboriginal organization. His advocacy for the broad human rights of his people included their right to practise historic ceremonial and spiritual ways. His advances in this area aided the eventual revitalization of ceremonial practices through the efforts of his grandchildren and great-grandchildren. Francis did not live to see these successes, but this seems to be the fate of so many great individuals who set in motion actions that—to the benefit of all of us today—long outlast them.

Thirty Thousand Islands

This story was told to me by Francis Pegahmagabow's youngest daughter, Marie Anderson, in the winter of 1998. Marie and I had been talking about a land origin story I had discovered in Diamond Jenness's book. In this account, the legendary cultural hero Nanabush was hunting the giant white beaver Waabmik. Seeking its hiding place, Nanabush smashed the rocky shore, the shards of which became Georgian Bay's famous chain of Thirty Thousand Islands; Waabmik himself climbed partway out of the water before being forever turned to stone. Marie had visited Waabmik's resting place with her father and acknowledged that, though this story was likely true, she had also heard the following account from him about how the islands came to be.

6. Marie Anderson. Photo by Brian McInnes.

Francis once befriended an old Thunder Bay–area Indian, also of the Caribou clan, during the years he was travelling the Great Lakes as a crewman. This old man recognized him as kin and shared both food and stories with him. Traditional Nishnaabe people treated those of the same clan as blood relatives. This gentleman also gave Francis the medicine pouch that later protected him throughout much of the First World War:

> When I was at Rossport, on Lake Superior, in 1914, some of us landed from our vessel to gather blueberries near an Ojibwa camp. An old Indian recognized me and gave me a tiny medicine-bag to protect me, saying that I would shortly go into great danger. The bag was of skin, tightly bound with a leather thong. Sometimes it seemed to be as hard as rock, at other times it appeared to contain nothing. What really was inside it I do not know. I wore it in the trenches, but lost it when I was wounded and taken to a hospital.[2]

The old man told him the following story after Francis shared details about his home community. It was an old story from legend time when the earth was still taking shape and animals and people had the ability to communicate freely with each other. Creation of the Thirty Thousand Islands is profiled in this narrative.

7. Georgian Bay Islands in the famous Thirty Thousand Islands chain. Courtesy of thom morrissey photography.

Mii giiwenh gaa-zhiwebdogobanen mewnzha.
This is what must have happened a long time ago.

Odi nake wenji-bngishmod giizis dbiyiidog gwa naa odi ensawhigewaad giw Nishnaabeg.
Somewhere off toward the setting sun is where the people had built their homes.

Mii aazhgo maanda kendaagwak wii-ntaawgid maaba gwiiwzens.
It was known that a certain boy among them would soon reach adolescence.

Mii aazhgo shkinwens wii-aawid.
For already he wished to be a young man.

"Ahaaw," kina gii-maawnzhooshnawaad gow getzijig gii-maajiinaawaad wedi megweyiing wedi megeyaakwaa gii-ozhitoowaad wodi nsawhigan.
"All right, then," they said, and so the elders all gathered and took him out to the middle of the forest, and over there in the woods they built him a lodge.

Mii dash gii-gnoonind gii-bi-dgoshnoon gwa en'sa-giizhgak niw gchi-yaawid nini ji-bi-gnoon'gwad waa-ni-naadzid niigaan wii-ni-bmaadzid.
He was given a talk by someone who would come to see him every day—an elder would speak to him about how he was to live and what his future life might be like.

Oonh gesnaa maamiikwendam maaba gwiiwzens gesnaa gchi-kinoomaagzi sa naa waa-zhi-niihged kina go gegoo gii-waabndagaaza waa-zhi-gtiged waa-zhi-zhaabwinaad oniijaan'san pii binoojiinyan wii-yaawaawaad.
So very happy and appreciative was this boy, for he was instructed about trapping and shown everything about how to farm and provide for his own should he one day wish to have a family and children.

Mii sa iw kina gegoo maanda gii-kinoomaajgaazod waa-zhi-ndawenjged kaa memkaaj baashkzigan.
He was even taught about how to hunt without a gun.

Mii go maanda waa-zhi-nsaad niw wesiinyan giishpine aabdeg geget noondezid ji-debnang waa-miijid gii-kinoomaajgaaza.
For only if he was truly in need of something to eat should he take the life of an animal.

Oonh gesnaa maamiikwendam miinwaa gegoo aagiman waa-zhi-zhihaad gii-kinoomaajgaazod.

He was so grateful for this instruction, and snowshoes were another thing he was taught how to make.

Kina go gegoo.

Everything he needed for life.

Naasaab gwa shkiniikwe pii ntaawgid kina gewiin gegoo kinoomaajgaaza.

It was the same for a young woman at adolescence, she too was taught about everything she would need.

Mii sa iw.

And that was it.

"Mdaaso-giizhgadoon aabdeg maa ga-mkadeke maanpii nsawhigaansing," ni-jigaaza sa. "Kaa go ngoji ga-zhaasii."

"For ten days you will fast right here in this small lodge," he was told. "You are not to go anywhere."

Mii eta go nibi gaa-ndaadzid miinwaa aapji go bangii bkwezhgan gnimaa go naa ngo-emkwaanens nginadog ow bkwezhigan.

Only on water was he to live and on a little piece of bread perhaps no bigger than a teaspoonful.

Mii go eta go mnik gaa-wiisnid ngo-giizhig.

This was all he was allowed to eat on a single day.

Mii sa iw aapji esnaa geget naagadawendam mii sa aazhgo pii wi-naakshing nbaad, oonh geget sa naa gchi-yenaabndam bwaajged.

He was to really think deeply about his life while he was there, and when it was time for him to lie down and sleep he was blessed with tremendous visions in his dreams.

Mii sa iw.

And that was it.

Aazhgo miinwaa bi-gshkozid kaa go gbeyhiing mii aazhgo bimandawetoonid niw waawiijiihaagojin waa-bi-dbaajmotaagojin kina gegoo epiitendaagwak kina gegoo.

He was not asleep too long when he awoke from the sound of someone walking toward him—this was the person who was going to help him and tell him about all the important things that he would need to know.

Mii sa iw. Gesnaa gchi-nendam.

That was it. He was so happy and grateful.

"Geyaabi ngo-dbik mii ji-giizhiitaayin maanpii ngwisenh," ni-jigaaza sa.

"In one more night, you will be finished here, my son," he was told.

Oonh aapji esnaa geget maamiikwendam mii dash go geget sa naa bkade.

He was excited about this but was also very hungry.

Mii go aazhgo ni-bngishmod giizis mii go maaba ni-maajaad maa ni-zaagdosed gaa-bi-kinoomaaged getzid bskaabiid neyaab odi endaad.

As soon as the sun went down, this elder who had come to teach him left that little lodge and returned home.

Baamaa miinwaa gzhebaawagak mii dash kina ji-bi-zaagjisewaad gow Nishnaabeg ji-bi-nkweshkwind gii-giizhitood iihow mkadekewin.

For later the next morning all of the people would leave their lodges to greet this boy when he completed his fast.

Gchi-gtaamgwaadkamgak gchi-feastkewag kina maawnzo-wiisniwaad.

It would be quite an event, and a great feast was prepared for everyone to gather and eat together.

Oonh gesnaa maamiikwendam mkwendang maanda miijim waa-miijid.

This boy was quite excited, thinking about all of the food that he would eat.

Mii dash gwehow gii-wi-naakshing wii-ni-nbaad megwaa gwa nbaad oonh gesnaa gtaamgwawewebideni omsad bkade.

He lay down to sleep, but all the while his stomach growled frightfully from hunger.

"Aanh daga-sh go!" nendam sa.

"All right, then!" he thought.

Mii go aazhgo wii-bi-waabang. "Nga-baa-zhaa maa besho nga-baanda-waabndaan waa-miijyaan."

It was now already near morning. "I will just walk around close by and look for something to eat."

Oonh ge baa-zhaad maa eshkam go waasa odi mii sa aazhgo bi-waabninig mii aazhgo zegzi wii-bskaabiid odi.

He went farther and farther, but by now it was already getting light out, and he was afraid to go back.

"Oonh besho go geyaabi maa nga-ni-zhaa."

"I will just go on a little more."

Mii sa maa gii-kosdood niw mtigoonsan ziibiins maa bmijwang—gii-kosdood kina maa mtigoonsan aapji go sigaakwaani gaa-zhisdood niw mtigoonsan.

He piled up some sticks along where the stream ran—and as he piled those sticks up he made sure they were tightly intertwined as he placed them there.

Mii maanda gaa-zhi-kinoomawind kaa dash go gbeyhiing mii aazhgo maa gii-debnaad maa giigoonyan.

This was how he had been taught, and it was not too long until he caught a fish.

Oonh gtaamgwa nakii sa naa maa miinwaa shkode giizhitood mii go wii-mnazwaad niw giigoonsensan gaa-nsaajin mii sa gii-mwaad.

He then set out to make a fire there to cook that little fish he had killed and promptly ate it up.

Oonh gmaapii go miinwaa wodi gii-ni-zhaa mii miinwaa odi bnewan gii-ni-nsaad.

And after a little while, again he went out and this time killed a partridge.

Oonh gesnaa maamiikwendam. "Oonh kaa memkaach ndaa-bskaabiisii kina aazhgo go gegoo ngii-kinoomaagoo—kaa memkaach miinwaa gegoo ge-kinoomaajgaaziiyaambaan wedi gaa-bi-njibaayaan."

He was so excited about this. "Oh, I don't need to go back home, for I have already been taught about everything—there is nothing else they can teach me back there where I came from."

"Mii go ge-ni-piiskaayaan nga-ni-ndawenjge."

"I'll just continue along with my hunting."

Miinwaa shkiniikwensan aapji gii-bwaanaan ensa-dbikak gii-bwaanaan shkiniikwensan.

And it was that a certain young woman came to appear in his dreams—every night he dreamed of her.

Oonh esnaa gwanaajwi shkiniikwens mii maa now ngoding giizhgak waa-nkweshkwaajin.

This young lady was quite beautiful, and he knew that one day he was going to meet her.

Mii sa iw kina gow mziwe maa gii-ni-nsaan zhiishiiban ge gii-ni-nsaan kina go gegoo gii-ni-ntoon mii sa ko mnazang mii go miijid.

He went around everywhere killing ducks and other animals, and everything that he killed was cooked and eaten.

Mii dash maanda gaa-zhiwebzid gaa gii-bzindzii.
This is what became of him because he didn't listen.

Kaa daa-gii-zaagdosesii odi gaa-nji-mkadeked mii-sh go en'sa go gegoo miijid mii go gii-maajiigid.
He wasn't supposed to leave that lodge where he had been fasting, and now he grew with everything that he ate.

Oonh eshkam sa naa gchi-nini eshkam sha go naa washme gnoozi shigwe epiichiwaad giw mtigook odi megeyaakwaa.
He gradually became a giant man—more and more so until he was taller than all the trees in the forest.

Oohn mshi sha go naa odi naaniibwi odi.
He eventually stood out from all else.

Aansh kaa go gegoo, kaa gegoo aazhgo gii-giizhendam gaa wii-bskaabiisig odi gaa-nji-kinoomaajgaazod odi gaa-nji-mkadeked.
He realized he could not to go back to where he had been given teachings throughout his fast.

"Mii gwehow ge-ni-piiskaayaan—oonh aapji go ndebsinii aapji go nmino-yaa."
"I'll just carry on with how things are for now—I am so full and very content right now."

Oonh bmosed.
And so on he walked.

Manj go naa mnik nsagwan gaa-bmosegwen miinwaa bmi-nda-waabndang waa-miijid mii dash maa zaaghigaansing maa gii-ni-dbewed kina go gii-ni-dbewe ni-naagahdood waa-miijid.
It is not known exactly how many days he must have walked along looking for things to eat, but he eventually came to a small lake and tracked something to eat along the shore.

Mii sa gmaapii, "Oonsh gdaaki wodi nga-zhaa." Nendam gdaaki wodi gii-zhaad.

After a while, he thought, "Oh, I will go up to the top of that hill." And so up that hill he went.

Mii waabmaad wedi gwaya wodi jiigbiig wodi nigaam.

He then saw someone over on a beach, just off the lake.

Kaa mshi wodi ni-zhaasii oonh gwaya sa go odi naaniibwiwan.

He had not yet gone this way, but there was definitely a person standing over there.

Oonh waawaatgoge ow shkiniikwe waawaatgohmwaan iihow nake.

A young woman was waving her hand, beckoning him to come that way.

Gegaa go nisidoonawaan.

He seemed to almost recognize her.

"Ngii-kenmaa maabam," nendam sa. "Ngoji gwa ngii-waabmaa ow."

"I know this person," he thought. "I have seen her somewhere."

Aansh aapji go aangwaamzi gchi-nini maa naa zaam gwa gaachiinyi odi naaniibwid ow kwe odi.

This giant had to be so careful as the woman standing over there was quite small.

Mii dash maanda enendang. "Giishpine, negaaj go nga-ni-naazkawaa, giishpine ge shko go odi ni-zhaayaan odi nga-zegaa," mii maanda enendang.

He decided, "If I approach her I must go slowly, if I just go right on over there, I will surely frighten her," he thought.

Aansh mii sa gii-ni-dgoshing odi oonh noondwaan sa go naanoondaagzi ow kwe.

When at last he arrived, he could hear that woman calling out.

Kaa-sh go gnage nisditwaasiin aansh go gtaamgwaanmad wodi shpiming aansh mii sa gii-waagjiitaad maa wii-bzindawaad.
He could not understand her because of the strong winds that were blowing in the sky, so he bent over to listen to her.

Mii sa maanda ekidod ow kwe. "Giin sa gaabaadziiyin! Ggiibaadiz aapji!"
And this is what that woman said. "You are a fool! You are so very foolish!"

Aapji go mii gaa-nendang wii-zegaad now wiin dash gii-zegigoon wjaanmigoon maa naa ge kaa gii-bzindzii!
He thought he was going to scare her, but it was now he who was afraid because she knew he had not listened!

"Mii maanda wenji-zhinaagziyin maanda," wdigoon.
"This is why you look like this," she told him.

Oohn gesnaa zegzi kaa ge wii-kenmoonaasiin niw shkiniikwen aapji zegzid zegigwad.
Oh, he was so afraid, but he didn't want the young woman to know he was afraid or that she was the one frightening him.

Mii sa iw.
And that was it.

Aansh naa iidog nendam sa gii-jijiingnitaad maa bzindawaan dash gwa mii sa gii-wiindmawaad, "Gii-waabmin mii gwa en'sa go wi-naakshinaan nbaayaan gii-waabmin."
He thought it best to bend down on one knee to listen to her, and he told her, "I have seen you before, every time I lay down to sleep I saw you."

"Genii go gii-waabmin," wdigoon sa.
"And I have seen you too," she said to him.

Mii sa iw gwejmaan, "Aaniish maa gaa-bi-nji-baayin?"
He then asked her, "Where did you come from?"

"Gegwa gegoo gwejmishken," aapji go maaba shkiniikwe maanaadendam.
"Now, don't you ask me anything," she said, for this young woman was troubled by something.

"Gegoo na gwa ge-zhichgeyaambaan ji-wiidookawnaan maa go naa gegoo gdaa-zhi-mina-doodoon?" wdinaan sa ow shkiniikwen.
"Is there anything that I can do to help you or anything good that I can do for you?" he said to that young woman.

"Kaa go naa gnimaa," kida shkiniikwe oonh zhaagooj maa nosed maa bngwiing ow shkiniikwe.
"Not likely," she said as she paced back and forth along the sand.

Aapji go gwanaajwan maa bngwi maa bagwaayaashkaamgak maa iihow nibi.
That sand was quite beautiful, having been washed down by the water as it had.

Oonh zhaagooj maa now nosed maa mtaakzide ge miinwaash mii sa ekidod ow shkiniikwe, "Aansh gnimaa—gnimaa gwa."
As she was walking back and forth there in her bare feet, she said, "Perhaps—perhaps there is something."

Mii sa maaba inaabid maa jiigbiig was go wodi gii-ni-zhaa mii sa odi gii-waabndang iihow aapji gwa gegaa gwa mkadewaamgad iihow bngwi.
She looked around and travelled far down the beach where she had seen sand that was almost black in colour.

Mii iw gaa-daapnang.
That is what she took.

Gchi-ngo-ninj gwa gii-daapnaan dinamwaan dash maa now gchi-niniwan iihow.
She took a big handful of that sand and handed it to the giant.

Mii dash ekidod maaba nini, "Aaniish dash maandan?"
And so said this man, "What is to be done with this?"

"Maajaan. Daapnan maanda." Mii sa gii-tinamwaad maa ninjiining.
"Leave now. And take this." She then placed the sand in his hands.

"Gii-gwejim en'gwen gegoo waa-zhi-mnadoodgwewnen. Mii sa maanda gaa-naabndamaan genii wii-bi-dgoshnan."
"You asked me if there was anything good that you might be able to do for me. This is what I saw in my dreams: that you would one day arrive here."

Mii sa ekdod maaba kwe, "Mii sa waa-zhiwebziiying maanda wii-gdimaagziwag gdooshkniigiimnaanig."
Then said this woman, "This is what will happen to us, our future generations will become so poor in all ways."

"Aapji go wii-baa-gwiishwiiyaawag aabdeg dash ji-mkamwaad mii maa naa maanda wendaadziiying maanda giigoonkeying miinwaa ndawenjgeying wii-wiisniwaad gniijaan'sinaanig. Mii dash maanda ezhi-bgosenminaan ji-naagdawenman wedi nakeyiing ningesh go wodi nakeyiing waabnong ji-naagdawenman."
"They will just move around here and there, but they will need to find a place where we can live by fishing and hunting, such that all of our children will have food to eat. So I am hoping that you can look after what needs to be done over there toward the east—that you can take care of this."

Mii sa gii-naaniibwid maa gaa-nji-jijiingnitaad mii dash go wodi nakeyiing enaabid bi-nji-mookang giizis.

He stood up from where he had been kneeling there before her and looked off toward the direction where the sun rises.

Mii sa gii-zhi-nkenid wodi oonh biiwaasnini gwa bngwi mii go ni-baateg maanda bngwi epiitaanmak wedi shpiming.
He raised his arms in that direction, and the sand started to blow that way—having been dried by the strong winds up there in the sky.

Mii sa gii-boodaajged kina wodi eko-naabid odi gii-ni-swe'aasinini ow bngwi.
Then he blew that sand as far as he could see, and it scattered about from the wind.

Oonh gchi-niimi sa naa maaba shkiniikwens yimbigwaashkni.
Oh, this young woman danced around, jumping up and down.

"Mii sa iw gii-zhiwebak gaa-zhi-bgosendmaan," kida. "Gchi-miigwech mii sa ji-debnamwaad gdooshkniigiimnaanig waa-dnizwaad."
"What I was hoping for has happened," she said. "Thank you so, for now our future generations will have a place to live."

Mii-sh naa ge maaba gaa-zhi-bwaajgegwen maaba sa kwe. Gchi-naanbaawe oonh gchi-naanbaawe sa naa.
This woman must have dreamed it would happen this way. Then she yawned, oh, did she ever yawn.

Mii go gewii maaba, maaba Nishnaabe mii go waabmaad naanbaawenid niw mii go gewii oonh aapji go naa ge-yekzi—esnaa yekzi gii-gtaaji gego ngoji wii-wi-naakshing wii-nbaad.
And when this man saw her yawn, he too felt very tired—but despite his fatigue he was afraid to lie down to sleep.

Mii dash maaba ekidod maaba shkiniikwens, "Kaa miinwaa nindawenmisinoon wii-gtaajiiyin."
Then said this young woman, "There is not again any need for you to be afraid."

"Gego gegoo gtaajken, nweshman."
"Do not be afraid of anything, now you must rest."

"Nmadbin maa gdaa-wi-naakshin ge gwa niin nga-kowaab. Kaa gegoo ga-zhiwebzisii nbaayin."

"Sit down, for you can lie here, and I myself will keep watch. Nothing will happen to you as you are sleeping."

Mii dash maaba Nishnaabe ow gesnaa gchi-naanbaawe mii sa gii-wi-naakdabid maa.

Then that Nishnaabe yawned loudly and sat down there.

Aapji go naa geget yekzi.

He was very tired.

Mii sa maaba gii-wi-naakshing maaba Gchi-nishnaabe.

And so this Giant lay down to go to sleep.

Mii sa naagadawendang ow Nishnaabe ntam go maa gii-wi-naakdabi maa. "Daga-sh go ga-gwejmin, wenesh gaa-nji-ndawenman maanda wii-sweswemgak maanda bngwi?"

The Giant was still really thinking about it when he first sat down there. "Please let me ask you something, why did you want this sand scattered about that way?"

"Mii sa iw ge-dnakiiwaad ndanshinaabemnaanig. Mii dash maanda ge-zhinkaademgak Thirty Thousand Islands daa-zhinkaadaan ow Zhaagnaash," kida shkiniikwe.

"This is where our people will live. And this is what it will be called—the Thirty Thousand Islands is what the Whiteman will call it," said the young woman.

"Miinwaa maanda mii go noongwa maa nkweshkwadaadiying mii go noongwa maanda maa ji-ni-mnjimenjigaademgak."

"And what has happened here, this meeting of ours, shall now always be remembered."

"Ahaaw, mii go eta go waa-kendmaan," kida Nishnaabe pane gaa-ni-wi-naakshing.

"Okay, that is all that I wanted to know," said this man, and so he lay down.

Mii gwehow kaa miinwaa gii-nshkaasii.
And never again did he get up.

Mii go ge-aapji-wi-naakshing iihow.
He lay down there forever.

Mii dash maaba Sleeping Giant wedi debaajigaazod.
This is the Sleeping Giant that is spoken of.

Mii maanda gaa-zhiwebdogobanen.
This is what must have happened.

Mii dash noongwa maa kina Georgian Bay maa ni-daawag kina maa Nishnaabeg.
And now this is why Georgian Bay is still home to the Nishnaabe people.

Enh, mii gaa-zhiwebak.
Yes, this is what happened.

Indigenous Life and **Community in Georgian Bay**

> *Niibna gegoo maa gii-bi-zhiwebad shkweyaang go naa nake gii-mno-bmaadziwag maa naa ge-wiinwaa Nishnaabeg gii-mno-yaawag nshike wedi gii-daawaad.*
>
> There were many things that happened long ago, and they lived good lives—the people were very well off living there by themselves.
>
> —Duncan Pegahmagabow

Weshkad—"The Beginning"

The story of the Ojibwe people in the Great Lakes region began when a mass exodus from the eastern seaboard left their communities in search of a prophesied homeland. A great spiritual vision would direct the Ojibwe Nation westward over mountains, rivers, and the Great Lakes to a special place where the "food grows on water."[1] The great wild rice lands at the far end of Lake Superior, the envisioned spiritual home of the Ojibwe Nation, took numerous generations and thousands of miles to reach. It was a journey filled with beauty and hardship and a steadfast belief in the original vision. Seven major stopping places were foretold, each of which would be marked by some kind of spiritual revelation.

Prophecy necessitated that the people pay attention to spiritual and physical markers (*kinoowaachiganan*) that would reveal themselves along the way. The reappearance of a great shell that rose out of the water was the greatest affirmation and signpost of their path westward. As noted by Ojibwe writer William Warren in 1885,

> while our forefathers were living on the great salt water toward the rising sun, the great Megis (sea-shell) showed itself above the

> surface of the great water, and the rays of the sun for some long periods were reflected from its glossy back. It gave warmth and light to the An-ish-in-aub-ag (red race). All at once it sank into the deep, and for a time our ancestors were not blessed with its light. It rose to the surface and appeared again on the great river which drains the waters of the Great lakes, and again for a long time it gave life to our forefathers, and reflected back the rays of the sun. Again it disappeared from sight and it rose not, till it appeared to the eyes of the An-ish-in-aub-ag on the shores of the first great lake.[2]

This great shell would appear at each of the seven stopping places throughout the journey. As affirmed by Edward Benton-Banai, "the Megis was to appear and reappear to the people throughout their history to show them the Path the Creator wished them to follow."[3] The great migration would lead the majority of the Ojibwe Nation to the far western side of the Great Lakes. This did not, however, include everyone. Several splinter groups, including the direct ancestors of Francis Pegahmagabow, remained at key places along the route. In this way did the Ojibwe and other related tribal groups come to inhabit the lands throughout the Great Lakes region.

The migration of the Ojibwe people was exceptionally difficult. The terrain was vast and new, and wintering in unfamiliar territory was hazardous in the best of years. Although there were seven major stopping places, the duration and extent of the journey necessitated more: such was the reality of moving an entire nation of people by foot and canoe across thousands of miles of unmapped wilderness and water. Famine, sickness, and even war were ever present. But the earth was rich in resources, and the people were skilled travellers. Even the most daunting of landscapes and war parties did not deter their sacred journey.

The entry into Georgian Bay proved to be one of the westward journey's most challenging. Although regarded as a part of Lake Huron in contemporary geography, Georgian Bay was a distinct entity among the Great Lakes (*gamiin*) to First Nations peoples. It was also a terrain unlike any other the Ojibwe had experienced on their sacred migration. Although abundant with food and other resources, the miles of uneven rock and swamp made for a humble progression. The local forests were equally daunting to traverse. The enormous trees of the pre-contact area made it difficult to navigate by either sunlight or starlight. Early maps made by settler cultures describe the landscape of "immense forests":[4] that is, prior to the logging era, which nearly destroyed this unique ecosystem.

8. Georgian Bay shoreline. Courtesy of Thom Morrissey Photography.

The waters of the bay proved to be an efficient means of travel during segments of the great migration westward. Elders of both Wasauksing and Shawanaga regarded the Waubano Channel as a great historical Nishnaabe water highway. Many area islands were even said to have had permanent teepee poles or lodges used by travellers.[5] Although travel was quicker by boat, it was also dangerous in moments; the same waters remain legendary for how quickly and powerfully they can change. The trials of the journey did not overshadow the direction of the spirit-led quest. The combination of land and water travel served the people well, and the area was rich in markers directing the migration westward. Even today many of those places continue to be remembered and honoured with gifts of tobacco and other articles by resident First Nations people. It is the continuing belief of the Nishnaabeg that such sites were not made by humans but placed there long ago in anticipation of their arrival and the events to come (see "Thirty Thousand Islands").

The lands and waters of the Great Lakes region were rich in spiritual presence, which the Ojibwe learned to embrace and live alongside. Such spirit beings, the *mnidoog,* themselves had various forms and responsibilities. From those who occupied the four cardinal points, to the mer-beings of the waters, to the thunderbirds of the skies, and to those who looked after the various parts of the land, life for the Nishnaabe people was based on reverence and respect for both the physical and the spiritual dimensions of life: "Youths came to learn about the manitous—their origin; presence; dwelling places; services and purposes; and kinship with all living beings, including plants, Mother Earth, animals, and human beings. The manitous were just as much a reality as were trees, valleys, hills, and winds."[6] It was perhaps this special connection that earned Georgian Bay distinct status not only as a Great Lake of the Ojibwe but indeed as Mnidoo-gami, "the Great Lake of the Spirit."

Travel was slow and further complicated by a persistent and formidable challenge from the mighty Haudenosaunee Nation. Always in pursuit, the Haudenosaunee were a worthy adversary. The strength of the Six Nations Confederacy was well regarded in pre-contact North America. The conflict between the Ojibwe and the Haudenosaunee in Georgian Bay proved to be the longest of any such encounter during the migration. When the Ojibwe finally reached the shores of Manitoulin Island, where the great shell again appeared to the people, many of the greatest warriors and leaders stayed put.[7] It was necessary for a sizable contingent to remain in parts of Georgian Bay to stave off the inevitable Haudenosaunee attacks from behind. The rich local hunting grounds provided great incentive for the Six Nations to continue their quest to control the resources of Georgian Bay. The Ojibwe had developed long-standing peaceful relationships with the resident Huron Nation, a harmony broken by decimation of the Huron by their Iroquoian relatives.[8] Control of the bay would alternate for generations until the Ojibwe and their allies finally developed the united strength to permanently drive the Haudenosaunee out of the region.[9] By this time, the promised lands west of Lake Superior were no longer a destination for the Ojibwe of the region: Georgian Bay had since become home. It was from these people that Francis Pegahmagabow descended, and in his own time he would demonstrate the truth of what it meant to be an Ojibwe warrior and leader.

Georgian Bay became a robust community of numerous Ojibwe bands in the period following the great migration. Kinship ties were strong, and the Ojibwe were blessed with large and bountiful hunting territories. Even after the forced move to permanent reserve settlements, the Nishnaabe of these communities retained a special connection with each other from a shared history of story, land, and blood. Francis was the direct descendant of old eastern Ojibwe families on both his mother's side and his father's side. His great-great-grandfather Bebagamigaabaw was a chief of the Muskoka band, one of the last free-moving and uncolonized Ojibwe groups in the region. Although Francis was born and raised in Shawanaga, his paternal relatives had made their home on the Parry Island Reserve (Wasauksing) ever since his great-grandfather James Pegahmagabow Sr. assumed chieftainship there;

it was in this community that Francis ultimately made his home and raised his family.

The place known as Wasauksing is directly connected to the story of the migration, particularly to the appearance of the great shell in Georgian Bay. Both the contemporary meaning of the word and its exact boundaries remain subjects of debate. It has been suggested for at least the past century—back to the time of Francis himself—that Wasauksing is a form of an older name: Waaseyaakosing, the "place that shines brightly in reflection of the sacred light." This name was shared with community members in the 1980s by Edward Benton-Banai, an Ojibwe historian and spiritual leader. Although local elders were not immediately familiar with the older term, there was a general consensus that this might have been the original name of the area, an agreement reinforced once the migration story, and the story of the great shell rising from the waters of Georgian Bay, were again recounted in the community.

By all accounts, it was at Mnidoo-mnising ("Island of the Spirit"), known more commonly today as Manitoulin Island, that the great shell revealed the fourth stopping place to the people during the migration west.[10] Emerging from the waters close to present-day Cape Croker Reserve, the *miigis* ("sacred shell") moved across the bay toward its destination above Manitoulin Island. A brilliant light was cast upon the eastern shore during its journey across the bay. In witnessing the light of the *miigis* and the way it was reflected by the land, rocks, and trees, the people were compelled to call this place Waaseyaakosing, a name now preserved in the present-day name Wasauksing.

The migration story is one of many significant events in the history of Georgian Bay that predates European arrival. Precious few details of this history, once passed down intergenerationally through the oral tradition, survived the near eradication of the First Nations cultures and languages by governments, churches, and education systems. The continued history and legacy of the First Nations in this territory need to be remembered as much as any of the documented events of the past 200 years. Recovering a comprehensive and authentic early historical record is difficult now because of the almost silent voice of the oral tradition, the often erroneous reports of early settlers and missionaries, and the desecration of Indigenous teaching and learning systems that once ensured the continuity of such knowledge:

> A thorough understanding of Ojibwe culture in the pre-European contact period is difficult to obtain. No written records were

> made by those who lived within the culture at that time. Our knowledge, therefore, is based partly on the accounts of explorers, missionaries, fur traders, soldiers, and government officials. They wrote about these people often years after European cultural contact had taken place. Their accounts are biased, and are often misleading and incomplete. They incorrectly viewed the Indians as a static, unchanging people, rather than a people in transition. Yet in the first two centuries of contact, a good case could be made from the existing European sources to indicate that the Ojibwe culture was evolving at a more rapid pace than the European. Unfortunately, no Ojibwe wrote about their culture and history until long after it had changed dramatically. Even then, the oral traditions they collected were written in the English language. This in itself was indicative of the European bias which had been thrust upon them.[11]

There are few reliable accounts of pre-contact history. The migration story itself represents but a small part of the experience of Indigenous peoples in Georgian Bay. But understanding some history of the people Francis Pegahmagabow came from helps us to understand the life of the man himself. This includes knowledge of the places where his people made their homes and lived their lives. In the traditional Ojibwe world view, knowing where one comes from might be as important as knowing one's name or clan. It is why any formal Ojibwe introduction still includes the name of one's community of origin, for it immediately creates a connection to a network of kinship, interrelationship, and history that helps to frame one's place in the world. The name, clan, and family relationships of Francis Pegahmagabow are explored in later chapters; here I include a discussion of the places he came from and valued above all others.

Conventional histories that begin with the arrival of European settlers to an area do a profound disservice to the legacy of the First Nations who first made their homes there. This "beginning of history" actually meant many significant ends with respect to First Nations cultural and environmental sustainability. The Indigenous peoples of Georgian Bay had developed long-standing successful and sustainable relationships between humans and the local environment. Although human habitation inevitably has impacts on the landscape, it is not always necessarily destructive. The abundant flora and fauna in pre-contact North America, particularly the old-growth forests that flourished alongside Nishnaabe communities, are direct evidence of

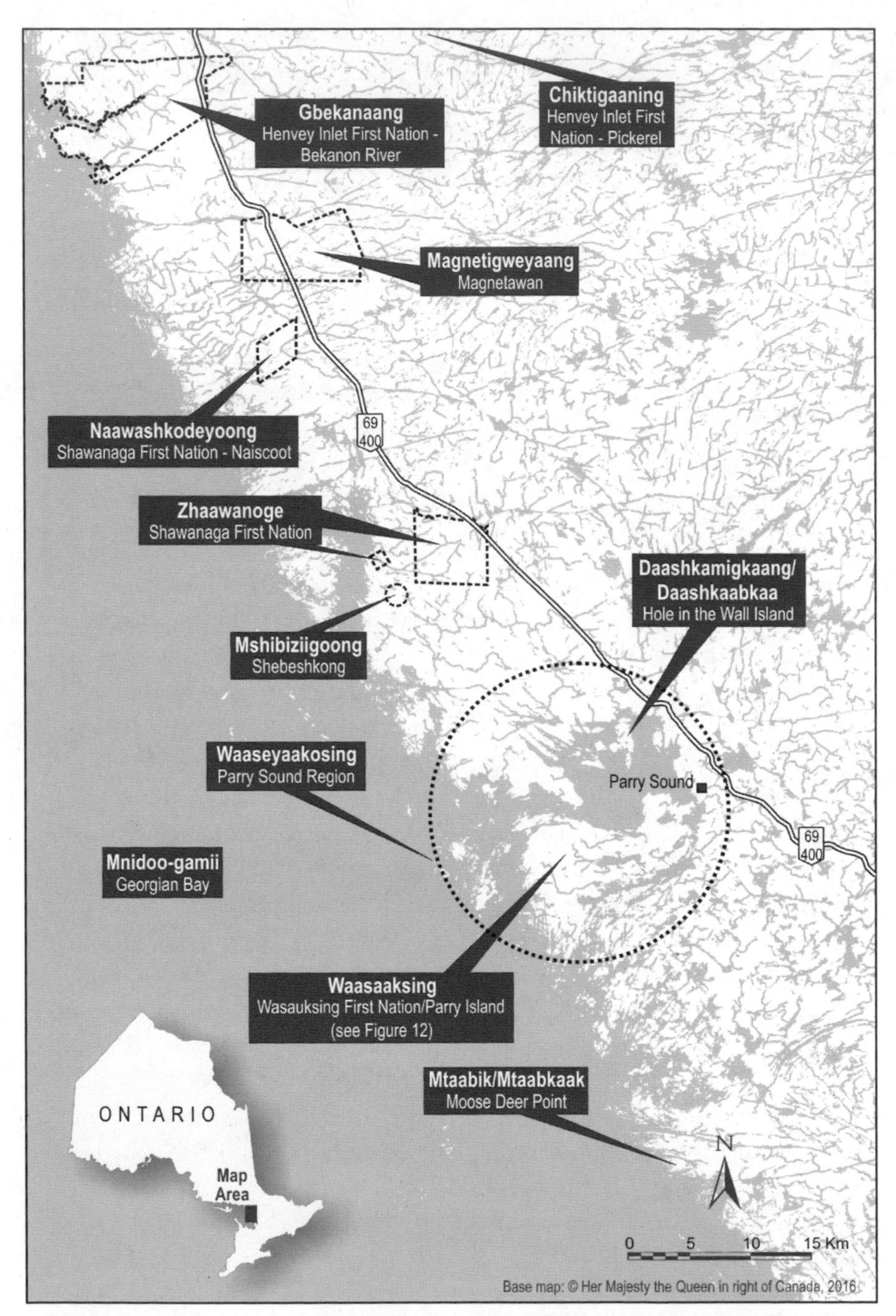

9. Waaseyaakosing and the First Nations of the Eastern Shore. Map used with permission of Angus Leech and Brian McInnes. Design by Weldon Hiebert.

Table 1. Waaseyaakosing and the First Nations of the Eastern Shore.

Location	Common Name	Meaning
Chi-ktigaaning	Henvey Inlet First Nation—Pickerel	At the Big Garden
Daashkamigkaang/ Daashkaabkaa	Hole in the Wall Island	The Place where the Rock is Split
Gbekanaang	Henvey Inlet First Nation—Bekanon River	At the End of the River
Magnetigweyaang	Magnetawan	River that Bends and Folds
Mnidoo-gamii	Georgian Bay	Great Lake of the Spirit
Mnjigan-mnis	Rose Island	Deer run island
Mshibizhiigoong	Shebeshkong	Place of the Great Cat
Mtaabik/Mtaabkaak	Moose Deer Point	Place of Bare rock
Naawashkodeyoong	Shawanaga First Nation – Naiscoot	The Place Where There is a Meadow in the Center
Waasaaksing	Wasauksing First Nation/ Parry Island	Where it is Reflecting/ Shining off Poles Lying Across
Waaseyaakosing	Parry Sound Region	Place that shines brightly in reflection of the sacred light
Zhaawanoge	Shawanaga First Nation	Pointing to the South

positive human presence. With the inception of mass logging in the region, the respectful system of environmental management and strategic long-term resource use established by the First Nations people was abolished.

The extraordinary beauty and ecological diversity of pre-contact Georgian Bay was celebrated in the stories and songs of the Ojibwe. Huge old-growth forests, a bountiful fishery, clean water, and large animal populations were all characteristic features of the landscape. Franz Koennecke notes that the earliest detailed description of Parry Island (Wasauksing) originates in an 1856 report made by W.H.E. Napier of the Indian Department:

> The coast is for the most part high and rocky timbered with Pine and Hemlock, but the interior is compound [sic] of much fine open hardwood land with occasional Tamarac, Spruce and Black Ash swales—there are many very excellent flats of open hardwood Beech, Maple, Elm, Ironwood, Birch and Ash, interspersed with occasional groves of large Pine of good quality. The Island is well watered by numerous creeks running nearly across it thro [sic] rich beaver meadows and the soil is rich sandy loam. The Eastern part of the Island is more rocky but well timbered and has many inlets all navigable for vessels of moderate draught.[12]

It is difficult to imagine the number of places in Georgian Bay that have been devastated ecologically and spiritually over the past 150 years of European settlement. Colonial life introduced a very different way of relating to the earth than that known by local Indigenous peoples who had learned to live in balance with both the abundance and the limitations of their homeland.

Waaseyaakosing: Land and Relationship in Georgian Bay

The original territory of Waaseyaakosing was well known and loved by its people. This was a place of legend and prophecy. It was also one of everyday life, suitable for hunting, fishing, planting, and the gathering of roots, berries, and other supplies necessary for community maintenance. Extensive knowledge of both the waterways and the intricate network of trails and roads that ran throughout the pre-contact forests was shared among the Ojibwe communities of the region. Members of the ceremonial societies looked after and protected the sacred places. Healers knew best where to hold purification lodge, shaking tent, or drum dance ceremonies. The people also designated or found areas conducive to child birthing, fasting, healing the sick, and burying the dead. This was all in addition to those places the people knew and respected based on great migrations, spiritual occurrences, ceremonies, and even wars. The landscape was shared not only by birds and animals but also by various orders of spiritual beings:

> The Place of Visions was a long way from the village.... The old people said it was formed by neither man nor by nature but by some other cause: by Pau/eensag (Little Dwellers of the Forest). Such an origin gave the glade a mystic character. It belonged to the spirits who inhabited the earth. Here, far from men and women, they could preside over their affairs without disturbance. And the Anishnabeg respected the sanctuaries of the deities. These were special places. The only time that it was regarded as permissible to enter the domain of the spirits was during the quest for vision. On these occasions it was said that the spirits welcomed the visitor and aided in the quest.[13]

The Waaseyaakosing region, accessible through a well-established system of interior forest trails and water ways, was an active and well-known stopping and trading place for the local Native bands. People from the interior were able to find expedient travel along the Seguin River, while those from more distant places could take advantage of the established water routes that ran along Georgian Bay, described by Koennecke as "a water highway, stretching from the Manitoulin Islands in the northwest for 120 miles to Wasaga Beach in the southeast."[14] There was a utilitarian purpose behind much of the journeying that occurred along this route, with much of the activity directed toward the maintenance of a vast intercontinental trading network of copper, pipestone, furs, tools, flint, and seashells, which began as early as 700 BC.[15] This was the antithesis of a vast, empty land with no history. It was a productive and dynamic society that strove to find a balance between physical and spiritual needs as a people living respectfully with the earth.

Waasaaksing: A Changed Name and Place

The swift settlement of the region in the late 1800s, and the even faster exploitation of the timber resources, began a rapid transformation of the local landscape and culture. The resident Ojibwe bands found themselves amalgated into a number of fixed settlements or permanently driven out of their homeland. It was in this era that the community of Waaseyaakosing was relocated to Parry Island.[16] Although this reserve is now officially known by the name Wasauksing, the current boundaries encompass but a fraction of the original territory once held by the band. A number of systematic injustices have removed much of the community's original land base, which extended from its current location on the shores of Georgian Bay to as far inland as the Haliburton Highlands; on a south-to-north continuum, the people were intimately familiar with the lands that ranged from Moose Deer Point to the Pickerel River.[17] A local example of such exploitation is the territory adjacent to the Seguin River, long a place of settlement for the Nishnaabeg and one of the first areas designated as reserve land. In negotiations over Parry Island, the band was deceived into ceding this territory, and despite numerous protests it has never regained control of this land: "The Anishnabwe did not become aware of the loss of their reserve until in 1856 ... William Milnor Gibson, a former land surveyor, purchased the surrounding timber limits and built a saw mill at the mouth of the Seguin River. The band had to leave their settlement and move to Parry Island. As Francis Pegahmagabow explained in 1923, his forefathers went on the island, because some of the early settlers told them to get out."[18]

The first people to officially settle on the reserve included the descendants of two local bands of Ojibwe. This was after the signing of the Robinson-Huron Treaty and the establishment of the reserve boundaries. Many of these first inhabitants chose to settle at two main locations, now known as Upper Village and Lower Village.[19] By the 1880s, two additional settlements included Potawatomi and Ojibwe immigrants residing at the Middle Village, with a group of Odawa living at Nenabozhnaang or "Nanibush town."[20] Many of these people had fled from the United States, likely in response to the forced relocations that began in 1830 with the passing of the Indian Removal Act. It is possible that some of the Odawa moved to Parry Island as early as the 1840s.[21]

Around the turn of the century, the various tribal peoples who had made their way into one of the four major settlements at Parry Island found themselves entering a time of tremendous change. Many of the transformations to their lives were physical, such as the increased use of cotton, European farming equipment, and other tools. A major transition was the shift from a semi-nomadic lifestyle over a far-reaching area to one confined to only about twenty-seven square miles or seventy square kilometres of their former lands.[22] With this restriction of their movement came basic lifestyle changes, which meant, for the people of Waasaaksing, an increased dependence on agriculture compared with the relatively balanced combination of fishing, hunting, gathering, and limited planting practised prior to European contact.[23] Dietary changes and increased participation in the wage economy also had significant effects on the local culture.

What is remarkable about this general period of change is that the cultural fabric of the Nishnaabeg remained basically intact. Modified sustenance activities and participation in the wage economy meant marked lifestyle changes. Social interrelationships, however, remained relatively consistent until the mid-1900s. The forced institutionalization of educational and religious domains of life presented significant additional challenges, but the Nishnaabeg were determined to preserve their identity and social structures. The same resilience was broadly observed among the Ojibwe in resisting or adapting to forced innovations: "Radical change was required to adjust to the incursions of the Europeans, yet, as the eminent anthropologist Ruth Landes observed, 'they must yet resemble psychoculturally their forebears.'"[24]

Nishnaabe-bmaadziwin—"Nishnaabe Life"

> *Mii waa-dbaajdamaan maanda gaa-bi-zhi-kendmaan pii be-shkiniigiyaan nake gaa-bi-zhi-kooganigooyaan maa shkoniganing.*
> I want to speak of what I came to know when I was young, the way that I was raised here on this reserve.
>
> *Aapji go bkaan ezhi-yaamgak.*
> It was so very different here.
>
> *Aapji go naa gii-yaawag gow Nishnaabeg ngii-nendam go naa aapji go weweni nake gii-bezhgo-gaabwiwag maamwi.*
> Of those people who lived here, I thought of them as always standing together in a good way.
>
> *Gaawiin waawaasa gii-naaniibwisiiwag.*
> They did not stand so very far apart from each other.
>
> —Duncan Pegahmagabow

In the years following the war, Francis took up permanent residence at Wasauksing. The community had extensive contact with non-Native peoples during this period, and almost all Nishnaabe children were attending school with some regularity. After years of proselytizing, the church had also become an accepted local institution. Most community members belonged to either the Catholic or the Methodist faith.[25] Many continued to follow traditional religious practices such as the Midewiwin or "Way of the Good-Hearted" despite the outlaw of such practices under the Indian Act. This was necessarily a secret observance. Although full-lodge ceremonies were no longer held, those who had once joined the *Mide* society remained loyal to its healing and life-restoring rites.

Traditional Nishnaabe cultural practice remained important for those who had converted to Christianity. Tobacco was generally offered by community members when the thunders were heard (see "*Nimkiik*—The Thunders"), before a long trip across waterways, or when one was in need of a successful hunting or fishing excursion. Like many of his fellow community members, Francis also decided to join the Roman Catholic Church. His profound devotion to his new faith was well known. He never abandoned the cultural practices he grew up with, such as making offerings of food and tobacco to the local spirits for protection and well-being. The ritual of fasting or visioning also continued to be observed by many at Wasauksing as a rite of passage. Francis had done this often as a boy and encouraged his children to do the same. There remained a deep-rooted belief in traditional Nishnaabe spiritual ways and practices even though most families had already made the formal conversion to Christianity.

The inevitable transition to reserve life was faced by the Wasauksing people with both resilience and adaptability. With many of their former lands now appropriated and movement generally restricted to the reserve, agriculture became a core sustenance activity.[26] People still travelled around as much as possible in pursuit of hunting, fishing, or gathering practices, but life became increasingly sedentary. In many local stories, such as "When My Father Went Home," the family garden became a hallmark of each homestead. Gardens became a significant source of interaction among families as visitors often exchanged or gave away part of their harvests as gifts. The custom of visiting, common in traditional times, remained important for reinforcing social ties and relationships.

The increased agrarian tendencies of the Waasaaksing people did not deter hunting and fishing practices. They were primarily for the immediate sustenance of the family since there seems to have been some degree of cultural prohibition against the selling, or at least the excessive selling, of meat and furs. Francis once told Duncan about how a respectful hunter would share his success:

> *Gii-nendaagzi sa gwa ji-nsaad niw waawaashkeshwan ji-miin'gozid iihow ji-giiwewnaad ji-shamaad niw mii go naa gewiin enchiwaad.*

> It was meant for him to kill that deer; he was blessed with it to take home and feed however many were in his family.
>
> *Miinwaa go naa ge-ni-shkosed maabam waawaashkesh daa-miigwe go odi ngoji ni-miigwe gwa ow wiiyaas ji-wiisniwaad giw aanind Nishnaabeg.*
>
> And that which was left over of the deer he would give away—he would go around and give away that meat so that others may eat. (from "*Enendaagwak Bmaadziwin*—What Is Expected of Life")

In the Nishnaabe world view, animals were not mere commodities to be bought and sold beyond moderation. Animals were a vital part of the natural world, regarded as the older relatives of the people themselves. Each Nishnaabe person was born with a clan animal through one's paternal line. Families honoured their clans and took special pride in their extended clan family membership.[27] All were considered relatives, though, in the community context. After particularly good harvests, or successful hunting or fishing expeditions, people distributed their excess food to neighbours and families in need.[28] Community members were assured that their extended families and fellow Nishnaabeg would help them through adversity even in hard times.

Community gatherings and ceremonies remained means of both establishing and maintaining a sense of cohesiveness. The annual remembrance feast, for which the community gathered in commemoration of their departed loved ones, was one such cornerstone event. An annual post-Christmas gathering, called Little Christmas, was also broadly celebrated by local families. Community members gathered to exchange food and hold a giveaway at this time. This was in recognition of the January moon (*Shki-mnidoo-giizis* or the "New spirit moon"), which marked the rebirth of the thirteen-month moon cycle. Although this gathering was eventually replaced by the Christian holiday, Christmas became a way to maintain traditional practice in a time when the Indian Act forbade it. Other ceremonies for which community members continued to gather, despite formal pressure to do otherwise, included naming ceremonies and feasts that celebrated the completion of a person's fast or vision quest (see "Thirty Thousand Islands").

For the people of Waasaaksing, traditional lifeways and sustenance activities remained important despite the alternatives imposed by Western society.[29] Community members continued with traditional practices such as making nets and other tools, and they expanded their carving and woodworking activities when European tools became available. Basket making,

10. Parry Island families selling traditional quillwork baskets and wall hangings to tourists. National Museum of the American Indian, Smithsonian Institution, N14411. Photo by Frederick Johnson.

rug weaving, and quillwork remained key practices, as did the tanning of hides and various forms of leatherwork.[30] The Nishnaabeg made a very successful synthesis of their traditional lifeways and those introduced by the Europeans. In everything from spirituality to dietary habits, a careful balance was established between traditional and European ways, such that life was progressive yet distinctly Nishnaabe. The Parry Island Fair, held for many years in the community, attracted visitors and competitors from far and wide, and it was a testament to the success of the people in blending a foreign way of life with their own.

Nimkiik—The Thunders

The "thunder beings" (*nimkiik*) were a strong spiritual part of the world of the Ojibwe. Francis Pegahmagabow's great-great-grandfather Bebagamigaabaw, a Muskoka band chief from whom the family surname originated, was named in part for the power of both thunder and wind spirits. So too was Francis's great-grandfather James Pegahmagabow Sr. (Beskinekwam or "The Thunder That Sets Things on Fire"), also named from the thunder spirits. As Francis related to Jenness in 1929, "When my great-grandfather was a baby his father joined a war-party against the Indians to the south. One day when the sky was almost cloudless a bolt of lightning set fire to a tree near the home camp. Then the people knew that the party was engaged in battle, and they named my great-grandfather *Beskinekwam,* 'the thunder that sets things on fire.'"[31] Thunder is animate in the Ojibwe language and a respected part of the natural world. Its presence inspired offerings of tobacco and the quiet attention of the people while its cleansing and healing energy was brought to the earth.

Although Francis did not grow up with his relatives at Parry Island, his adoptive family made sure he was exposed to all the rites of passage common in Ojibwe tradition. Fasting was one such practice that helped young people to find direction in life and often the blessing of a helper spirit. Francis himself was blessed by the thunder spirits while fasting as a boy. He had long forgotten about this, however, until he found himself on the front lines during the Great War. He was reminded that they would never abandon him, even in a place he did not expect their help: "During the great war Pegahmagabow was overtaken by a terrific thunderstorm. He felt the air flap his face as though moved by the wings of a mighty bird. Previously he had not believed the story of a thunderbird, but on this occasion at least it seemed to him that it must be true."[32] After this experience, Francis would describe the sound of a coming storm with the word *biidweyaangwe* ("the coming sound of a thunderbird's wings"). On other occasions, he would use the word *bmakwazhiwewin* ("the sound the thunder beings made as they rowed across the sky"). The thunder spirits were powerful defenders, and Francis told his children one could sometimes hear the sound of their "war clubs" (*bgamaaganan*) echoing in the distance. The Ojibwe believed the thunders had their own language. Few, however, were able to interpret their message.

While it was during the war that Francis would remember his blessing from the thunder spirits, it was also his war experience, somewhat ironically, that would corrupt this relationship. When he returned home, he sometimes found the sound of a thunderstorm reminiscent of the chaos he experienced during his many years on the front lines. Always the protector, Francis would go off on his own should the sound of a coming storm induce the memory of war. He also learned to listen to the thunders and appreciate the gifts of cleansing and renewal they brought to the earth. The following story from Duncan affirms that Francis continued to find value and blessing when the thunders sounded their voices.

Mii naa dazhindmaan mewnzha ko gaa-bi-naadziwaad Nishnaabeg.
I am speaking about how the Nishnaabe people were long ago.

Mii ko gaa-zhichgewaad ngitziimag iihow pii gchi-nimkiikaamgak.
This was what my parents did whenever there was a thunderstorm.

Waasa go naa odi aazhgo kaa maa gaawaanh go naa gnoondwaag biidwewdamwaad giw nimkiik.
Over there in the distance, you could just barely hear those thunders sounding their voices as they came this way.

Mii aazhgo maa bi-yaa ndedem gii-bi-yaan gwehow naagaans gaa-aabjitood zkamwaajged.
This was when my father would approach them, taking a small bowl that he used to make his tobacco offering in.

Mii zkamwaajged niw yahaan nimkiin.
For this tobacco offering was for the thunders.

Nmishoom'sinaanig maa naa go—giw nimkiik—nmishoom'sinaanig.
They are our grandfathers—those thunders—they are our grandfathers.

Mii-sh gwa zkamwaajged gwa.
And so he would make his tobacco offering to them.

Gchi-nendam ko mnookmig ntam giw bebi-yaajig go bi-bgamak.

He was so glad in the spring when those first thunders came rolling in.

Mii ko memdige zkamwaajgepan mii iw gchi-nenmaad niw miinwaa bipskaabiinid niw nimkiin.

He especially offered tobacco then, being so glad that those thunders had returned.

Mii-sh ko gaa-zhichged go ndedem iihow biptaamgwak zkamwaajged.

This is what my father did whenever a storm came in, he made an offering of tobacco.

Pane gaa-zhi-kendmaan zhichgewaad iihow Nishnaabeg mewnzha zkamwaajgewaad.

For as long as I can remember, the Nishnaabe people of long ago would offer tobacco during these times.

Zkamwaajgewaad ge niw yahaan nimkiin.

They made an offering to the thunders.

CHAPTER 3

Wind, Rock, and Water: Maps and Names at Wasauksing and Shawanaga

> *Mii sa naagadawendang ow Nishnaabe ntam go maa gii-wi-naakdabi maa. "Daga-sh go ga-gwejmin, wenesh gaa-nji-ndawenman maanda wii-sweswemgak maanda bngwi?"*
> The Giant was still really thinking about it when he first sat down there. "Please let me ask you something, why did you want this sand scattered about that way?"
>
> *"Mii sa iw ge-dnakiiwaad ndanshinaabemnaanig. Mii dash maanda ge-zhinkaademgak Thirty Thousand Islands daa-zhinkaadaan ow Zhaagnaash," kida shkiniikwe.*
> "This is where our people will live. And this is what it will be called—the Thirty Thousand Islands is what the Whiteman will call it," said the young woman.
>
> —Marie Anderson, "Thirty Thousand Islands"

Growing up in Georgian Bay meant mastering a beautiful yet rigorous landscape. The heavy granite base of the Canadian Shield—the oldest rock on earth—gradually gave way to the wind and water to form a unique and special place. The elegant bent pines, wind-swept rock faces, white-sand beaches, and tens of thousands of small islands remain characteristic features of a landscape with more than 12,000 years of continuous Aboriginal occupation and stewardship. Growing up with traditional Nishnaabeg meant that Francis Pegahmagabow would inherit millennia of environmental, cultural, and spiritual knowledge that connected the people to the land.

11. Wind, water, and rock in the land of the Georgian Bay Ojibwe. Courtesy of Thom Morrissey Photography.

Although many regions of Georgian Bay experienced an influx of Odawa and Potawatomi families in the generations preceding his birth, Francis himself came from the Ojibwe bands who had inhabited the area since the time of the great Ojibwe migration. He grew up steeped in the cultural traditions of his ancestors, and the way he lived his life reflected that experience. Born and raised in Shawanaga, Francis had many fond memories of this smaller reserve that shared much history with the people of Wasauksing, where Francis was a member. He would relocate to Parry Island as an adult and raise his family and spend the majority of his days there.

This chapter discusses the significance of some local stories and place names in the region of Georgian Bay that Francis made home. It was in this landscape that he hunted, prayed, worked, and raised his family. Although I describe some place names at Shawanaga and the surrounding area, my focus remains on the Wasauksing First Nation, where Francis felt he most belonged.

Shkoniganing—"On the Reserve"

The Wasauksing community is located on Parry Island in the heart of Georgian Bay's Thirty Thousand Islands. This was the territory that Francis would come to know best. Since the time of Chief James Pegahmagabow Sr., generations of his family have lived on this First Nation territory. It was in this spirit that Francis identified himself as *Waasaaksiiwinini* ("a man of Wasauksing") throughout his adult life.

The second largest island in Georgian Bay, Parry Island is a place of great fascination for many. The sandy beaches, interior waterways, swamps, forest stands, and variety of flora and fauna are just some of the reasons why this island has captured the interests of both Native and non-Native peoples over the years. The once burgeoning town of Depot Harbour, built on reserve lands appropriated by the Department of Indian Affairs, has left one of the most historic ghost towns in North America. However, the commanding presence of the land here is perhaps best expressed in the incredible rock faces that show themselves at every turn. The time-shaped rocky face of Wasauksing remains one of its most characteristic features.

Wasauksing was long known among area Native peoples as a great spiritual place for many years. Even before its selection and designation as reserve land, local tribes placed great value on this island. The land was not nearly as hospitable as the traditional mainland sites (the current town of Parry Sound) or as fertile.[1] There was also little choice in the matter. Parry Island had been historically known to the First Nations of Georgian Bay as the "Great Medicine Island" (Gchi-Mshkikii-Mnis). Community elder Ted Wheatley had always heard that the island had been a great place of storytelling and ceremony prior to its designation as an Indian reserve.[2]

Ezhnikaadeg Maa Kiing—"So Named Is This Earth"

Evidence of North American Indigenous history and presence is often found in the innumerable place names of Native-language origin that fill our maps. Although these names are often written incorrectly, and their stories long forgotten or erased, they represent the continuing legacy of First Nations. Georgian Bay remains one of those territories replete with such names and stories. Although much of this knowledge has been lost, these names serve as a map of the original history of our shared country. There is much that we can learn from the original place names of the land. Even though Native peoples may no longer live in all of these places, the names remain a lasting testimony to the founding presence and knowledge of the original peoples of this land: "No place names distinguish a region, a province, or a country better than those derived from Aboriginal designations, descriptions, and legends. Ontario's various Aboriginal languages have given many of its place names a certain distinctiveness and venerable beauty. Many of the Aboriginal names are derived from Algonquin languages, especially Algonquin, Ojibwe, Cree, Mississauga, and Ottawa."[3] Examples of Nishnaabe place names in Georgian

Bay include Waubamik (*waabamik* or "white beaver"), Manitouwabing (*manidoowaabing* or "where one may see as a spirit"), Shebeshekong (*zhiibaashkaang* or "to go through a narrows, waterway"), and Keewaydin (*giiwedin* or "the north wind, the north spirit). Like much of the documented history of the Nishnaabe in Georgian Bay, many of the names from maps and other written sources are plagued by misrepresentation and error. The majority of these names, such as Kashegaba, Waubashene, Musquash, Cognashene, or even Magnetawan, the name of both a local reserve and a township, were all recorded so poorly that the proper reconstruction of the original place names is difficult in the present—especially when the stories might have also been lost. There is perhaps no territory in North America that does not have some part of its original history represented in names of Indigenous origin.

The resurgence of historical First Nations place names in the present is part of a broader movement of reclaiming Aboriginal history and relationship with the land. Changing the name of the Parry Island Reserve back to Wasauksing was one such example. The reclamation of a name is both a cultural and a political process that helps to restore an appreciation for the history of the first peoples of this place. It is also a valuable indicator of the relationship between people and the land. This is especially important in an age when the unsustainable economic development of Aboriginal lands and waters is increasing. Traditional notions of stewardship over place—meaning the original cultural understandings of use and respect—must be balanced with economic interests. Remembering the meaning of place is one way Indigenous peoples have traditionally maintained such a perspective and sustainable relationship with their earth mother.

A place name represents several things for First Nations people. Fundamentally, it is a symbol and reminder of relationship. Native languages are highly descriptive, often with a rich vocabulary for talking about geographical terms and phenomena. Much of the descriptive capacity of the Ojibwe language is verbal, with the use of proper names being comparatively rare. The existence of a place name shows how important that site was to the lived experience of the people or the spiritual legacy of the land itself.

Wasauksing and Shawanaga Community Place Names

Francis would have become intimately familiar with the Ojibwe-language place names of Georgian Bay growing up at Shawanaga. Whether named after "a large clearing in the land" (*wezhaawen'gaag*) or "the long, narrow bay" (*waazhiwaan'gaag*), this close-knit community had the same cultural traditions as the people of Wasauksing and many of the same Muskoka band ancestors. Francis grew up in the heart of the reserve and played along the Shebeshkong River with his adopted siblings. It was a place rich in resources and the characteristic landscape of Georgian Bay.

His adopted family, the Kewaquados, taught him essential survival skills such as hunting, trapping, fishing, and how to find and use plant medicines. The rich variety of geographical terms that make the Ojibwe language so unique and descriptive would have been among his first words. Francis learned that rocks and waves were animate, even when sand and water were not, and that the sun, earth, moon, and thunder all shared the same respective kinship terms with his human relatives (father, mother, grandmother, grandfather). Like all Nishnaabe people of that era, he learned a deep respect for a world full of spiritual powers and sacred places; humans were always welcome, but were always mindful of the true owners. The Kewaquado family often visited the great rock turtle at Carling (*mshiikenh-zhiibigweshing* or "turtle lying there with his neck extended") and left offerings of tobacco, gifts, or food as Nishnaabeg had done for centuries. This place was one of the most significant *kinoowaachigan* or "landmarks" that had guided his forebears in the great westward migration centuries before.

When I first attempted to document Francis's homeland in the Ojibwe language, there were few maps or records that were helpful. I discerned a handful of terms from old documents, but the writing was always hard to decipher, and the locations were often mismatched. The two maps in this book (Figures 9 and 12), documented first in the Ojibwe language, are the products of many years of work. I am indebted to many community elders from both Wasauksing and Shawanaga who helped me to recreate a model of the community and landscape as Francis would have known them in his time. I once asked elders if this was knowledge that should be reserved only for community members or Indigenous peoples. They replied that once these names had been known and used by even local non-Native people and that it should be this way again. Sharing these maps is one step toward that goal.

Numerous place names were collected at Wasauksing (Parry Island), Shawanaga, and the greater region once known as Waaseyaakosing. Although more than one place name was sometimes found for a given place, there remained a general consistency among those consulted: "In any community, the meanings assigned to geographical features and acts of speech will be influenced by the subjective determinations of the people who are using them, and these determinations, needless to say[,] will exhibit variation. But the character of the meanings—their steadier themes, their recurrent tonalities, and above all, their conventionalized modes of expression—will bear the stamp of a common cast of mind."[4] Many of these conversations about places of importance and their names occurred over two decades ago. Culturally sensitive and sacred locations are not included out of respect. The names included on the present maps were rechecked with contemporary elders, but there was no significant change to the original information.

For many local Nishnaabeg, the vast majority of names have long since disappeared from memory. Wasauksing and Shawanaga elders remembered hearing innumerable place names when travelling throughout Georgian Bay as children. Places of importance were located both along the shore and deep within the Muskokas. The widespread settlement of non-Natives in the area made travel to these locations increasingly difficult. As the Nishnaabe people's lives became more sedentary, these places and their names became lost—seemingly as irrecoverable as the immense forests and unaltered shorelines they must have once described. Most elders had not heard many of the names I documented since they were children. This would have been the era when Francis was raising his family and travelling around the region.

The majority of the documented place names are locations on Parry Island (see Table 2). A number of other locations in the immediate area were also documented, but the focus remains on current Wasauksing (see Table 1). The use of English names for certain places was becoming common when Francis was living in the community. Many residents of the island—particularly in the town of Depot Harbour—were increasingly non-Native, and the suppression of traditional Nishnaabe religion and storytelling traditions hindered the transmission of traditional knowledge. Many places of historic importance and common use acquired English names during this era, and these names sometimes became more regularly used than the Ojibwe versions (e.g., Blackie's Island, Johnny Bay, Painkiller Lake). Generally, only Ojibwe-language-derived place names are included here.

Place Name Origins

Ojibwe-language place names have numerous origins. Some of the oldest were documented in stories preserved on birch bark scrolls, in petroglyphs, or within the oral tradition. Many of these original names—what elders at present-day Wasauksing recognize as the "old names"—were contained in stories of creation or the great migration. Such names were said to be in existence before humankind, derived only from the spiritual traditions of the people. Maintenance of these places and their stories was part of First Nations' stewardship of the land.

As traditional knowledge societies went underground because of the imposed restrictions of the Indian Act and pressure from both religious and educational institutions, the maintenance of such knowledge became harder. Reading the old birch bark scrolls or recounting legends in public settings was no longer possible. These "old names" often faded from memory as the stories became more difficult to tell and the storytellers became branded as sorcerers or witches. Some place names might even have been preserved in a "variant" form so as to protect their meanings or true locations. Francis lived throughout this era of underground ceremonial expression, and he witnessed first-hand how many of the old teachings and stories were fast fading away in Georgian Bay. His travels throughout the Great Lakes as a crewman provided opportunities to learn from Ojibwe people in many other regions where ceremonial practice and traditional knowledge had not yet significantly diminished. Francis endeavoured to learn as much as he could about these stories and traditions before they disappeared.

Duncan and Marie remembered how trips with their father were filled with stories about the places they were travelling through. Such stories became a regular part of evening conversations with him. Both Duncan and Marie remembered that few things made Francis smile more broadly than their successful recitation of a story he had told them earlier. It was not simply enough to remember the name of a place. It was its story that contained the special meaning. Perhaps most important to Francis was that the stories continued to be shared. This was why Duncan and Marie principally wanted me to write this book.

Many of the places described here were named based on local use of a natural resource by families or the larger community. Certain animals, fish, or plants often inspired place names. Spiritual entities were also sources of many place names. One such example is the *memegwesiwag,* "a tribe of little people" that lived along the rocky shores of the bay. The Ojibwe had great reverence for their homes, and non-Native travellers were taught to respect such locations. Duncan and Marie recall Francis telling a story similar to that told to Jenness by John Manatuwaba:

> At the north end of Parry Sound, in what white men call Split Rock channel, there is a crag known to the Indians as *Memegwesi's* crag. Some natives once set night lines there, but their trout were always stolen. At last one of the men sat up all night to watch for the thief. At dawn he saw a stone boat approaching manned by two *Memegwesi,* one a woman, the other bearded

> like a monkey. The watch awakened his companions, and they pursued the stone boat, which turned and made for the crag. Just as the thieves reached it the woman turned around and called to the Indians, "Now you know who stole your trout. Whenever you want calmer weather give us some tobacco, for this is our home." The boat and its occupants then entered the crag and disappeared; but the Indians still offer tobacco to these *Memegwesi* whenever they pass their home.[5]

Other places on the island were named for the presence of other spiritual entities known to inhabit that locale. Names relating to "thunderbirds" (*bine-siiwag*), "merpeople" (*nbaanaabeg*), "great serpents" (*mshi-gnebigook*), the great "underground/underwater cat" (*mshi-bizhii*), and various tribes of little people were all once broadly known to community members. These were the kinds of names that could not be documented here. Duncan and Marie remembered their parents leaving offerings of tobacco if they journeyed close to one of these locations. People would never stay at them for long. If they ever had to travel close to one, they always passed by quickly out of respect.

A significant historical event also resulted in many unique names still found throughout the bay. The long series of wars between Ojibwe and Haudenosaunee peoples in Georgian Bay left behind a number of names, such as Nbo-mnis ("Death Island"), Kowaabi-mnis ("He-Who-Watches Island"), and Bapekoondibeneyaashing ("Skull Island"). One of Duncan's favourite stories was about the Martyr Islands located west of Parry Island. After a fierce battle with the Ojibwe, the Haudenosaunee raiding parties managed to escape to these islands, changing themselves into pink snakes to avoid capture. No strangers to medicine powers or battle tactics, the Ojibwe bound their enemies to their changed form and stole their canoes to ensure they would never escape. Duncan said you can still see these snakes today. These were the stories that filled the names of many such places throughout Georgian Bay.

Some distinct categories of names emerged among those found at Wasauksing. There were many more places of importance that the Nishnaabe people would have recognized a century ago. It is also likely that in the past the place names themselves would have been distributed differently among the following categories. The names that could have been elicited in the early 1900s might have more closely reflected the distribution of plants, animals, and spiritual entities than the large number of names reflecting human habitation and family use in the current summary. So too would there have been a greater number of names rooted in mythological origins than the few noted here.

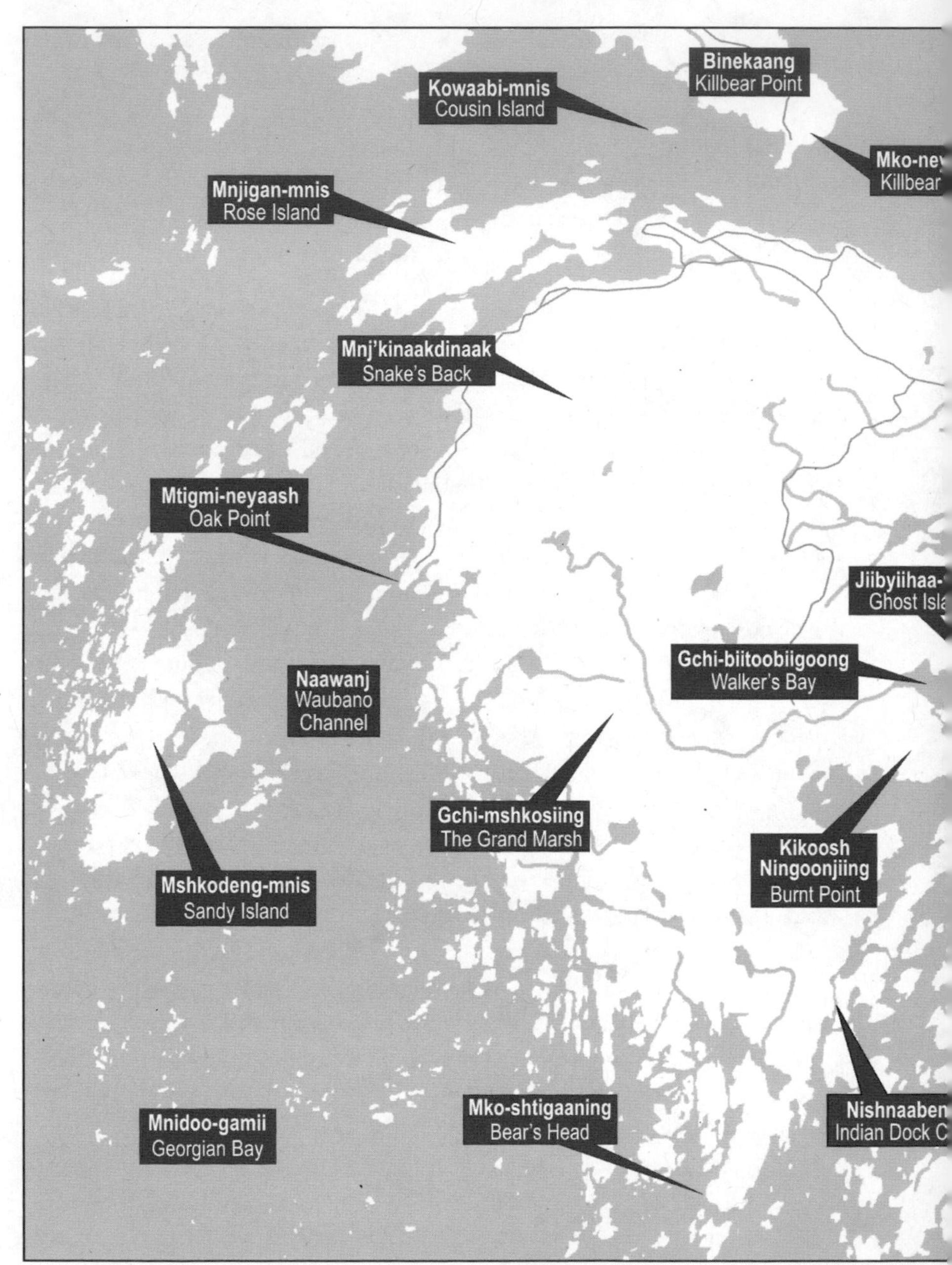

12. Traditional Place Names: Wasauksing First Nation/Parry Island Band. Map use with permission of Angus Leech and Brian McInnes. Design by Weldon Hiebert

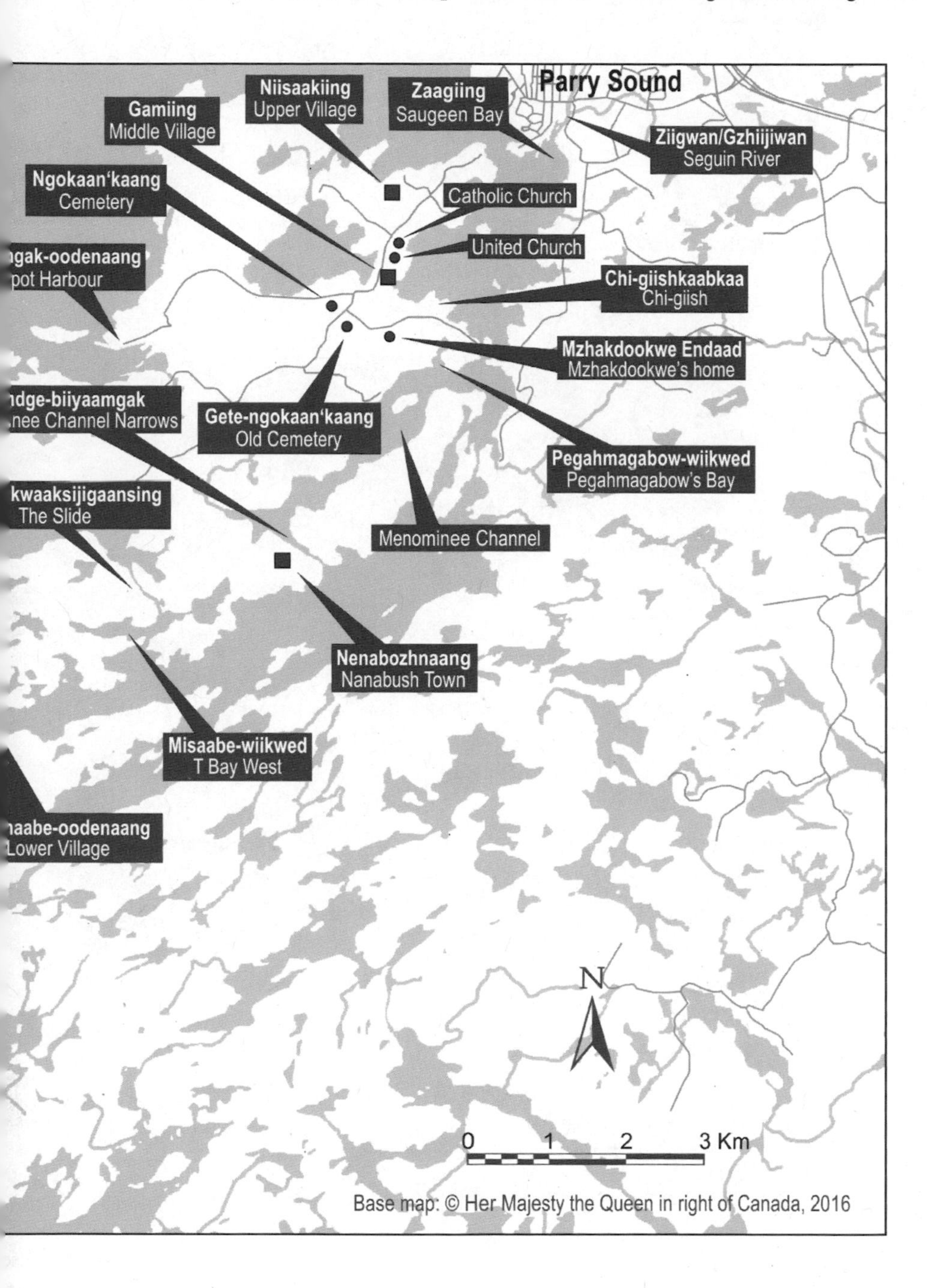

Parry Sound
Niisaakiing
Upper Village
Zaagiing
Saugeen Bay
Gamiing
Middle Village
Ziigwan/Gzhiijiwan
Seguin River
Ngokaan'kaang
Cemetery
Catholic Church
United Church
gak-oodenaang
pot Harbour
Chi-giishkaabkaa
Chi-giish
Mzhakdookwe Endaad
Mzhakdookwe's home
dge-biiyaamgak
nee Channel Narrows
Gete-ngokaan'kaang
Old Cemetery
Pegahmagabow-wiikwed
Pegahmagabow's Bay
kwaaksijigaansing
The Slide
Menominee Channel
Nenabozhnaang
Nanabush Town
Misaabe-wiikwed
T Bay West
aabe-oodenaang
Lower Village
N
0 1 2 3 Km
Base map: © Her Majesty the Queen in right of Canada, 2016

Table 2. Wasauksing First Nation/Parry Island Band Place Names.

Location	Common Name	Meaning
Binekaang	Killbear Point	Partridge Abode
Biindge-biiyaamgak	Menominee Channel Narrows	The Place it Comes to Enter/The Narrows
Catholic Church		
Chi-giishkaabkaa	Chi-giish	The Great Rock Cut
Demiimgak-oodenaang	Depot Harbour	At the Deep Water Town
Gamiing	Middle Village	At the Lake
Gchi-biitoobiigoong	Walker's Bay	At the Great Marsh
Gchi-mshkosiing		At the Great Swamp
Gete-ngokaan'kaang		The Old Cemetery
Location	**Common Name**	**Meaning**
Jiibyiihaa-mnis		Ghost Island
Kikoosh Ningoonjiing	Burnt Point	Where the Old Kettle is Hanging
Kowaabi-mnis	Cousin Island	He Watches in Wait Island
Menominee Channel		
Misaabe-wiikwed		Giant's Bay
Miizhashk-wiikwed/ Mnidoo-wiikwed	Hay Bay	Hay Bay/Spirit Bay
Mko-neyaash	Killbear Point	Bear's Point
Mko-shtigaaning	Bear's Head	At the Bear's Head
Mnidoo-gamii	Georgian Bay	Great Lake of the Spirit
Mnj'kinaakdinaak	Snake's Back	Fench-like Ridge of Earth
Mnjigan-mnis	Rose Island	Deer Run Island
Mshkodeng-mnis	Sandy Island	Clearing Island
Mtigmi-neyaash	Oak Point	Oak Point
Mzhakdookwe Endaad		Mzhakdookwe's home

Naawanj	Waubano Channel	Out on the Bay
Nishnaabenaang	Indian Dock Channel	Nishnaabe Place
Nishnaabe-oodenaang	Lower Village	At the Indian Town
Niisaakiing	Upper Village	Upper Village
Nenabozhnaang/ Aabtooyihiing		Nanabush Town/ The Half Way Point
Ngokaan'kaang	The Cemetery	The Cemetery
Pegahmagabow-wiikwed	Pegahmagabow's Bay	Pegahmagabow's Bay
United Church		
Zaagiing	Saugeen Bay	At the Inlet/Where the river comes out
Zhooshkwaaksijigaansing		The Slide
Ziigwan/ Gzhiijiwan	Seguin River	The Early Spring/ Fast Flowing River

Table 3. Origins of Wasauksing Place Names.

Place Names Based on Family Residence	
James-wiikwed	James's bay
Judge-gtigaan	Judge's farm
Kegzhiihaange-wiikwed	Kegzhiihaange's bay
Medweyaash-gtigaan	Medwayosh farm
Misaabe-wiikwed	Misaabe's bay
Mnidoowaabi-gdaaki	Manitowaba hill
Mnoomini-neyaash	Rice point
Nenabozhnaang	Nanibush place
Pegahmagabow-wiikwed	Pegahmagabow bay
Waabgiizhig-wiikwed	Waabgiizhig's bay
Zaagaankwad-wiikwed	Zaagaankwad's bay
Place Names Based on Geographical Features	
Biitoobiigoong	Where the ground is floating
Biindge-biiyaamgak	Where it comes to enter (channel)
Chi-giishkaabkaa (Chi-giishk)	The great cut rock
Daashkamigkaang/Daashkaabkaa	Where the rock is split
Gamiing	At the lake
Gzhiijiwan	Fast-flowing river
Gchi-biitoobiigoong	A great mass of floating land

Gchi-mshkosiing	The great swamp
Gchi-pwakwadnaamgad	The great mound
Gchi-waanaang	At the great rounding of the shore
Gwekwekjiwang	Where it flows back and forth
Miizhashk-wiikwed	Hay Bay
Mko-neyaashing	Bear Point
Mko-shtigwaaning	Bear's Head
Mtigmi-neyaash	Oak Point
Naadwe-bgaskdiyehaagwad	Waves slapping the enemy's rear
Naawanj	On the bay
Niisaaki	Down the hill
Tkibi	The coldwater spring
Waanaang	The rounding of the shoreline
Waasaaksing	The shining of the leaning poles/ shining rocks
Waasgwanjiing	The light/shining object that is floating
Wiikwedoonsing	The small bay
Zhiibaawdaangaak	Sand bar that goes across
Zaaghigaanzhish	The small lake
Zaaghiganing	At the lake

Place Names Based on Human Habitation/Use of Landscape

Aabtooyihiing	The halfway point
Nishnaabenaang	Nishnaabe place
Nishnaabe-oodenaang	Nishnaabe town
Nishnaabe-ziibiins	Nishnaabe creek

Place Names Based on the Presence of Fish/Animals

Binekaang	Partridge abode (Killbear)
Bineshiinh-wiikwed	The bay of birds
Mko-neyaash	Bear point
Mnjigan-mnis/Mnzhigan mnis	Deer run island
Nit-neyaash	Spear point

Place Names Based on Historical Events

Kowaabi	He-who-watches-out
Kowaabi-mnis	He-who-watches island
Naadwe-bgaskdiyehaagwad	Waves slapping the enemy's behind

Place Names Based on Spiritual Occurrences/Entities	
Jiibyiihaa-mnis	Ghost Island
Mnidoo-gamii	Spirit Lake
Mnidoo-gdaaki	Spirit Hill
Mnidoo-wiikwed	Spirit Bay
Mnidoo-zaaghiganing	Spirit Lake
Shkodeng-mnis	Fire Island
Waasgwanjiing	The light/shining object that is floating
Waaseyaakosing	Land shining from the reflection of sacred light
Ziigwan	The maiden of spring
Zhaawshko-neyaash	Green Point
Place Names Based on Mythological Occurrences	
Daashkaabikaang	Where the rock is split
Kikosh ningoonjiing	Where the old kettle is hanging
Mnj'kinaakdinaak	A ridge of earth/sand shaped like a fence

Table 4. Variations of the Wasauksing Place Name.

Documented Name	Meaning	Location
Waasaaksing	Shining rock	Parry Island
Wausakwasing	Shining rock	Parry Island, Parry Sound Harbour
Wah-sah-ko-sing	White all around the shore	Parry Sound, the Big Sound
Wasauksing	Something white in the distance	Hulett's Bay, Parry Island
Wasoksing	White stakes you can see in the distance	Parry Island
Wasquising		Sandy Island
Wausakwasene	Distant view, distant outlook	Parry Sound, Saugeen (Zaagiing) Bay
Wau-sah-wa-sene	The distant view	Parry Sound Harbour/Port
Wau-sak-ah-sing	Shining light	Parry Sound/ Bay Area

Source: Adapted from McInnes (1999, 55).

Wasauksing

Perhaps the oldest, most significant, and most complicated place name was that of Francis's home reserve itself: Wasauksing. Both its exact English meaning and its specific location have provoked much debate. Written sources seem to reflect only some of these general opinions, summarized in Table 4. The only general consensus among local elders is that the name Wasauksing is a variant of some former term.

The name Wasauksing is often attributed to Sandy Island, also known as Mshkode-mnis ("Clearing Island") or Shkode-mnis ("Fire Island"). Many have also contended that Wasauksing was the name of a mainland Nishnaabe settlement in existence until sometime in the 1850s.[6] This village was generally understood to span the territory from Belvedere Hill to the east side of the Seguin (*gzhiijiwan* or "fast current") River—the present location of the town of Parry Sound.[7] However, other sources,[8] and the vast majority of elders asked over the past quarter-century, contend that Wasauksing was best directly identified as Parry Island:

> I, James Edward Wheatley, a member of the Wasauksing First Nation of Parry Island, solemnly declare that I am 91 years of age, ... that I have lived most of my life on Parry Island, ... that the name for Sandy Island translated in the Ojibwe dialect of Parry Island means michkodang [or] "level land without too much timber," ... that the Wasauksing location was the tip of Parry Island across from Sandy Island, that the definition of the word Wasauksing is "shining object seen from a distance," and that this Ojibwe word Wasauksing was given to this specific area when the Ojibwe used this place as a land-mark.[9]

Although permanent settlement of Parry Island did not occur until 1870–80, there had been continuous use of the territory by Nishnaabe peoples since at least the great migration. Koennecke refers to the observations of a Methodist missionary, who commented in 1836 that the inhabitants of camps located at Parry Island were absent.[10] Napier, a secretary of the Indian Department, is also cited in Koennecke for his observations in late 1850: "The southern and western parts of Parry Island had been settled by Indians before. He recorded a number of abandoned and overgrown clearings totalling close to one hundred acres."[11] This is consistent with local descriptions of past historical ceremonial locations.

13. The Wasauksing swing bridge, built in the late 1890s, a well-known area landmark. Courtesy of Parry Sound Public Library.

Francis once told his children about a trip he made to the island with his adopted family as a small child. He vividly recalled crossing the huge swing bridge and travelling to Three Mile Lake (Mnidoo-zaaghigan) in the middle of the reserve. Francis witnessed one of the last full Midewiwin lodge ceremonies held on the island at that time. He remembered the songs and other

14. Shining white rocks and wood at Wasauksing. Photos by Brian McInnes.

ceremonial rites but was most fascinated with the fire whose flames seemed to alternate with all the colours of the rainbow while the old men narrated sacred legends. This history, connected to that of the great migrations, wars, spiritual revelations, and centuries of use by their ancestors, made Wasauksing of enduring value to the Ojibwe people. Whether by shining logs, rocks, or sand, or the cumulative reflection of all parts of the earth when the great shell lit up the shore during the migration, Wasauksing was always a place of light and life for Francis, as it had been for all those who had come before him.

Nishnaabemwin— Language of the People and the Land

This short reflection was recorded during the fall of 1995 at an Ojibwe-language conference in Sault Ste. Marie. Duncan was describing how important it was for Nishnaabe people to retain and use their Ojibwe language before the use of English or French. Like his father, Duncan believed that even contemporary business should be discussed in the Ojibwe language so that a calmer and more respectful discourse might ensue. As a spiritual language, Ojibwe provided the people with a special connection to their identity and purpose. Only through the language, Duncan believed, could we be sure that our thinking was reflective of the values and teachings given to the Nishnaabe people in the beginning.

> *Geget sa nii go nishin—Nishnaabewaadziwin.*
> It is indeed so good—this traditional Nishnaabe way of life and belief.
>
> *Mii go ge-giinwind gaa-zhi-miin'gozying iihow daa-giisaadendaagwad wnitooying iw.*
> We too were given something special, and it would be tragic if we lost this.
>
> *Mii go gewiin maabam Mnidoo gaa-zhi-miin'goying iihow ji-naadziiying iihow nake mii gaa-zhi-miin'gozying iihow gegoo enweying.*
> For it was the Creator who gave to us this way of life and blessed us with this way of speaking.
>
> *Aapji shpendaagwad maanda enweying ge-giinwind ji-kendmang ji-moozhtooying geget gwa nishnaabewiying.*
> This beautiful language is worth more than anything and is what truly lets us know and feel what it means to be Nishnaabe.
>
> *Mii ezhi-yaamgak iihow nishnaabemyin mii go ge-zhi-moozhtooyin iihow eyaawiyin geget gwa.*
> This is how it is when you are speaking the Nishnaabe language, you can truly feel who you are.

Naan'godnong ge-ni-kidyaan iihow kaa ndaa-nsitaagoosii kidyaan iihow.

Sometimes, when I speak my language today, I am not understood at all.

Kina gwa, kina gwa enchiiying—kina sa go naa eyaawiying ji-moozhtooying iihow geget gwa Nishnaabewiying gdanishnaabewendam.

To be Indian is to talk Indian—for all of our people, we would feel and understand what it truly means to be Nishnaabe and what it means to think as Nishnaabe.

Language, Culture, and Story

Gegoo-sh ko ndizhiyaa pii gaa-kwaandwiyaan odi gijiyihing go daa-naaniibwiyaan gegoo-sh ko ndizhiyaa en'gwen gwa.
I felt something when I climbed up there to the top; as I stood there, I am sure that I felt something.

Manj go naa iidog.
I really don't know what it was.

Gnimaa go naa gii-mkwendmaan iihow gaa-bi-naajmotawiwaad giw kiwenziiyag.
Maybe because I was thinking about all the stories those old men had told me.

—Duncan Pegahmagabow

Learning the language, culture, and stories of the Nishnaabeg was a natural part of community life for Francis Pegahmagabow. He would be among the last to grow up with the older generations whose lifeways were not significantly influenced by settler culture expectations, institutions, and implements. Hunting, gathering, and farming were primary means of sustenance for the Nishnaabeg even as some participation in the wage economy became necessary for most.[1] Government control of the lives of the Nishnaabeg tightened significantly at the beginning of the twentieth century, and the cultural and social norms of home and community life underwent significant change.[2] Communities were still comprised of family collectives that openly shared resources with each other and had limited contact with settler populations. Francis experienced some of those original models of Indigenous spirituality, socialization, and learning.

Reconstructing his stories was beset with challenges, even for a family member with a long-time interest in his life. I never had the opportunity to meet Francis, and virtually everything I know about his life came from written or verbal accounts of others. Neither source was easy to come by or interpret. Written materials were often hard to find or access and usually meant obtaining complex permissions and driving long distances to find little new information. But every corroborated fact, name, or event seemed to be a victory over the foreboding cloud that obscured the life and achievements of this man. His limited English-language skills made his letters difficult to decipher even if one was familiar with the unique style of English that had developed among the Ojibwe. Even harder was learning how to read through the interpretations of non-cultural members who did not share the same world view or perspective of the Georgian Bay Nishnaabeg. Learning how to read through the words—or between the lines, if you will—would become as important a skill as any other.

The oral stories of Francis Pegahmagabow proved at times to be just as difficult to collect and interpret. Family members shared what they knew, but a critical shift in language use (from Ojibwe to English) affected the transmission of the old stories from one generation to the next. These stories seemed to be embedded in an older era, as if somehow bringing them into the present, and even into the English language, would be incongruous with their substance. Elders thought that looking at the stories through any vantage point other than the linguistic, cultural, and even social lens of the historical Nishnaabeg would be a misinterpretion of the people and their life. Duncan and Marie were the best sources of information about their father's experience and stories. Although the stories collected here were not directly told to me by Francis, he thought them important enough to make sure his children remembered and would hopefully share them with others.

Members of both the Wasauksing and the Shawanaga communities provided invaluable sources of insight into Francis's life and history. I sometimes presented content from the Jenness book as a means of engaging discussion but generally found doing so unhelpful. Local reactions to his 1935 ethnography were mixed. Although he authentically captured many words and stories of community members, he also drew conclusions that seemed to be both judgmental and predetermined. Community members generally participated in his study, though they were clearly dedicated to protecting each other and more intimate details of local culture.

Although community life in the 1990s was markedly different from that of Francis's time, there remained a strong ethos about safeguarding the dignity of a community member no matter which historical disagreements took place between individuals. My relationship to Francis as a great-grandson was an important factor; the sincerity of my request for information was real, yet there was enough distance for non-relatives to speak openly about their experiences with him. I quickly learned how to balance both commendations and criticisms in the formation of my own opinions and perspectives.

I had a special relationship with Francis's two youngest children, Duncan and Marie. Their stories provided me with an honest and heartfelt look into the life of their father and the challenges he experienced. The stories featured in this book are the ones they wanted shared with everyone. Francis was a man of the world. He was well travelled and friends with people of many ethnicities and origins. These stories are meant for all of the communities and peoples Francis cared about. I think what I value most from the many years of working with Duncan and Marie was their insistence on speaking to me in Francis's Ojibwe language as they told me our family stories. Although Francis had learned enough English and French to successfully interact with Euro-Canadian society, he always thought it was only through his own language that he could express his true self. One of the beliefs he imparted to Duncan was the connection among language, culture, and identity. Duncan shared his father's opinion of the Ojibwe language in the following way:

> *Aapji shpendaagwad maanda enweying ge-giinwind ji-kendmang ji-moozhtooying geget gwa nishnaabewiying.*
>
> This beautiful language is worth more than anything and is what truly lets us know and feel what it means to be Nishnaabe.
>
> *Mii ezhi-yaamgak iihow nishnaabemyin mii go ge-zhi-moozhtooyin iihow eyaawiyin geget gwa.*
>
> This is how it is when you are speaking the Nishnaabe language, you can truly feel who you are.

Francis observed many changes and adaptations in Nishnaabe communities throughout his lifetime. The broad loss of language was one he never foresaw. His oldest sons returned from the Catholic boarding school hesitant to use Ojibwe but still able to do so if they chose. What Francis could not have known was that English would almost exclusively dominate the lives of the people by the time of his grandchildren and great-grandchildren. This almost total loss of language, Duncan once commented to me, would have hurt him more than any injury sustained in the Great War. It was his father's unique love of Ojibwe that inspired the following commentary on his Native language and why his stories are featured first in Ojibwe throughout this book.

Ojibwemowin—The Ojibwe Language

The Ojibwe language is believed by the Nishnaabeg to be something they were given as a part of their stewardship of the earth, as Duncan so eloquently remarked in the preceding narrative, "*Nishnaabemwin*—Language of the People and the Land." Ojibwe continues to be a valuable way of communicating about historical and contemporary frames of life. It also serves as the oldest and most substantial reservoir of cultural history indexing traditional items, ideas, and relationships that have been important to the people since time immemorial. Perhaps more succinctly, the Ojibwe language is a reflection of the way the people see the world and their place within it:

> There is no doubt, however, that there is a correlation between the form and content of a language and the beliefs, values, and needs present in the culture of its speakers. The vocabulary of a language provides us with a catalogue of things considered important to the society, an index to the way speakers categorize experience, and often a record of past contacts and cultural borrowing: the grammar may reveal the way time is segmented and organized, beliefs about animacy and the relative power of beings, and salient social categories in the culture....[3]

Studying a language is a means of examining the very roots of the culture itself. With culture changing faster than language, Ojibwe stands as a valuable source of cultural perspective and practice. The anecdotes, stories, and teachings of the people become ways of sharing the deeper meaning of the language and culture that, in its truest and total expression, reveals the quality and character of the people's Nishnaabe soul.

Language and communication patterns were quite different from the English and French languages imposed on the Ojibwe of Georgian Bay. Traditional Ojibwe speech was not characteristically marked by greeting routines, small talk, or leave takings. Language was not to be idly used, but there was great value in using language to build relationships.[4] The highly descriptive nature of Ojibwe allows for vibrant traditions of humorous speech and storytelling.[5] Silence was also a valued part of Ojibwe communication. Francis was known for long pauses of reflection during visits with his guests. Although this was familiar to his own Nishnaabe people, it could make his non-Native visitors quite uneasy. His children recalled that he would lightly chuckle or smile in these moments to reassure his guests should they become uncomfortable with the silence that often punctuated conversation.

Greeting expressions were comparatively rare in the historical day-to-day interactions of the Georgian Bay Ojibwe. Welcome and belonging were understood among the Nishnaabeg, and such conversational exchanges seemed to be unnecessary and even contrary to the spiritual engagement that occurred between individuals upon meeting: "When you meet a man on the road you should never address him until you have passed him, for your soul and his soul continue on their way and only your bodies and shadows stay to converse; if there should be disagreement between you it will pass away quickly for your souls are unaffected. (Even today the Ojibwa of Parry Island often pass one another in silence, then turn back to converse)."[6] Visiting was welcome, but gossip or malicious speech against others was discouraged. Discourse on practical matters of life and work was, of course, necessary and common. Weather and water conditions were always important topics of conversation, but they were always discussed in the sense of how to prepare for such circumstances and never in complaint or disrespect. Language had a spiritual function, and care was taken in its use.

A greeting term that the Nishnaabeg were known to use during formal or ceremonial settings was *boozhoo.* Many elders are surprised at the prevalence of this term in conversational Ojibwe today. It was formerly rare to hear it in the home, except when a relative or friend who had long been absent visited. Or when a soldier returned home. The word is derived from the Ojibwe name of the great cultural hero Nanabush (Nenaboozho) and is not a borrowing of the French term *bonjour.* Duncan eloquently described the significance of this word:

> *Boozhoo* is more spiritual in meaning. When you say *boozhoo,* you are acknowledging the good in that person when you see them. Like Nanabush. Nanabush is like our Jesus Christ. When you say *boozhoo,* you are acknowledging the Nanabush, or Jesus Christ, the good in that person, whatever way you want to interpret it. Usually with *boozhoo* you take their hand. You are acknowledging the Nanabush in that person. Everybody is good. With Nanabush, or Jesus Christ, he left a little bit of himself in each one of us. It is our mandate, our job, to find that little bit of good. That is our lifetime job. To one day say, "I can understand it." Then it all comes together.

Whether one uses the term *boozhoo* or *weweni boozhoo* ("in a careful way do I make this greeting"), a sense of mutual respect is implicit. Francis especially encouraged his children to greet those with whom they might have had disagreements. Seeing the good in others first was the way children were traditionally raised in the Wasauksing community.

Language, Culture, and World View

The ultimate significance of the relationship between language and culture is manifest in how one perceives and understands the surrounding world. Early major proponents of the idea that language has a direct effect on one's perception and cultural interpretation of the world included Edward Sapir and Benjamin Whorf.[7] Their conclusions were drawn from a comparison of different languages, including a number of Native American languages such as Hopi, Mayan, and Inuktitut. They determined that different languages tended to classify the world in unique ways and that these classifications played a role in both influencing and revealing the linguistic ideology of Native speakers:

> The categories and types that we isolate from the world of phenomena we do not find there because they stare every observer in the face; on the contrary, the world is presented in a kaleidoscopic flux of impressions which has to be organized by our minds—and this means largely by the linguistic systems in our minds. We cut nature up, organize it into concepts, and ascribe significances as we do, largely because we are parties to an agreement to organize it in this way—an agreement that holds throughout our speech community and is codified in the patterns of our language.[8]

The animate classification by Native speakers of drums, pipes, animal pelts, shakers, or tobacco is one such culture-specific classification that reveals how the Ojibwe uniquely perceive and know the world.

The term "world view" refers here to the sum total array of cognitive processes unique to the Nishnaabe mind. The Ojibwe language is both key and map to this unique way of perceiving and comprehending the world. One unique aspect of the Nishnaabe world view as revealed through the Ojibwe language pertains to the grammatical category of animacy. Everything in the Nishnaabe language is classified as either animate or inanimate. The animate/inanimate distinction in Ojibwe functions in a similar way to masculine/feminine classifications in other languages. As in many other cultures, animate and inanimate distinctions are generally determined based upon the quality of biological life. Thus, trees, animals, fish, amphibians, and insects are considered animate. Biological parameters are not always the sole determinant of animate status. A number of inert or biologically inanimate objects such as pipes, pots, boards, and shells are classified as being grammatically animate. That is, these objects are spoken of in ways similar to biologically living objects such as fish, animals, or trees.

That snow, nets, or beads are described in the same way as humans, animals, or trees, and not in the same way as other inert objects such as buildings, books, or plates, is often problematic for cultural outsiders to understand. Ojibwe speakers don't necessarily view a grammatically animate pipe as being like a bird, insect, or fish. Activities such as breathing and eating are not necessarily limiting or defining factors. Elders at Wasauksing have long contended that a degree of spiritual quality or relevance is an important part of the distinction. The animate state of an object might be as dependent on an associated spiritual quality in the Ojibwe world view as on a biological parameter.

All of the following terms were collected on Parry Island and are representative of categorizations familiar to Francis Pegahmagabow (see Table 5). These words were subsequently organized into a number of categories based upon physical or functional similarities. Terms for humans, animals, fish, amphibians, and insects, all animate, are not included. Terms for plants, which vary greatly in their animate or inanimate designation, are listed here.

Table 5. Irregular Animate Terms in Ojibwe.

Ceremonial/Religious Instruments	
pipe	*pwaagan*
Midewiwin pelt	*Mide-wyaan*
shaker	*zhiishiigwan*
whistle	*gwiishkojigan*
drum	*dewehgan*
sweat lodge stone	*madoodoosin*
small round stone	*siniins*
beads	*mnidoominens*
cowrie shell	*miigis*
shell	*esens*
cross	*aazhodeyaatig*
Spiritual Beings	
spiritual being	*mnidoo*
ghost	*jiibay*
his/her soul	*ojichaagwan*

water lynx	*mshi-bzhii*
large serpent	*gchi-gnebig*
little person	*memegwesi*
mermaid	*nbaanaabe-kwe*
merman	*nbaanaabe*
windigo	*wiindigoo*
flying skeleton	*baagak*
Celestial Bodies	
sun	*giizis/nmishoomis*
moon	*dbiki-giizis/nookmis*
star	*nangoons*
sundog	*nwaachige-giizis*
rainbow	*nimkii-naabkwaagan*
thunder/thunder being	*nimkii*
sky/heaven	*giizhig*
Utilitarian Instruments/ Tools	
bow	*mtigwaab*
net	*sab*
mortar	*bootaagan*
pen/writing instrument	*zhibiihganaak*
pencil/writing instrument	*zhibiihganaatig*
arrowhead (barbed)	*sawaan*
file	*siboojgan*
flint	*biiwaanag*
grindstone	*zhiigwanaabik*
net sinker	*sinaabiig*
Geography/Weather	
snow	*goon*
ice	*mkwam*
clay	*waabgan*
Transportation	
airplane	*mbaasjigan*
bicycle	*biimskowebshkigan*
car	*daabaan*
ski	*zhooshkjiwaanaatig*
sled	*zhooshkjiwe-daabaans*
snowshoe	*aagim*
toboggan	*nbagdaabaan*
train	*shkode-daabaan*
wagon	*det'bisenh-daabaan*
motor	*biiwaabik*
wheel	*detbise*

15. Julia and Clara Medwayosh of Parry Island using mortar and pestle. National Museum of the American Indian, Smithsonian Institution, N14452. Photo by Frederick Johnson.

Why all such seemingly inert objects have been designated as animate is unclear. Some of these questions might have found interesting extended answers among the Nishnaabeg of Francis's time. Spiritual relevance is a connective element in most cases and the capacity for movement and growth in others. One is left to wonder why other culturally or spiritually important entities such as the heart, hair, teeth, drumsticks, or even sweetgrass are not designated as being animate. But mystery has always been a part of the Spirit itself and, for the Nishnaabeg, something to be accepted.

Language and Culture Shift

Linguistic and cultural worlds of reference were beginning to shift for the Ojibwe of Francis Pegahmagabow's time. Like many of his contemporaries, Francis learned at least one other language and culture throughout his life. His French-language proficiency was reportedly as good as his command of spoken English because of early interaction with French Canadian families, traders, and merchants. For the Ojibwe, mastery of language was absolutely vital to understanding the cultural world view. Over time, this would even become equated with Nishnaabe identity itself. As Duncan once directly remarked, "to be Indian is to talk Indian":

> *Kina gwa kina gwa enchiiying kina-sh ko naa eyaawiying ji-moozh-tooying iihow geget gwa Nishnaabewiying gidanishnaabewendam.*
>
> For all of our people, we would feel and understand what it truly means to be Nishnaabe and what it means to think that way.

Multilingualism was not uncommon in pre-contact North America. The Nishnaabeg placed great historical value on their relationships with neighbouring tribes, who often spoke entirely different languages. Learning settler languages proved to be important in this regard and was a task at which the Native peoples of Georgian Bay excelled. The challenge was not to let settler cultures and languages take the place of Indigenous ways of living and speaking.

Traditional people and elders at Wasauksing continue to affirm their belief in the spiritual dimension of language by insisting that prayers or traditional speeches be made in Ojibwe rather than English. This can still be observed in community gatherings and local ceremonial activities. Translating the Native language into English is difficult when trying to capture the meaning intended by the speaker. The hardest part of translating the narrative art of Duncan and Marie was that it seemed to destroy the finer meanings that could not be expressed by English. Everything was factually communicated, but the deeper feeling, the love that came through their words, seemed to evade my English-language renderings—even with their help. This did not dissuade me from presenting an English translation alongside the Ojibwe original in the hope that it would inspire interest in the deeper messages of the story that eluded representation in this book.

Stories as Life

It was Francis Densmore who once remarked that the Ojibwe have a song for everything. So too it seems that the Ojibwe have a story for everything. From the creation of the earth to the most basic of moral lessons, stories seem to touch on every part of life and experience. Francis Pegahmagabow himself had a particular affinity and love for stories. This might have been engendered growing up in a community of great storytellers in which long winter nights were spent listening to epic tales of the cultural hero Nanabush and his adventures in the world. Although it was common enough to help out a community elder by bringing her fresh game or firewood, a young Francis often found his efforts rewarded by the stories he was told. He would one day tell his children that he learned how to live a good life and be a good person by remembering what the stories had to teach him.

Perhaps it was these early experiences listening to the stories of others that made Francis such a reflective and careful listener. The stories inspired within him a love of history and attention to good values. He had a deep respect for tribal elders and the wisdom they carried; ironically, this would one day work against him in political forums that perceived such interest in traditionalism as antithetical to progress. Diamond Jenness made the following observation of Francis in his 1935 ethnography:

> Being of profoundly meditative temperament, he began to write down the lore of his people, but later lost the notebooks in which he had jotted down their customs and traditions. He was elected Chief of the Parry Island Indians after he returned from the war and held the position for two years, when he stirred up some opposition by urging the old men and women to narrate in the council house the earlier customs of the people. Although comparatively young, and more travelled than most of the Indians, he was more saturated with their former outlook on life than the majority and more capable of interpreting the old beliefs. Occasionally his interpretations may have been a little more advanced than the average Indian would have given, yet they were a logical development of the lay beliefs such as were possible to any philosophically minded Ojibwa before the coming of Europeans.[9]

If the tribal council hall was not a place for the old stories, then Francis made sure that his home was. His children recalled not just hearing stories but also growing up on them. Marie remarked to me once that listening to her father was "like our television back then." The highly descriptive and verb-rich nature of the Ojibwe language made listening to stories a colourful experience. Stories were both fun and entertaining but could also be poignant and serious. "Knowing the story of something changed it somehow, it changed you," Duncan once said. "They were important for life."

There are two particular styles or genres of storytelling that Francis's children best remembered. The first genre includes those stories classified as *dibaajmowin,* best described as one's personal or general stories of life. These *dibaajmowinan* ("stories") can be told at any time, though some narrators prefer to wait until evening before reciting certain ones. The second style includes traditional legends or myths, commonly known as *aadsookaanan.* Such legends are generally told to demonstrate a moral lesson or explain the origin of something in the world. Two such examples of legends contained in this book are "Thirty Thousand Islands" and "*Gchi-Ngig*—The Giant Otter."

Many stories have their own protocols or conditions under which they can be shared: this is particularly true of the *aadzookaanan* that can be told only in winter and only when there is snow on the ground. I remember visiting Duncan one December evening to talk about traditional legends (*aadzookaanan*), and I had brought him tobacco and a gift, as is customary. This was in late 1997 during the El Niño weather phenomenon that held back the ice and snow almost all winter. When I asked him if he might be able to tell me a few legends that evening, he looked out the window and remarked, "*Gaawiin goon bi-sii*" ("There is no snow on the ground"). We had a pleasant evening visiting, but no legends were told that night or any night that particular winter.

I once asked Marie if she had ever heard anyone tell a legend in the summer months. Her immediate reaction was that she had not, but she later remembered that two of her older brothers had once told legends while on a fishing trip together. They were young men by this time and allowed to camp overnight on their own. Francis warned all of his children that telling a legend out of season was to risk having a frog crawl into their beds later that night. Marie had always thought this was just a silly expression. That was until her older brothers spent a rainy summer evening in a tent recounting their favourite legends to each other. The frogs seemed to be unusually loud that night, and the boys had a hard time sleeping. When finally they drifted off, they were awakened by the sound of a particularly large bullfrog scratching on the side of their tent. This continued all night. The boys vowed never to tell stories out of season again and implored their siblings not to repeat their mistake. Marie said her father even looked a little surprised when they reported this to him the next day. "He believed in all those old teachings," Marie said, "and that is what kept us safe."

16. Biindge-biiyaamgak—Menominee Channel Narrows. Photo by Brian McInnes.

The stories featured in this book are primarily *dibaajmowinan* that frame aspects of Francis Pegahmagabow's experience in the world. Within them are embedded simple lessons about life as well as truths about the spiritual and cultural world view of the Nishnaabeg. They provide insight into the kind of man Francis was at his core and the way he knew the world to be. Whether we accept each of these stories as truth or find it the equivalent of a "frog in the bed" allegory, they all contribute to understanding the broader world view of the First Nations of that era. Francis was fiercely loyal to his Nishnaabe identity and the way it shaped his belief system. These stories reveal something about why being Nishnaabe was so meaningful to him and how and why he lived his life as he did.

Gchi-Ngig—The Giant Otter

This story was told by Francis Pegahmagabow to Duncan when he was a young boy living at Nenabozhnaang, a small village on the Parry Island Reserve. While on a fishing excursion, Duncan asked his father about how a channel they had just passed through had been made. His father answered his question with this story. Duncan heard the same story told almost identically by his uncle Levi Nanibush many years later.

Mii dash go wedi nake aazhwiyhiing iihow waa-dbaajdamaan yahaa Jim Nanibush gaa-nji-mdaabiimtood.
I am going to tell a story about a place on the other side of where Jim Nanibush had a landing.

Aazhwiyhiing go wodi nake odi iihow Nenabozhnaang neyaash maa yaamgad yahaa go maa bdakshing Zhingwaak.
Over on the other side of Nanibush town there is a point of land on which stands a pine.

Mii maa ngoji gaa-daad ow yahaa Giiwedin ow Jim Nanibush.
This is the place where Giiwedin lived, Jim Nanibush.

Mii maa ngoji gaa-daad.
This was where he lived.

Mii dash iihow wedi aazhwiyhiing go maa nake neyaashiins biindge-biiyaamgad odi.
Now over there on the other side of this little point is a narrows.

Mii-sh go naa maa daawaad maa giw Nishnaabeg Nenabozhnaang.
This is where those people were living—at Nanibush town.

Mii-sh giiwenh iw gii-oodetoowaad ezhaawaad odi Parry Sound gii-ni-kwiinwidgenag go naa gii-ni-wiijiiwndwaad go naa.
One day they made a trip to town; they all went together to Parry Sound in one large group.

Mii-sh giiwenh gii-nganindwaa odi giw yahaag binoojiinyag mii-sh giiwenh gaa-nindwaa giw binoojiinyag.
They left their children there at home, but those children were also apparently given some instructions.

"Gego zhaakegon odi ni-biindge-biiyaamgak," jigaazwidogenag giw binoojiinyag.
"Don't any of you go over there to the narrows," those children were told.

"Ga-bzaanyaam maa."
"You are all to stay here and be quiet."

"Mii eta go maa endaaying maa ji-ni-baa-dzhiikeyeg."
"You are to only play around our homes here."

"Gego zhaakegon odi."
"Don't go over there."

Mii-sh go naa ezhi-yaad maaba bemaadzid.
For this is how a person is.

Mii gegoo enind kaa ezhichgesig mii go ge-o-zhichged iw.
If one is told not to do something, one will go ahead and do it anyway.

Aansh naa giiwenh gii-baabiihowag giw binoojiinyag mii nake gii-ninkewekzhiwenid niw wgitziimwaan.
And so those children waited until their parents had gone out of sight in the boat.

Mii-sh giiwenh wii-maajaawaad gii-zhaawaad odi ge-biindge-biiyaamgak gaa-ni-dgoshnowaad giiwenh odi gtaamgwaadkamig ezhi-gwanaajwang.
They then set out on their journey over to the narrows, and when they arrived there they were amazed at how incredibly beautiful it was.

Wewenі yaamgad go naa.
It was very pleasant.

Kaa aapji gnwiindmaasinoon.
The water wasn't deep at all.

Weweni maa bngwi go naa.
And the sand was so very nice there.

Mii-sh maa naa gnimaa maa bi-niisaabkaamgak go maa.
The rocks gently sloped downward there too.

Aapji go naa geget go naa gwanaajwan maa bngwi go naa.
So truly beautiful was that nice sand beach there.

Mii-sh maa baa-dzhiikewaagwen mii sa ek'dowaagwen giw binoojiinyag, "Mii sa maanda gaa-nji-kidwaad gaa maa ji-bi-dzhiikesiwang maa ezhi-gwanaajwang."
The children must have played together there a while before eventually remarking, "This was why they said this, that we were not to come and play here as it is so beautiful."

"Mii gaa-nji-gooying iihow," kidwidogenag giiwenh.
"This is why we were told this," those children must have said.

Oonh gii-tkaabaawziwag mbiigziwag.
They swam around there making a tremendous racket.

Oonh tkaabaawziwaad giw binoojiinshag.
Those silly children swam around there together.

Kaa gii-noondwaasiiwaan niw.
They didn't hear anyone else around at all.

Baamaa pii go naa wiikaa gii-noondmowaad iihow ayhii sin eyaamgak mdwe-shkaamgad miinwaa niisaabkiseg go naa ge niw siniin.
It was not until much later that they heard the loud sound of the rocks falling to the ground.

Mii gii-naabwaad odi gii-waabmaawaad odi bi-dpoodenid niw yahaan gchi-ngigwan.

As the children looked over toward that great rock face, they then saw a giant otter crawling out.

Mii iidog gii-zegziwaad.

They were so afraid.

Gtaamgwaadkamig giiwenh engokwaanig maaba shtigwaan gchi-ngig.

It was said to have been a frightful sight, just how big this giant otter's head was.

Miinwaa ezhi-biigbidood niw siniin.

He was breaking up those rocks.

Mii gwa ezhi-daashkbidood niw siniin.

In fact, he was splitting apart those rocks.

Mii-sh gii-dpooded.

He then finally crawled out.

Wewiip iidog gii-bi-maajii-pahwewaad giiwenh gii-giiwe-pahwewaad giw binoojiinshag.

Those silly children ran away so quickly, they must have run straight home.

Oonh gosaawaad zeginaagzinid gchi-ngigwan.

They were so frightened by that scary-looking giant otter.

Gtaamgwaadkamig enginid.

He was such a terrible size.

Gii-giiwe-pahwewaagwen go maa go naa epiichi-zegziwaad gii-giiwe-pahwewaagwen.

The children ran right home, they were so afraid that they ran straight home.

Mii gaa-ni-dgoshnawaad odi endaawaad mii gii-bi-biindge-pahwewaad odi endaawaad go naa.

When they finally arrived at their houses, they ran right inside their homes there.

Mii dash giiwenh wiikaa go naa baamaapii bi-dgoshnidgenag giw gaa-oodetoojig.

It was only much later that the adults who had gone to town again returned.

Mii giiwenh gii-ni-mkawaawaad odi niw wniijaan'siwaan.

That was when they must have found their children there.

Oonh gtaamgodemwag giiwenh.

The children were crying terribly.

"Aaniish naa ezhiwebziiyeg?"

"Now what has happened to all of you?"

Mii sa gii-wiindmaagewaagwen, "Ngii-zhaamin niinaa wodi gii-zhiyaang ji-zhaasiwaang."

The children then told them, "We went over there where you told us not to go."

"Mii odi gaa-zhaayaang mii dash gii-waabmangid odi gchi-ngig."

"We went over there, and we saw this great otter."

"Mii gaa-zhi-baapaasbidood niw siniin mii go gaa-bi-dzhi-dpooded iidog odi."

"He was cracking up those rocks as he was crawling out over there."

"Gtaamgwaadkamig engokwaanig iihow shtigwaan."

"So fearful was the size of his head."

"Mii sa gaa-nji-gooyeg—kaa daa-zhaasiweg odi," jigaazwag giiwenh.

"This is why this was said to you all—you should not have gone over there," they were told.

Mii dash go noongwa waya zhaad odi mii go ge-zhi-waabndaman niw siniin gaa-baashksegin wii-gzhiibaajiwang noongwa odi.

Now today if someone goes over there, you can see how the water spins about where those rocks were blasted apart.

Mii odi nake gaa-bi-nji-dpooded ow yahaa gchi-ngig.

It is like this now because of the way that he crawled out of there, that giant otter.

Mewnzha ngii-noondaanaaban maanda gaa-kidwaad giw Nishnaabeg.

Long ago I heard this story being told by those old Nishnaabe people.

Mii-sh go noongom naa wenji-zhaabiiyaamgak mii odi gaa-bi-dpooded ow.

This is why today the water flows through there, where he crawled out.

Aapji-sh go naa gwanaajwan.

It is so very beautiful.

Mina-biiyaamgad geyaabi maa bngwi naambiing naabyin temgad.

It flows in so nicely, and you can still see the sand there under the water.

Aapji-sh go naa gwanaajwan.

It is so very beautiful.

CHAPTER 5

Learning from Stories

> *Mii-sh go naa ezhi-yaad maaba bemaadzid.*
> **For this is how a person is.**
>
> *Mii gegoo enind kaa ezhichgesig mii go ge-o-zhichged iw.*
> **If one is told not to do something, one will go ahead and do it anyway.**
>
> —Duncan Pegahmagabow, from "*Gchi-Ngig*—The Giant Otter"

Duncan Pegahmagabow told me the story "*Gchi-Ngig*—The Giant Otter" while I visited at his home in early December 1998. I was allowed to record this story after making an offering of *semaa* ("tobacco"). Duncan first talked a little about life with his family at Nenabozhnaang, an old settlement on Parry Island where he had grown up during his early years. He demonstrated remarkable recall of this story, not having heard it in over half a century himself. As a young boy, he often wondered about how a particular channel between two major local water bodies had been formed. His father told him this story in response to his question about the channel's origin.

"*Gchi-Ngig*—The Giant Otter" is rich in moral lessons, Nishnaabe philosophies of the human-land relationship, and some striking verbal artistry. It shows the profound teaching capacity of the storytelling tradition and was one of many ways Francis taught his children about the history of the land and expected human behaviour. This story is of particular interest since it is neither fully a *dibaajmowin* ("general narrative") nor an *aadsookaan* ("legend"); it seems to possess features of both types of story, which makes it unique. Duncan began by saying he would tell a story but did not specify that it would be a legend:

> *Mii dash go wedi nake aazhwiyhiing iihow waa-dbaajdamaan yahaa Jim Nanibush gaa-nji-mdaabiimtood.*

> I am going to tell a story about a place on the other side of where Jim Nanibush had a landing.

Most elders and community members who heard this story agree it is more like a traditional legend than any other type of story. The presence of an unusual or sentient non-human creature (the giant otter), the underlying moral lesson, and the explanation of how a landform came to be are all characteristic of such stories. The relatively contemporary setting, though, is a contrast to the distant past, in which most such legends take place.

"*Gchi-Ngig*—The Giant Otter" takes place close to the historical Parry Island village of Nenabozhnaang or "Nanibush town," inhabited until the 1950s. The largely Odawa population who lived in this community had escaped from the United States in the early to mid-1800s during the Indian relocation era. These people were learned in traditional ways and maintained a small but progressive settlement for many years. All of Francis's children were born in this village with the help of his wife's extended family.

In the story, all of the parents and other adult community members (collectively identified as the Nishnaabeg) make a day trip to the town of Parry Sound. This is a surprisingly large outing, all of the adults of the village travelling together. The children are left behind with instructions to play close to their homes. The adults give them an explicit warning not to venture to one specific location. No sooner are the adults out of sight than the children rush over to this place. It is a stunningly beautiful spot that seems to be an ideal place to play. The children unknowingly awaken a "giant otter" (*gchi-ngig*) that has a den inside the large rock face. Crawling out of his den, the otter breaks apart the rock and opens the channel into the larger bay. The resulting narrows formed in this story are those which can be seen today.

The children are terribly frightened by the huge otter and his sudden emergence from the rocky wall. They flee back to their village hoping the otter is not in pursuit. Even after reaching the safety of their homes, they are compelled to hide until their parents find them that evening. The children confess their failure to heed the warning they were given and that a terrible calamity ensued as a result. The adults remind the children that their failure to listen was the cause of all the troubles that befell them.

Narrative Structure Outline

"*Gchi-Ngig*—The Giant Otter" is structured like a classic legend in many respects. There is both a sign-on and a sign-off, a plot devoted to teaching both a moral lesson and the human relationship with the world, and a

17. Opening of Menominee channel into the south channel at Biindge-biiyaamgak. Photo by Brian McInnes.

mysterious event unlikely to happen in the present. The story is structured by three major changes of place that signal important transitions of action and plot. From the initial instructions given in the first part of the story to the subsequent defiance, consequence, and resolution phases, the children's actions are mirrored in the landscape as the narrative progresses. The following structure seems to best characterize the course of events featured in this classic Wasauksing story:

Part I, scene one: Leave taking
- a. Setting of scene at Nenabozhnaang
- b. Parents give warning to children
- c. Parents leave

Part II, scene one: Arrival
- a. Children arrive at Biindge-biiyaamgak
- b. Children explore and play

Part II, scene two: Complication
- a. Emergence of otter/opening of narrows
- b. Children escape

Part III, scene one: Return home
- a. Children arrive at their homes
- b. Parents arrive home and find children
- c. Children explain to parents
- d. Parents remind children of earlier instructions

Epilogue:

a. Audience encouraged to visit the narrows
b. Reminder of how giant otter formed the narrows
c. Qualification of narrator to tell the story
d. Final description/appreciation of place (sign-off)

Story Notes

Duncan discusses the local landscape throughout the story. In its orientation, body, and epilogue, there is considerable effort to provide the listener with a strong sense of place and the major geographical features. The orientation is devoted to establishing the exact location of the place spoken of, even before the events of the story begin:

> *Mii dash go wedi nake aazhwiyhiing iihow waa-dbaajdamaan yahaa Jim Nanibush gaa-nji-mdaabiimtood.*
> I am going to tell a story about a place on the other side of where Jim Nanibush had a landing.
>
> *Aazhwiyhiing go wodi nake odi iihow Nenabozhnaang neyaash maa yaamgad yahaa go maa bdakshing Zhingwaak.*
> Over on the other side of Nanibush town, there is a point of land on which stands a pine.
>
> *Mii maa ngoji gaa-daad ow yahaa Giiwedin ow Jim Nanibush.*
> This is the place where Giiwedin lived, Jim Nanibush.
>
> *Mii maa ngoji gaa-daad.*
> This was where he lived.
>
> *Mii dash iihow wedi aazhwiyhiing go maa nake neyaashiins Biindge-biiyaamgad odi.*
> Now over there on the other side of this little point is the narrows.

If this were a classic legend, one might expect the story to be explicitly set in the distant past. Duncan, however, dates the story with respect to the life of Jim Nanibush and the existence of Nenabozhnaang. And while this village has been abandoned for almost sixty-five years, it is not the characteristic "time before memory" within which many legends take place.

A number of different locations are mentioned throughout the story. From the town of Parry Sound to the enigmatic "other side of the island" (*aazhwiyiing*), there is one definitive place of action in this narrative: the "narrows" (*biindge-biiyaamgak*). Duncan masterfully focuses on this location by gradually directing our gaze from one location to the next. From directing our attention to the far side of the island, past the boat landing and home of a well-known community member on the south channel, until we finally arrive at the village of Nenabozhnaang, Duncan takes us on a visual tour. However, it is the single point of land with the pine tree growing on it that truly helps to direct our attention to the closed channel where the children were told not to go.

It is significant that Jim Nanibush—alive at the time these events took place—is mentioned in the orientation of the story. He was perhaps better known by his Ojibwe name Giiwedin or "North wind." Jenness documented him to be about ninety years old in 1929 and that he moved to Parry Island when he was about five years old.[1] This meant that the Nanibush family arrived on Parry Island from the United States around 1844. This group of people, all of Odawa ancestry, were part of a mass relocation of people that began in the 1830s: "During the 1830s and 1840s, several thousand Algonquian-speaking Indians living in the United States immigrated to Upper Canada. The United States government passed the Indian Removal Act in 1830, permitting it to relocate eastern American Indians."[2]

Since the Odawa did not arrive on the island until at least this time, and since Parry Sound itself was established as a town, the events at Biindge-biiyaamgak could not have occurred until at least the late 1860s. Jim Nanibush might well have been one of those parents or adults who made the trip to town that fateful day; the fact that Nanibush is a possible participant in the story is rare indeed. The human characters in such stories are seldom identifiable. It is entirely possible that Nanibush himself was the original raconteur of this story as Duncan's great-uncle and namer.

Topography

There is particular care in detailing the locations of key events throughout the story. Such attention to detail extends from the introduction through the main body to the epilogue. Twenty-four of fifty-four lines in "*Gchi-Ngig*—The Giant Otter" are devoted to descriptions of places. There are important reasons why a narrator might expend considerable effort in framing the location and any key geographical features or changes that occur in a story. As noted by Lisa Philips Valentine, "the connection of the aatisoohkaan to a known landmark is no mere setting of the stage; it is the land that validates the legend-myth.... The presence in the here and now of such landmarks proves that the aatisoohkaanan are true, which in turn legitimizes the message of the legend-myth for use in the present."[3] This story could be described as an etiological story in that it describes the origin of the narrows in this location. In this way, the land becomes a confirmation of story—and story a confirmation of land. Francis always believed in the importance of knowing the stories of the land, and this story serves that purpose.

The central place of the story is identified throughout as Biindge-biiyaamgak ("The place where it comes to enter"—a narrows). This location is first mentioned by the narrator in the orientation as a preface to the eventual action. Duncan provides a rather picturesque description of this place by drawing on the verbal imagery of the language and saying each detail in isolation with the use of sequenced pausing. The effect is to leave the audience hanging until the next sentence is delivered:

> *Weweni yaamgad go naa.*
> It was very pleasant.
>
> *Kaa aapji gnwiindmaasinoon.*
> The water wasn't deep at all.
>
> *Weweni maa bngwi go naa.*
> And the sand was so very nice there.
>
> *Mii-sh maa naa gnimaa maa bi-niisaabkaamgak go maa.*
> The rocks gently sloped downward there too.
>
> *Aapji go naa geget go naa gwanaajwan maa bngwi go naa.*
> So truly beautiful was that nice sand beach there.

Everything about this place seems to be ideal. The waters do not grow dark and deep there, and the nicely sloped rocks ease gently down into the water. The sand is both beautiful and evenly distributed; the white sand beaches of Georgian Bay have attracted scores of visitors since long before the giant otter's awakening. Duncan further comments on how exceptionally beautiful the sand is to refocus our attention from memories of warm summer days on Georgian Bay's beaches to the sequence of events taking place at Biindge-biiyaamgak that fateful day.

The opening of the channel would have been of great advantage for the people of Nenabozhnaang. With a clear channel to the larger surrounding waters, both fishing and transportation would have become much easier. Regardless of whether in the distant past or the near present, giant animals were always worthy of respect and caution. Giant snakes, bears, beavers, and dogs were all a part of the narrative tradition—and sometimes lived experience—of the people of Wasauksing. Such encounters were not necessarily bad or frightening and could even bring blessings to those who experienced them. But seeing such unnaturally large creatures could unnerve even seasoned Nishnaabeg, as Francis once shared with Jenness:

> My father and another Indian named *Micikkan,* "Turtle," shot a deer one morning a little north of Parry Sound. As they were paddling back to their camp my father, who was sitting in the bow of the canoe, called out, "Look." Both men saw the back of an enormous turtle protruding from the water in front of them. The monster raised its head and gazed at them, its eyes shining like large mirrors. The Indian in the stern lost consciousness and fell forward, but my father turned around in his seat and steered the canoe to the camp. Neither man received any medicine power from this experience because it was only an accident.[4]

The known presence of a giant otter suggests that the place be better left alone. For this reason the children might have been told to avoid that area. They unfortunately do not heed the instruction and awaken the great creature from its slumber through their play.

The channel is created by the giant otter as he crawls out of the great rock where his den is located. That there is no other apparent entrance suggests that he has been there since ancient times, when such giant animals freely roamed the world. This was the time of the ancient legends. Duncan refers six times to the otter's breaking out of the rock and the subsequent transformations of the rock as the otter emerges. The rock is first described in the story as gently sloping down into the water. Eventually, the children hear the sound of the rock cracking (*mdweshkaamgad*) and the pieces falling down the slope. The otter fully captures their attention through the varied ways he breaks apart the rock in which he has been sleeping.

> ... *ezhi-biigbidood niw siniin*
> ... he was breaking up those rocks
>
> ... *ezhi-daashkbidood niw siniin*
> ... he was splitting apart those rocks
>
> ... *gaa-zhi-baapaasbidood niw siniin*
> ... he cracked apart those rocks

The rock is later described as virtually having been blown apart: "*niw siniin gaa-baashksegin.*" Duncan skilfully employs the verbal resources of the language to illustrate the obliteration of the former barrier to the larger bay. This otter would have had to be truly gigantic in order to manipulate solid Georgian Bay rock in the ways suggested by these verbs of breaking.

Duncan's rich verbal artistry is not reserved for sand or rock alone; the water is also given the same kind of descriptive attention. Even the name used for the narrows, Biindge-biiyaamgak ("Where it comes to enter") is descriptive of the passage of water into this place. Once the rock has been blasted apart by the emergence of the otter, a small channel or narrows is formed between these two previously separated bodies of water. Duncan describes the resulting flow of water through the narrows with the terms *gizhibaajwan* ("where the water spins") and *wenji-zhaabiiyaamgad* ("where it flows right through"). He ends his depiction of Biindge-biiyaamgak by commenting that the water there flows in "so pleasantly today" (*mina-biiyaamgad*). The description of place proves to be as important in this story as plot or character development. Many community elders have commented that listening to a good story should be like "watching a picture show in your mind."

Characters

There are three major characters—or groups of characters perhaps—who appear throughout the story. Duncan makes some intentional contrasts among these groups in order to emphasize the particular role each plays in the story as well as the nature of their interrelationships. The central characters in the story are the children. The number of direct references to them (seven) indicates their principal status in the story. Lesser but still important characters include the parents/community members and of course the giant otter.

Duncan begins the story by introducing a number of community members planning a day trip away from their village. They are always identified as a collective, and no individual is ever singled out in the story. All of their actions are performed together as a group, and they even speak with a common voice—a classic feature of many Wasauksing legends and reflective of the community's self-identification as a collective of individuals living and working together for a common purpose over time.

The same might be said for the children, introduced early in the story. Throughout the story, they act and speak as a group, with no singular reference ever made. In this legend, the children are referred to most often as "the children" (*binoojiinyag*), "their children" (*oniijaan'siwaan*), or even "the silly children" (*binoojiinshag*). This last reference is particularly interesting because it shows a definite sense of evaluation by Duncan, rather rare, but not unheard of, in the telling of an *aadsookaan.* The pejorative noun *binoojiinshag*—which occurs twice in the text—indicates that the narrator considers the children to be somewhat foolish in their actions.

The third and final character to make an appearance in the story is the giant otter. Although he never speaks, he plays a key role. He represents a direct connection to the old world—a time when giant creatures and mythological happenings were common: *aadsookaan* time. It is the presence of the giant otter that inspired many elders to view this story as a legend despite the relatively contemporary setting of the events. Duncan gradually introduces this character, successfully building a degree of suspense by identifying the otter only with the enigmatic fourth-person pronoun *niw* ("that one"). We know this is intentional since it is the only example in the story of a pronoun being used without a direct reference. It is not until several lines later that we learn who this mysterious creature is.

The Ojibwe language has a rather unique way of marking or referencing two or more third persons in discourse. Characters in focus are referred to as being proximate, and their perspective is assumed at any given point in the discourse. Proximate characters, as well as any verbs that might be associated with their actions, are grammatically unmarked. Third persons said not to be in focus are said to be obviative, a grammatical category that might even stand as a fourth person of sorts. Such obviative nouns or verbs are marked with a special suffix, typically *-wan, -an,* or *-n.*

In a story, the main character is typically in focus for most of the discourse. Secondary characters can become proximate should the narrator choose to adopt their perspective at any given point, but this is less common. In "*Gchi-Ngig,*" out of forty-three lines of story text (excluding the introduction and epilogue, during which no character is in focus), the children are proximate actors in thirty-three lines. Duncan takes the perspective of the parents for six lines, while the otter is in focus for only four lines.

Narrative Voice and Asides

Duncan performs the dialogue in accordance with the emotional and vocal emphasis expected of a given character in the story. He does not attempt to approximate the voice of any character at any point in the dialogue. For instance, he speaks with a level of concern characteristic of any parent returning from a long absence to find his children hiding in the home or with a degree of nervousness expected of children forced to admit wrongdoing to their caregivers. But there is no attempt to emulate the actual voice of a young parent or child. Direct discourse in this story is more a "taking on of words" than a "taking on of voices" (a finding also reported by Philips Valentine of Severn Ojibwe narrative at Lynx Lake).[5]

There are two clear instances of narrator asides in the story. In the first example, Duncan makes a direct comment that relates general human behaviour to the actions of the children. This aside brings the meaning and purpose of the story much closer to the audience by directly referencing the kinds of choices we face every day. The following aside occurs immediately before the children disobey their parents:

> *Mii-sh go naa ezhi-yaad maaba bemaadzid.*
> But this is how a person is.
>
> *Mii gegoo enind kaa ezhichgesig mii go ge-o-zhichged iihow.*
> If one is told not to do something, then that one will just go ahead and do it anyway.

This aside serves multiple functions. It prepares the audience for some deviation from an ideal course of action and provides some comic relief. Both Duncan and I burst into laughter when this comment was made. It is a simple human truth but one I did not expect to hear so directly within the stated confines of the story. Laughter is a vital part of Nishnaabe storytelling culture, and even in a serious and informative narrative such as this it is welcome and perhaps even necessary.

Duncan and I were the only two present when this story was recorded. He did have a broader audience in mind when he told it. He knew this story would be included in a resource with wide distribution. It was one way of ensuring "*Gchi-Ngig*" would be shared with as large an audience as possible and in a medium people could understand. Within this context, his aside is understood to have greater meaning and extension and to exemplify the classic Nishnaabe communicative strategy that values indirectness as a way of making a point.

The audience is not directly addressed again until the epilogue. Although it could be argued that the epilogue is in fact a comment to listeners, there are only two sentences explicitly directed toward listeners:

> *Mii dash go noongwa waya zhaad odi mii go ge-zhi-waabndaman niw siniin gaa-baashksegin wii-gzhiibaajiwan noongwa odi.*
> Now today if someone goes over there you will see how the water spins about where those rocks were blasted apart.
>
> ...

> *Mina-biiyaamgad geyaabi maa bngwi naambiing naabyin temgad.*
> It flows in so nicely, and if you look you will see the sand there under the water.

Note how second-person verbs are used in both closing lines: *ge-zhi-waabndaman* ("you will see how") and *naabyin* ("if you look"). These are the only examples of direct address of the audience in the whole story. Shifting the focus to the second person at the end of the story reminds the listener that he or she has some relationship to the story and its events. The listener is encouraged to go and see the landscape first-hand. In so doing, he or she can witness the evidence of the story in the land and develop an enhanced relationship with that place.

Story Epilogue

Duncan reserved many important features for the epilogue. The audience is alerted to the fact that the story is coming to a close by a deliberate shift in tense marked by the word *noongwa* ("today"). As noted above, Duncan then shifts the verbal focus to the second person; the audience is not simply encouraged to remember the story as told but actually to travel to the narrows and witness both the opening made by the otter and the continuing beauty of the land. Just as suddenly as the audience is moved to the present, Duncan again changes tense and returns to the distant past. The word *mewnzha* ("long ago") is the first direct time reference in the story itself. Although Duncan is referring to when he first heard this legend from his father and uncle, it does give the story some further contextualization.

Duncan uses most of the epilogue to reinforce the connection between story and place. Although the channel is opened because of the children's failure to listen, the land itself is not marred by any lasting negative sentiment. The area is still very beautiful. But it is a changed beauty. The lovely sand the children find so carefully distributed on the shore when they first arrive at Biindge-biiyaamgak is now located under the water. And the great rock wall now lines the edges of the channel where the water spins about as it flows in. It is still a special albeit different place.

An interesting feature of the epilogue is that Duncan does not use any kind of formulaic sign-off. It is common in Ojibwe narrative for a story, teaching, or other related communicative event to end with a phrase such as *mii iw* ("that's it") or, in Duncan's case, *Mii ko gaa-zhiwebak* ("This really did happen"). Although it is hard to represent in written form, each of the last six lines takes on a different voicing quality and pacing from the rest of the story. Each sentence is said more slowly, and the pause after each sentence increases. Sentence length also decreases. The effect is that each line comes to stand as a separate event of sorts, and the story concludes in almost poetic fashion. The contented silence that fills the air after the last line brings the story to a fitting and conclusive end.

Enawendiying—We Are All Related

Duncan Pegahmagabow told me this story after I asked him to comment on a quote he once made in a military publication citing his father's respect for the natural world and how we should work hard to live in harmony with all living things.[6] Duncan thought, if you did not know his father's astonishing sniper record of 378 kills, you might not believe it was the same person. Francis Pegahmagabow had great reverence for living things. He was true to the teachings of the Nishnaabe about honouring all life, particularly when it must be taken for food or medicine. War, however, was a different situation altogether. His children remember Francis to have been entirely at peace when travelling throughout the forests or waters of Georgian Bay. When it was necessary to take life, he dutifully offered sacred tobacco and words of prayer. *Gaawiin nishaa gii-zhichgesii* ("He didn't do any of this for nothing") was how Duncan and Marie each described their father's practices respecting life. Francis truly believed that all beings in the natural world shared a relationship to the Creator and therefore deserved respect in both life and death.

> *Mii-sh go naa maaba Nishnaabe miinwaa iihow ezhindawendaagwak iihow kina gegoo ji-gchi-piitendang kina gegoo bmaadziwin.*
> The Nishnaabe was taught about the importance of everything, so that he would have respect for all life.
>
> *Maabam Nishnaabe kaa go wiin go eta bmaadzisii giw mtigoog, miishkoonsan ge gwa waawaaskonensan.*
> A human being needed to understand that he was not the only one to have life, for there are the trees, grasses, and flowers as well.
>
> *Mii gegoo gewiin waya en'goons ezhi-gaashiinyid gegoo go gewii maa gii-nji-nijigaazo nshke go giw aanind giw yahaag wesiinyag.*
> And also the ant who is so small, there is a reason why he too was placed here as it is for all of those other animals.
>
> *Aapji gwa gchi-piitendaan iw bmaadziwin mii maaba ezhindawendaagzid maaba Nishnaabe nake gewiin ji-naadzid iihow.*

To value and respect life, that is what is expected of a human being in the way that he moves through the world.

Kina go gegoo bemaadziimgak.
For everything has life.

Kina go niw wesiinyan—niijkiiwenyan go niw wesiinyan.
All of those animals—those animals are like his brothers.

Miinwaa go waya mtigoon ge gwa mii go wiijkiiwenyan.
And those trees, they too are his brothers.

Mii bezhig gaa-noondwag ekaad kidad iihow.
I once heard my father say this when he was a little older.

"Dbiyiidog odi ge-baa-inaakoomwanen waasekmig."
"Sometime when you are travelling in an unfamiliar place deep in the woods."

"Kaa go nshike gdayaasii."
"You are not alone."

"Yenaabin, mii ji-waabmadwaa gow gwiijkiiwenyag enawemjig."
"Look around, and you will see your brothers, your relatives."

"Mii kina gdinawendaaganag gow mtigoog miinwaa ge gow wesiinyag."
"They are all your relatives, those trees and those animals."

"Kina go giin gow gdinawendaaganag gow."
"They are all relatives of yours."

"Kaa go ngoji gdaa-n'saan'zisii nshike ngoji baayaayin."
"So there is no place that you will ever be lonely when you travel."

Ngii-noondwaapan kidod.
This is what I heard him say.

Mii-sh go geget ezhi-debwed iihow.
He was most certainly speaking the truth.

Family

> *My clan is the caribou. I have never visited Temogami, but I have heard there are caribou people there also, and if I ever wish to spend a winter in that district I shall seek them out and ask them to use their influence with their band so that it will assign me a good hunting-ground. They are my relatives and will certainly help me.*
>
> —Francis Pegahmagabow[1]

Much of the history of Francis Pegahmagabow continues to be shrouded in mystery. It is like reading a manuscript that has lost many pages to the wind. In this, one of the names he carried—Bnaaswi—holds true to what is remembered of his life. An Ojibwe pronunciation of Francis, the name Bnaaswi can also mean "that which has blown off in the wind." And many details of his life have irretrievably scattered to each of the four winds. Yet much of his story remains known to his family and community, and it is a task of the present to ensure this much survives into the future. Such is the way we should honour our ancestors.

Francis's story began with the founding of the great Ojibwe territories along the Georgian Bay shoreline and interior. The local bands coordinated their leadership using a clan system of governance. Each member of the nation was born into a patrilineally inherited clan. The inherent traits of one's clan had a role to play in maintaining the well-being of the community. Edward Benton-Banai writes that the clan system was a gift from the Creator that provided "a framework of government to give them strength and order."[2] Each clan had general roles and responsibilities in the maintenance of community life. Some of the roles identified by Benton-Banai include leadership (Crane and Loon clans), teaching (Fish clan), guardianship (Bear clan), and housing (Hoof clan). Several of the clans common to the Ojibwe of the Georgian Bay and Muskoka region included the Caribou (*Adik*), Bear (*Mkwa*), Beaver (*Amik*), Otter (*Ngig*), Wolf (*Mahiingan*), Eagle (*Mgizi*), Fish

(*Giigoo*), Hawk (*Gekek*), Sturgeon (*Name*), and Turtle (*Mshiikenh*). The clan system was important in the everyday life of the people. As extended family members, men and women of the same clan could not intermarry. Not only did this prohibition keep the bloodlines strong, but also it helped to maintain relationships among governing clan families across communities.

The Caribou clan from which Francis descended had strong ties to leadership among the Ojibwe of the Georgian Bay and Muskoka region. Those born into this clan were characteristically blessed with speed, stealth, a gentle nature, and the ability to vigorously defend themselves or their kin should it be necessary. His great-great-grandfather Bebagamigaabaw was chief of one of these small bands and perhaps one of the last to engage in direct battle with the Haudenosaunee. Francis translated his name for Jenness in explaining the origin of the family surname: "Pegahmagabow ... means 'it advances and halts, advances and halts,' and refers to the passage of a hurricane that seems to halt while it uproots the trees and bushes in its path."[3] Bebagamigaabaw—like the great standing wind his name described—was legendary for his ability to quickly travel great distances and then suddenly change his position. He was a formidable warrior and strong orator. His clan and many of his gifts alike passed through the generations to his great-great-grandson Francis.

Bebagamigaabaw would be among the last to live outside the enforced controls of the Indian Act. Like all of his predecessors, he would never adopt an English name or surname. The Midewiwin faith to which he belonged was universally strong among the Ojibwe and provided strength, healing, and direction to the people for generations unbroken. The increased presence of settlers in Bebagamigaabaw's lifetime would change the world in ways his forebears might never have imagined. His son James Pegahmagabow Sr. (Beskinekwam) would continue his father's traditions of leadership and traditional ceremonial practice. But with the old-growth forests cut down, the sacred territories of the Ojibwe seized and sold off, and virtually every aspect of life regulated by the Indian Act of 1876, Nishnaabe society was irrevocably changed. The outlawing of traditional ceremony dealt one of the most significant blows to the continuity of the old ways. Even the Pegahmagabow family homestead at Obaajiwanaang (Lake Joseph) was lost to land appropriation and the reallocation abilities of Indian Act–empowered government officials.

With the loss of the family territory in the Muskokas, and the subsequent reorganization of the Indian bands and their homelands, James Pegahmagabow Sr. and his family relocated to Parry Island. The island was known to the Ojibwe of the region more as a place to visit and not inhabit.

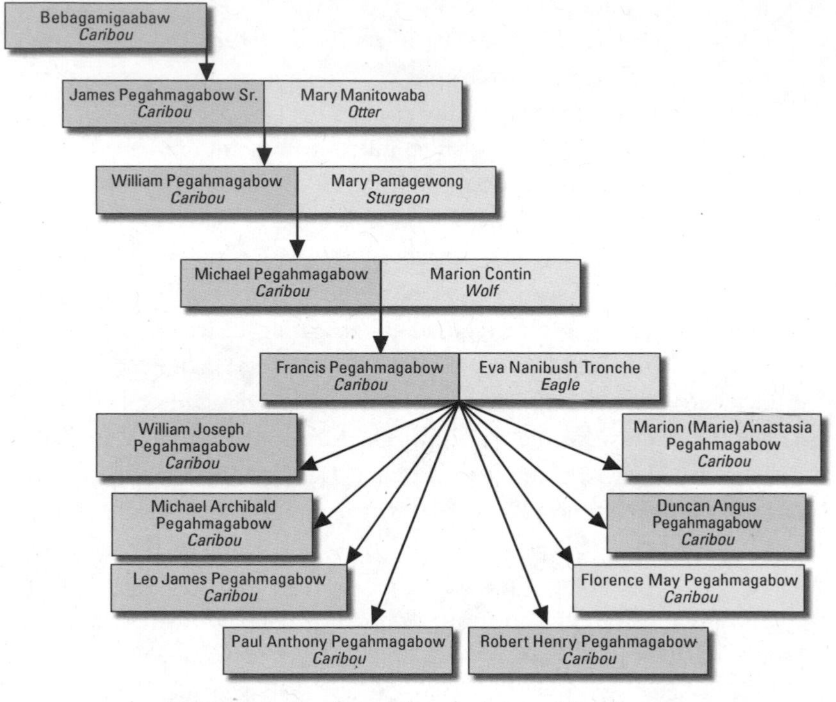

18. Francis Pegahmagabow's clan and family tree.

The forced relocation to Parry Island imposed certain hardships on the formerly semi-nomadic and autonomous Nishnaabeg. The land was not as fertile or as vast as their previous territory.[4] Hunting was limited, and the people needed to adapt to a new set of living conditions in a short period of time. James Pegahmagabow Sr. served as chief of the Wasauksing community for nearly twenty years. His son James Pegahmagabow Jr. would also later serve as band chief. Beskinekwam was one of few chiefs whose customary appointment was upheld by Indian Affairs.[5]

It is often referenced in periodicals and memorial tributes that Francis, like his father and grandfather before him, served as chief of the Wasauksing band. Francis would hold the office twice, first serving from 1921 to 1925 and then from 1942 to 1945. His father and grandfather, however, never had such an opportunity partly because of their untimely early deaths. His great-uncle James Pegahmagabow Jr. served as chief for many years and was a role model for young Francis. James's brother and Francis's grandfather, William Pegahmagabow, never aspired to political office and left his community to marry into the Shawanaga band. William married Mary Pamajewong, the daughter of a prominent family that also had Muskoka band origins. Mary's Sturgeon clan relatives endorsed the marriage to a member of the Caribou clan—particularly one with such deep roots of leadership and renown in the region. William relocated permanently to the Shawanaga community, where his only son, Michael, was born and raised.

The details of his father's and grandfather's lives were important to Francis. Although he would only know them through the stories of others, he honoured them by naming his first two sons after them. William and his wife died shortly after Michael was born, and the baby was raised by Noah Nebiniyanakwod, a maternal relative. Michael was welcomed in the Shawanaga community and lived there the rest of his life. A resourceful man skilled in negotiating with both French and English settlers, he showed great promise early on in becoming a leader. During his travels across Ojibwe country, Michael made many connections with the old families. He would eventually marry Marion Contin, a member of the Wolf clan, from the Henvey Inlet Reserve farther up the shore.

Although neither Michael nor Marion was a member at Shawanaga, the couple were accepted by the community and established a permanent homestead on Snake Island. Old family and clan connections were deep in Nishnaabe communities, and the people remembered their common historical roots. This was especially true for many Shawanaga and Wasauksing families who shared Muskoka band origins. Francis was born in 1889, and life for his family was prosperous and good. The Shawanaga community might have been where Francis lived his entire life had circumstances not greatly changed things for him.

Like that of his father, Michael Pegahmagabow's life was far too short. The circumstances of each man's death—like so many untimely passings in Aboriginal communities—remain mired in suspicion and uncertainty. Both men were young and in good health, self-sufficient, and had supportive and loving families. There are no reports or records of any investigation into the sudden demise of either William or Michael. The abrupt sickness that took Michael also afflicted his wife. Marion Pegahmagabow proved to be resilient despite becoming gravely ill after the death of her husband. A relative who retrieved Francis from Snake Island nursed him back to health while his mother recovered in isolation. She seemed to be so moribund that the man who retrieved Francis dove into the water with the small boy to wash them clean of any sickness. Marion entrusted Francis to the permanent care of his extended family at Shawanaga while she returned to her home community to recover. His adopted grandfather, Noah Nebiniyanakwod, found a long-term home for young Francis with Noah's brother and sister-in-law, Francis and Louise Kewaquado.

The Kewaquado home was a safe and secure place for Francis in such uncertain times. The community was facing increased pressures from settlers and the local Indian agent, and a few consecutive poor hunting seasons made day-to-day survival difficult. Francis struggled to understand the events of his early life. His father's sudden death was difficult to accept, as was the perceived abandonment by his mother. Little is known of her reasons for returning permanently to Henvey Inlet other than her expressed hope that she might one day return to claim her child when she was again well. Her subsequent remarriage, and the knowledge that Francis was well looked after by his extended family, were no doubt factors in her decision not to reclaim her son.

It was not uncommon for Nishnaabe children to live with or be raised by other family or community members. Francis, however, was so profoundly affected by the loss of both parents that he referred to himself as an orphan the rest of his life. It is uncertain whether he had direct communication with his mother again. His loss was somewhat mitigated by the birth of his two daughters, the youngest of whom he would even name after his mother in the spirit of love and reconciliation. Francis eventually built relationships with his half-siblings from Henvey Inlet later in life. His half-brother even offered to marry Francis's widow, Eva, after his death in accordance with Ojibwe custom.

Once a prolific and well-known family, many of Francis's paternal relations seemed to pass away over a short period of time. Francis shared with Jenness that his family had been the victims of deliberate attacks: "My father and grandfather had offended some of the Indians on Lake Huron, and these Indians destroyed by sorcery every member of their families except myself."[6] Whatever the source of the misfortune that afflicted his family, Francis was the last direct descendant. After surviving a near drowning, poisonous snake attack, and lengthy childhood illness, Francis relied on his own efforts for his well-being. Adrian Hayes cites how Francis would run between the village and shore as a boy in order to build up his strength.[7] The excellent care and rehabilitative medicine of his adoptive family helped to ensure his continued wellness. Francis was determined that the legacy of tragedy he had experienced would not continue any further and that the lives of his own children would be free of the burdens that had disadvantaged him.

Roots

Upon his return from the First World War, a young and optimistic Francis was determined to re-establish his family in the Wasauksing community. This seemed unusual to some, given that he had grown up in Shawanaga, but Parry Island had always been a place of intrigue to him. With no remaining close family members, Francis felt a strong imperative to create a family of his own; this seemed to be especially important given the imbalance of life and death he had experienced in the trenches. Establishing himself in the community meant finding long-lost relatives, a permanent residence, and employment. Francis struggled to attain a pension or significant compensation for his military service and incurred health conditions.[8] This was where growing up among the Nishnaabeg of Georgian Bay proved to be advantageous. The skills and work ethic he had learned from his own people ensured his well-being no matter how little support he received from the government or band council. Francis found a variety of local employment opportunities throughout his lifetime, including guiding for some of the Georgian Bay lodges and tourists. He exemplified an ethos and persistence true to the character of the Ojibwe, and his natural affinity for people won him many friends among local community members and townspeople.

Francis married Eva Tronche shortly after returning from the war. She was the daughter of his old friend Elijah, whom he had met before going overseas. The two men shared many interests and experiences. Both had lost family members early in life, had a strong work ethic, loved music, and found joy in the company of others. Like Francis, Elijah had not grown up on Parry Island. A member of the Saugeen Reserve, Elijah married a young woman from Parry Island's Nanibush family and subsequently made his home in the community. He and his wife, Mary, enjoyed many happy years living among her kin—Odawa who had relocated to Canada from the United States. The Odawa were provided with permanent sanctuary on Parry Island and were eventually made full members as the community consolidated.

Elijah and Mary had a single daughter, Eva, before Mary tragically died of polio. Eva survived the disease that claimed her mother but became permanently crippled in one of her legs. She fortunately had a large extended family that took special interest in her life and education. Although many of the local townsfolk were willing to hire Indians for occasional work, the pay was notoriously poor, and Elijah often found himself away from home. Eva's aunts ensured that Eva was well cared for and learned the basic skills important for life. When she reached her first menses, her aunts also ensured

19. Francis Pegahmagabow, posing here with Ted Stevenson, worked as a fishing guide for many years. Photo used with permission of Ted Stevenson family.

that the rites of *bkaangewin*—a ritual of teaching, fasting, and transformation—were completed for their niece, who became more like an adopted daughter. Eva's youngest daughter, Marie, described this practice as she remembered it:

> *Mii maanda mewnzha gaa-zhiwebak pii ntaawgid shkiniikwens.*
> This is what happened long ago when a girl matured into a young woman.
>
> *Oonh gnimaa naa thirteen gemaa fourteen piitzidog.*
> She would be about thirteen or fourteen years old.

Pii ntaawgid mii gii-o-zhichgaadeg odi gtaamgo waasa megey-aakwaa odi wiigwaamens mii sa wodi gaa-zhi-wanind shkiniik-we ten days wedi gii-gnawendizo odi megeyaakwaa.
At the time she became a woman, she was taken far into the forest, and a small lodge was put up; for ten days would she then look after herself out there in the forest.

Mii dash mnik maanda mdaaching mnik wodi gaa-yaad mii aazhgo kina gegoo gii-kendang gii-kinoomawind kina gegoo waa-ni-bmiwdood maa bemaadzid maa kiing.
And within those ten days that she was there, she would be taught about everything she would have to know throughout her life here on this earth.

Mii go kina waa-zhi-zhitood ge mkakbinaagaansan, gaawiikaa-jgaansan, miinwaa waaboowaanan waa-zhi-zhitood gii-kinoomaajgaaza kina go gegoo miinwaa baagaakooganan waa-zhi-ganawenmaad gii-kinoomaajgaaza wiingashk miinwaa go mnidoominensan waa-zhi-mzinaakshimaad maa pshkwegnoong gii-kinoomaajgaaza.
She learned how to make baskets, quill baskets, and blankets—she learned how to do all of this; she was also taught how to prepare black ash and sweetgrass, how to look after black ash, sweetgrass, and also how to thread beads onto leather.

Mii dash maanda gaa-zhiwebzid en'sa-dbikak ni-nbaad gii-nam-haa gnoonaad now Mnidoon.
This is how it was for her each night as she went to sleep, praying to the Creator for a blessing.

Mii dash maanda gaa-zhiwebzid, oonh aapji go naa gii-gchi-nendam gaa-naabndang gii-gchi-bawaajge.
And so this is how it happened for her—she would be so happy with the visions and dreams she was blessed with.

Eva's maternal aunts were protective of their niece and made sure her every need was met. They would one day fill the same role for Eva's children, serving as adoptive grandmothers in place of their lost sister. This was representative of traditional Nishnaabe family structures in which the extended family—even the broader community—participated in the care, education, and upbringing of a child.

20. Quillwork done by Eva and Priscilla Pegahmagabow. Photo by Brian McInnes.

The following story was one Marie loved to tell about her parents' courtship. I have paraphrased a number of the accounts she told in the English-language version below.

The Crow's Wedding

Like all returned veterans, Francis Pegahmagabow looked for a way to resume the life he had left behind following the completion of his military service. He felt compelled to return to the Parry Sound area in the hope of establishing lasting roots in the Wasauksing community. Finding permanent employment was difficult because of some unresolved health conditions from the war. After a brief hospitalization, Francis was ready for a new journey. He had spent most of his adult life working for non-Native interests and causes. It now seemed to be fitting that he find a way to better serve his own people and community.

Francis wandered into the Kipling Hotel on the long walk from the town hospital to Parry Island. The Kipling was a popular spot for tourists and townsfolk that also welcomed the local Ojibwe. The lounge was filled that afternoon with several parties engaged in animated conversation. One of those in attendance was Francis's old friend Elijah Tronche, whom he had met on Parry Island before the war. Fresh off a day of commercial fishing,

Elijah recognized his old friend, who seemed hesitant to come in. "*Aanii,*" Elijah called out, beckoning with his hand. Francis returned the gesture with a broad smile and promptly joined him at the table.

Elijah was enjoying a few moments of camaraderie with friends before returning to his home on the Wasauksing Reserve. He was still grieving the loss of his wife, Mary, who had passed away not two years prior. Life was difficult for the now single father of sixteen-year-old Eva. Work was hard to come by, and what employment he could find required him to spend long days out on the bay. He knew he could afford a little extra time that day since his daughter was visiting with her aunts. He depended on his wife's family to help him care for Eva during the times he was away. "*Aansh maa gii-bi-njibaayin?*" ("Where have you now come from?"), Elijah asked his old friend. Francis related that he had recently returned from the war and was looking for a place on the reserve to live and work. The two quickly renewed their friendship and enjoyed some spirited conversation. The hours flew by, and Elijah knew his daughter would now be at home waiting. "*Baamaa pii ga-waabamin niijii*" ("I will have to see you later, my friend"), Elijah said, getting up. He explained that the fishing boat he was working on left early in the morning and that he would have to be going. He bid his friend farewell and got up to leave.

Francis jumped up from his seat. "*Ga-wiijiiw dash!*" ("Well, then I will go along with you!"). Elijah invited his friend back to his home on Parry Island, realizing Francis probably had no place to go. It had been a long time since Francis had visited anyone on the reserve, and he was happy with the offer. He had few blood relatives, and even fewer close friends, so an invitation to the reserve was most welcome. It was important to him to earn the acceptance of the community. Proving himself to his military comrades had been comparatively easy; in truth, they had expected little of their Indian compatriot, so any accomplishment was ground won. The Wasauksing community, led by his relative Peter Megis, remembered the great leadership regimes of his predecessors, such as James Pegahmagabow Sr. and Jr. He quickly learned that his forefathers had inadvertently set a high bar of expectation.

Francis and Elijah found their way to the small, tidy home by early evening. The men enjoyed continued conversation over food and drink, reminiscing over their many shared adventures from years before. Elijah proved to be an excellent storyteller, and their conversation lasted well into the night. The men heard a bedroom door open during a short break in one of Francis's stories. The young woman who emerged from the room beckoned for her father's assistance. Elijah jumped up from his chair. "*Mii sa ndaanis*" ("This is my daughter"), he said. He helped her across the room and through the door to the outhouse. Although she had made steady progress, her recovery from polio had been slow. "*Nindoojaanmenmaa*" ("I worry about her"), he later said to Francis. When Elijah and Eva returned from outside, she helped her father by clearing the table, and then she retired to her room for the night. Elijah wished his daughter a good sleep, then returned to his guest. Francis was surprised to have just learned that Elijah had a daughter. She was quite different from the young women he had met in town or overseas. Eva was much like the girls he remembered from his boyhood years—quiet and reserved but with an unspoken strength and bravery. Her waist-long raven hair was freshly combed, and Francis admired her determination to walk without her father's help.

Elijah explained that his daughter's recovery had been trying. Losing her mother made the situation that much harder on his small family. His work schedule did not allow him to be home as much as he should. He was grateful to his in-laws for their mentorship and care of his daughter whenever he was away. Elijah told Francis not to worry about Eva, that she would one day recover and find work somewhere. Sickness and loss had compromised her education, and he hoped that her talents in sewing and basket making would allow her to sustain herself in the world. Elijah joked with Francis that he would be better to focus his attention on the pretty young women from the Kipling Hotel who had been making eyes at the returned soldier earlier that afternoon.

Francis was touched by the courage of Eva. She had defied the sickness that had claimed her mother, and she showed great determination to regain self-sufficiency. He appreciated her quiet disposition, for he had found the young women from town far too overbearing and forward. Prior experiences with non-Native women convinced Francis he would be better to take a Nishnaabe wife. Elijah suggested they retire for the evening since he would have to be up early to board the fishing boat. Francis agreed that would be good but asked his friend one question before retiring. "*Gdaa-miizh na gdaanis?*" ("Would you give me your daughter?")

Elijah laughed at the question, quite sure Francis was speaking in jest. A decorated soldier such as he could surely marry whomever he liked, and there were older, more established families on the reserve who would welcome such a union with one of their daughters. Elijah playfully responded, "*Enh, awi-maajiiwizh!*" ("Yes, please take her away!"). The men continued to joke about how soon a wedding could be held and about how angry Eva's aunts would be should they not receive an invitation. Elijah again petitioned Francis not to worry about his daughter, but Francis insisted he would like to get to know her a little better. Elijah agreed that Francis could remain at the house the next day to visit a little more with his daughter. But he would have to be wary of her aunt, who would be stopping in to check on her in the morning. With that he packed his lunch in the icebox, and the men retired to their sleeping quarters for the night. Eva lay awake in her bedroom wondering about the strange man in her home and the bizarre conversation that had taken place. The walls were thin, and she had been able to hear everything. Her father and the soldier were now long asleep, but she was unable to drift off. Life had been hard since her mother had died. Polio had claimed most of the mobility in her leg, but she was set on living as independently as she could. Fortunately for Eva, her aunts had stepped in where her mother had left off. All strong, independent women of the Nanibush family—traditionalists who had come to the community from the United States during the Indian Relocation Act era—her relatives knew how to overcome struggle. Her aunts encouraged her to be positive but also to remember that human life was beset with challenges. Eva would one day tell her own children the same words: "*Znagad bemaadzing*" ("Life is difficult"). Knowing and accepting the hardships made for a greater appreciation of the good things.

Eva had been concerned with her father's delayed arrival that evening. Elijah was seldom that late returning home, and she valued the few hours they spent together each evening. Her father worked hard and did his best as a single parent. She could see how much he missed her mother and how faithfully he tried to conceal that from her. The thought of having to leave him troubled her greatly, and her heart beat nervously as her father jokingly promised her hand to the visiting soldier. "Oh, my poor heart!" she would one day tell her daughters about that fateful evening. It would be a night that would change everything for her.

Eva awoke to the sound of her father readying himself for the long day ahead. It was still dark when she heard the door shut behind him, and she wished she could fall back to sleep. She wondered if the soldier had gone with her father to work on the fishing boats, but that hope vanished with the sound of rustling in the kitchen area. Francis rekindled the fire in the wood stove and set about preparing a morning meal. Eva dressed herself and nervously entered the main living area. She knew her aunt would be along shortly and that she had only a short time to visit with her father's guest.

Francis was already seated at the kitchen table when Eva came into the living room area. He greeted her with a nod, and she shyly did the same. "*Ondaas maa bi-nmadbin*" ("Come here and sit"), he gestured to her. Although hesitant, Eva accepted his offer and joined the soldier at the family table. Francis offered her a cup of tea he had just brewed and some biscuits he had brought from town. The two sat in silence enjoying their breakfast together. Francis smiled to himself, not wanting to frighten her. They would occasionally look at each other but shared very few words. Eva cleared the table after they had eaten and joined her guest in the living room to visit a little more.

Francis told her he would have to be getting along to town shortly and requested she thank her father for the hospitality. He shared his condolences for the loss of her mother and that he thought she was kind to help Elijah as much as she did. She nodded throughout the conversation, unsure of what to say. He was still a stranger to her, after all, and she was surprised her father had let him stay. To make matters worse, her aunt was already late getting there. The presence of an unknown man in the house might not go over well.

The soldier asked if there was anything he could do to help Eva. "*Gdaawiidookoon na gwa?*" ("Can I help you in any way?"). Eva was uncertain how to answer. She said nothing for the longest time, and he didn't rush her response. She finally commented that she would need water brought into the house at some point, and the soldier jumped to his feet, grabbed the water pitcher, and was back from the well in a flash. She had been dreading the long walk down the hill, and Francis made it look so easy. "*Miigwech*" ("Thank you"), she said. What Eva could not have known then was that this would be the first question Francis would ask her whenever he walked in the door the rest of their lives together: "*Nibi na te?*" ("Is there water?").

Eva was now beginning to enjoy his company. It was nearing mid-morning, and Francis asked if he might sit with her a little longer. Eva wished he could but was nervous about her aunt's arrival. "*Wii-bi-dgoshin nzigos*" ("My aunt will soon be arriving"), she said. Before she could warn Francis to go, her aunt loudly rapped on the door, having heard a strange man's voice inside. Eva and Francis looked nervously at each other.

Had Francis met Christine Nanibush in any previous encounter, he might have had second thoughts about daring to visit her niece without her consent. Unlike her deceased sister Mary and her beloved niece Eva, Christine was an outspoken woman with little concern for how others might perceive her. Many in the community actually feared her, worried that the old medicine knowledge the Nanibush family carried might one day be used against them. Christine, however, had no patience for those who attempted to use medicine power in negative ways. It was she, as recalled by both Duncan and Marie, who much later accosted a dog with a glowing mouth they had noticed hanging around the community: "That is no dog!" she told them, grabbed the animal by the ear, and forced its transformation back into human form. Christine promptly banished the exhausted witch, from a community across the bay. "She was afraid of nothing," Marie recalled, "and she was not afraid to tell anyone what she really thought." She was a role model of strength and integrity for First Nations women.

Chi-Christine ("Big Christine," as they called her) swung open the door to the house and found her niece talking to some strange man she had never before seen. Eva looked down. Francis's eyes grew wide. Christine glared. True to the clan to which she belonged, Chi-Christine burst into the house like a mother bear protecting her cub. "*Aansh maa enanokiiyin?*" ("Now what are you doing around here?"). "*Gdaa-ni-maajaa maa!*" ("You must leave immediately!"). Having survived a war, Francis had no intention of perishing that day. He smiled at Eva, tipped his hat to Chi-Christine, and quickly made his exit.

That would not be his last trip to the home. Francis did, however, pick more strategic times to come by. Eva now looked forward to the visits of the soldier and became ever more confident when he was around. Elijah noticed and supported his daughter's interest. Her aunts would prove to be a more discerning audience. Christine, Leona, Mary-Jane, and Liza-Jean all treated the soldier with great suspicion: "*Nshke gaawiin ndinenmaasiimin wii-bskaabii ow Nishnaabewish!*" ("We don't think this silly old Nishnaabe should be allowed to come back here!"). He was a source of great arguments for the family. But his persistence paid off, and before long Eva herself was asking her aunts if he could visit.

After one of the aunt-supervised visits, Francis left a note for Elijah. He expressed his interest in marrying his daughter but wanted to wait until she was at least seventeen. He also made a special visit to her aunts to reassure them that his intentions were sincere and that he would take good care of their niece. He demonstrated this sincerity by helping Eva find treatment for her leg. The progress she made convinced her aunts of his good intent, and he finally won the family's permission to marry her. Francis consulted with the clergy of the Catholic Church in Parry Sound and asked for their assistance in arranging a wedding. He left the non-Native church staff with the necessary money to purchase an appropriate outfit for his bride and asked them to help get Eva ready for their wedding.

Francis was both excited and nervous when the day arrived. He looked forward to starting his new life and dreamed of having a family of his own. He stopped in a little before the ceremony and found his bride-to-be Eva being attended to by church staff. He gasped when he saw her. Her beautiful

21. Wall portraits of Francis and Eva Pegahmagabow. Canadian War Museum, George Metcalf Archival Collection, CWM 20040035-006, CWM 20040035-007.

long black hair had been shorn to just above her ears, and she was dressed in a black suit the women had found for her in town. He asked the women what they had done with her hair. They responded it had been thrown away, and there was nothing he needed to worry about. Long hair is sacred in the Ojibwe tradition, and Eva had grown hers all of her life. Whether her hair had been cut in the spirit of giving her a new start, or perhaps something deemed necessary before this "pagan" Indian girl could enter the church in holy matrimony, it brought Francis great concern for his bride on this important beginning to their life together.

With the time nearly at hand, Francis asked for a moment with his wife-to-be. "*Aansh naa enenman, Peggy?*" ("What are you now thinking, Peggy?"), Eva asked him. He looked stunned. "*Gkendaan na enenmaan?*" ("Do you know what I am thinking?"), she then asked him. He shook his head no. "Short black hair, black suit, black shoes.... If this is the day you want to marry a crow, then so be it!" Francis broke out in that broad smile he was famous for and remarked, "*Aabdeg nga-wiidgemaa aandeg!*" ("Then I most certainly will be marrying a crow!"). They then laughed together and, after a few adjustments, proceeded with the ceremony. It would be a life full of challenge but also great happiness, love, humour, and fulfillment.

Children

Francis and Eva would be blessed with many children and happy years together. Their children, grandchildren, and community members alike remembered how compatible and well matched they were as husband and wife. They would have eight children in total, losing two sons to early childhood ailments. They cared deeply for their six surviving children and worked hard to ensure they had everything they would need in such a rapidly changing world. Francis understood how important it was to have the skills necessary for mainstream life. He also knew how essential it was for his children to know the traditions that would preserve their sense of self as Nishnaabe people, and he made sure they experienced major cultural rituals and rites of passage. Both he and Eva insisted Ojibwe remain the language of their home if English was going to be necessary for participation in all other frames of life.

William (Joe) and Mike would be very special to Francis, and there were very few places he would go without them. He shared the following with Jenness in 1929: "My two boys met me at the wharf yesterday evening and accompanied me to my house. Some time before our arrival my sister-in-law looked out of the window and saw the elder boy pass by. It was really his shadow that she saw, not the boy himself, for we must have been nearly a mile away at the time."[9] Francis would ensure his sons were proficient in all of the skills they would need to survive on the land, and the boys became skilled trappers, hunters, and fishermen. This included knowledge of the complex spiritual world order of the Ojibwe. They also showed great ability to remember stories, and Francis spent many hours each evening talking with his sons about the customs and legends of the people. Perhaps somewhat unconventionally, he would later teach his daughters Florence and Marie many of the same skills his sons were expected to know.

Eva and Francis offered tobacco to her great-uncle Jim Nanibush to give their children the customary spirit names that would strengthen their lives and help them to find purpose and direction. Marie offered the following thoughts on the importance and ritual of the naming ceremony:

> *Miinwaa gwa pii gwa bi-dgoshing maa mii gwa zhesjigaademgak iihow gchi-wiisni-waagan maawnzowag dabwag maa—nemdabjig kina getzijig ndanjigaazwaad.*
>
> And when a child is born, a great table is set, and they all gathered to sit there—all of those people sitting there would be elders who had been called.

22. Parry Island boys photographed in 1928. National Museum of the American Indian, Smithsonian Institution, N14449. Photo by Frederick Johnson.

Mii dash maa gii-taangaazod maa wiisniwaaganing gii-taa-naawaad maa now binoojiinsan gnoonaawaad maa gewii-sh go maaba shki-binoojiins giigda.
He was then passed around the table, they passed around this child, and they talked to him—and so too did this new baby speak.

Mii dash maandan ezhiwebak maanda bmaadziwin shki-dgosh-ing binoojiinh.
This is how it is to happen in life for a newborn child.

> *Kaa gwa nshaa maa bizhaasii aw binoojiinh gegoo go maa bi-nji-zhaa.*
> That child does not come here for nothing—there is a reason why he has come.
>
> *Aabdeg go gegoo maa nakiiwin maa dayaan maa waa-ni-nakiid.*
> There is most certainly some work that he has to do on this earth, that he will one day set out to accomplish.
>
> *Mii sa iw gii-shkwaa-taanind maaba binoojiinh gwyak go getzijig maa giiwtaahaakhdabjig maa wiisni-waaganing, "Ahaw, mii sa maaba" gaa-kidod "maaba gaa-bi-disgwayingid."*
> When the child was finished being passed around, one of the elders sitting around the table would say, "For this one here, this one who has arrived among us."
>
> *"Mii maanda ezhi-wiinzod, mii maanda ezhnikaazod: Mkadewaankwad."*
> "This is how he shall be named, this is how he shall be called: Black Cloud."

The bestowed name was often the product of a dream or vision the elder had received. A name could also confer healing or strength to a child who had previously suffered from sickness or disease. Francis's children were proud of their spirit or Indian names, and Francis encouraged their use in the home and community. He was reserved about using these names in church or with non-Native people; it seemed then they were best kept among the Nishnaabeg themselves.

The Matter of Leo James

One of the strongest messages that all of Francis's children imparted to their own families was how consistently kind and patient Francis was with all of them. Ideas about how to raise children were changing in this era because of the influence of both religious and educational institutions. The government had sweeping powers of control over Indian life, and children could be removed from Indian homes and placed in residential schools at the whim of the local Indian agent.[10] Francis wanted to ensure his children had the best of both worlds and worked hard to provide them with every opportunity. He was never known by any of his family or community members to have hit any of his children. It is for this reason that questions are raised about a story told in the biography by Adrian Hayes that implies Francis caused the death of one of his infant sons.[11]

All of his children were delivered by traditional midwives in the Wasauksing community. All of these births were successful, and Eva herself was inspired to become a local midwife. Their first two sons were strong and very seldom ill. Their next two children were quite sickly as infants and eventually succumbed to early childhood maladies despite the best efforts of the family to restore them to health. The remedies of both the local doctors and Eva's aunts proved to be equally ineffective. The older of these two children, Leo James, was born on 26 March 1925 and died only three months later. Paul Anthony was born almost a year later on 25 June 1926 and passed away shortly thereafter. The loss of these two boys was a devastating blow to the young family.

It would be a number of years until another child was born to Eva and Francis. Perhaps all Nishnaabe parents of that era viewed their children as gifts from the Creator and took responsibility for child rearing accordingly. Their next child's fate weighed heavily on the young parents. Robert Henry's birth was celebrated by the family, but his sickly constitution proved to be a source of great concern. The pain of their last two children's deaths was still fresh, and losing another child might be too difficult to bear. They considered putting the child through Midewiwin lodge ceremonial rites as a means of ensuring life-long health, but the practice had all but disappeared by that time on Parry Island. Their daily tobacco offerings were answered when the family received powerful visions of a spirit name that would restore the child to health. Francis related the following to Jenness: "Just after my baby was born a woman nearly related to me dreamed that it embodied the soul of a man named Blue Sky who had died many years before. My wife had a similar dream about the same time, so I named the baby Blue Sky, even though the original bearer of the name was unrelated to either of us. The name quickly showed its power, for the baby, which had been very sickly, gained strength immediately and is now quite healthy."[12] Two daughters and one son would follow Robert into the world and bring Francis and Eva much happiness. They are remembered as loving parents who would do anything for their children.

The story found in Hayes about Francis critically injuring one of his infant children is unfamiliar to any of his current descendants. The actual course of events is impossible to determine now. It has been suggested that this story shows evidence of his reported mental instability. Francis was the victim, after all, of residual wartime trauma and suffered many physical and emotional after-effects. He was known to get frustrated and even angry at others in political settings. However, he was such a loving and caring family man that the suggestion he might have seriously harmed one of his children is profoundly uncharacteristic. Neither Duncan nor Marie could ever remember their father striking any family member. Hayes describes the story told by Marie in the following way: "Although her father was usually quiet and peaceful, he may have been deeply troubled. One particular story involved the death of a sibling, Leo James Pegahmagabow, on June 30, 1925. A relative who dabbled in witchcraft told Francis that he had not fathered the three-month-old child."[13] The story suggests that Francis attempted to leave as the witch cited the baby's blue eyes as proof of Eva's infidelity. Such an observation would hardly require witchcraft. The accuser is identified as being an aunt, and—given that Francis had no living aunts and was living among his wife's extended family—it would have been one of Eva's own blood kin who so defamed the young mother.

It has already been noted how Eva was raised by her mother's sisters after the tragic death of Mary Nanibush. The protective spirit these women had for their niece shone through in Marie's story about her parents' courtship. The family patriarch, Jim Nanibush, had zero tolerance for witchcraft and once gave Francis and Eva protective medicine to stave off any such attacks on the family.[14] Bad medicine was not an acceptable practice, and it seems to be inconceivable that any of these women would have spread such malicious gossip about their beloved niece: "Sure enough when my dad walked in the house my mother said the first place he went was for the baby. He picked up the baby in the cradle and took the baby to the light. Sure enough the baby's eyes were light. He took this baby and threw the baby in the crib. This baby's not mine. It was the aunt that put that in his head. My mother didn't even have a chance to tell him that babies' eyes change."[15] Francis by nature was an extremely observant man who spent a great deal of time with his children. The greatest sniper in North American history would surely have noticed before three months if his son had been born with light-coloured eyes. Even if Leo's eyes had yet to darken, blue eyes would not have been that much of a surprise. The child's grandfather himself, Elijah Tronche, had blue eyes, the result of his mixed Ojibwe, Mohawk, and French Canadian heritage.

The little boy who wavered between life and death during his short time on earth, Leo James, would be buried on 1 July 1925. Records at the funeral home run by former Indian agent Alexander Logan show the cause of death as pneumonia. Indian agent J.M. Daly signed off on the documentation on 24 July 1925. Neither Logan nor Daly was a fan of Francis and undoubtedly would have pursued any irregularity with vigour. Francis never attempted to hide any details of his sons' deaths from family members; his children and grandchildren broadly knew the names and fates of their lost relatives for inclusion in remembrance ceremonies. Francis talked openly with Jenness about the deaths of his two children but also shared a story about Leo's passing that brought his family some peace: "We often heard a sound as of a saucer moving beside my first baby, and it seemed to us that some unseen presence was tending the child. Shortly before it died we could feel this presence near us trying to take the child away, and I dreamed that it was the soul of my wife's dead mother. So we did not grieve greatly when the baby died, knowing that my wife's mother would take care of it."[16] Francis and Eva continued on courageously from their losses with the support of their extended family and community. Although they would eventually build their own homestead on property given to them by Eva's grandfather David Nanibush, relationships with their extended family and community would always be important. Eva remained close to her aunts the rest of their lives, and they would regard her children the same way they did their own grandchildren.

Raising a Family

Francis and Eva's children were encouraged to pay attention to their elders and what they learned in their dreams. Francis would take his children to visit the old people in the community, and they were expected to listen attentively to whatever lessons, teachings, or stories might be shared. He would later ask them what they had learned before they fell asleep that night. He would also often be the first person they saw when they awoke, wanting to ensure they didn't forget any messages or lessons learned in their dreams: "Every morning, even now, Pegahmagabow lies beside his two boys, seven and nine years old, respectively, and asks them what dreams have come to them during the night."[17] His children failed to remember any moments when their father was truly angry with them. They remembered occasions when he seemed to be troubled about his relationships with government officials or other Nishnaabeg supportive of the local Indian agent. Francis always seemed to resolve conflicts in his home in a peaceful and quiet way.

Marie emphasized that her father was a very soft-spoken man who never raised his voice at them or his beloved wife. She said her parents would always talk through any challenges and seemed to be devoted to maintaining a calm and peaceful home. Life was difficult in those times, and the family was often poor. Their home was remembered as being happy and never without the basics. Marie recalled her parents as being rather comical and that Francis's trickster-like spirit would keep them all on their toes.

She remembered only one conflict in the family home as a child. Her older brothers returned home intoxicated one evening and soon began arguing. Their shouting came close to blows, and Marie recalled being afraid for perhaps the first time in her life. She said her father simply walked into the room, put his hands on his sons' shoulders, and calmly asked, "*Aansh naa ezhiwebziyeg?*" ("Now what is the matter with each of you?"). Whether it was their profound love for their father, or the gentle way he asked this question, the conflict between the two quickly de-escalated. Francis already served as a role model for his sons by never drinking or allowing alcohol in the family home. He reminded the boys how important it was to calmly find a resolution and that they were lucky to have each other. He poignantly stated he was all alone and had no family left in the world. Marie didn't remember any of her brothers fighting like that again.

The formal education of their children was a necessary part of life that Francis and Eva encouraged. With the near disappearance of the old ceremonial societies and the almost universal acceptance of Christianity in the community, the family became devout Roman Catholics. Not wanting his two oldest sons to be sent to any school that was influenced by the Indian Department, he did his best to educate his children at home. The boys eventually attended a Catholic boarding school that was not one of the Indian residential schools that community members feared.

Francis worked a variety of jobs to support his family. He would frequently take on seasonal work guiding or doing manual labour to support his family. Work was scarce, and as noted by Schmalz, "Indians were the first fired and the last hired."[18] Francis's efforts to procure the necessary resources to start a small farm or other enterprise were continuously blocked by Indian agents who feared his reputation and ability to organize the people might one day create problems for them.[19] It was easier to dismiss Francis as mentally incompetent than to take the kind of action he was demanding of them: to allow the people to authentically govern themselves, recover lost territories, and distribute the resources they were entitled to as they saw fit. Hayes cites Indian agent Logan in 1920: "This man is very hard to handle as he suffers from dementia and takes very strange notions."[20] It was perhaps a "strange notion" then that Indian people could govern themselves and look after their own affairs. It was certainly not safe for the average Indian to suggest—especially to a representative of the Indian Department who had so many controls over the life of the people.

Francis's relationships with the Indian agents would become progressively worse as the years went by. His experience working for townspeople, tourists, marine vessels, and the military had taught him respect for those who held positions of authority. It was an entirely different relationship, though, with the Indian agent, who held great unilateral power. It was as if the Nishnaabeg were like children to be managed, and if their behaviour was found to be inappropriate they were subject to punishment. Harold Cardinal describes the real control the agent had over people's lives: "The Indian agent ... actively worked against the leaders of the day.... He had many weapons.... Sometimes he openly threatened to punish people who persisted in organizational efforts. More often he used more subtle weapons such as delaying relief payments or rations to show the Indians which way the wind was blowing.... By spreading gossip or falsifying facts, the government officials often were able to undermine the leaders through their own people. It was made quite obvious to people on the reserve that it was not wise to talk to certain Indians."[21] Brownlie cites some of the complaints that Francis made about Indian agent Daly, "claiming that the agent had discredited the council, taken sides among the band, and discouraged people from associating with Pegahmagabow himself."[22] Daly further incited resentment from Francis by taking control of the disability pension he was eventually awarded and withholding it from the family if Francis was perceived to step out of line.[23] Francis would fight until his last day against the control of Indian Affairs over the ability of the people to manage their own business. The "puppet" tribal governments the Indian agents supported lost credibility over time. The traditional Ojibwe term for "chief" or "leader" (*gimaa*)—the very term advanced by Indian agents for the elected head of the local Indian government—would lose its revered historical meaning. Indeed, the Ojibwe of Wasauksing would come to refer to any non-Native as *gimaa* (the Indian agent in particular) based upon the control they seemed to have over the Nishnaabe people's lives.

Francis would often experience first-hand how vile the efforts of the Indian agent could be. His work on behalf of the emerging political movements of Indian people required him to travel away from home for extended periods of time. The family received several visits over the years from the Indian agent, who always came accompanied by others from town, when Francis was away. He thought these visits were in retaliation for his actions to help build Indian governments that might one day succeed the controls of Indian Affairs itself. Duncan and Marie credited their dog's attentiveness to oncoming strangers, their excellent hiding skills, and the Indian agent's inability to communicate with their mother, who did not speak English, as key reasons for their not being removed from their home to attend residential school. During one major trip to demonstrate in Ottawa in 1943, his family received two such visits. Hayes noted that Francis had gone against Indian agent Devlin's wishes, and one might suspect these visits were revenge for his rogue action.[24]

Francis loved his children dearly, and it was perhaps his only true fear in the world that they would be taken from him. He had heard accounts of the needless and wanton removal of Indian children from homes all across Nishnaabe country. It was a blessing for the Pegahmagabows that their family was not one of the thousands who lost their children to these insidious schools. Military medals did not restore what Francis had lost during the war, and employment or political office did not provide him with the sense of belonging that had evaded him all of his life. It would be the strength and love he found in his wife, and the enduring hope and happiness he found in his children, that would provide him with what he had been hoping for all along: a home and a family that would not abandon him no matter the circumstances.

Tkwaans—The Dead Branch

This story was told to me one late-summer evening by Duncan Pegahmagabow. We had been discussing the benefits of traditional medicines and the history of ceremonial societies at Wasauksing. Our visit was coming to an end when Duncan suddenly relayed this story as a means of demonstrating the power of belief when using plant medicine. It was also meant to address the long-standing question of whether Francis was actually able to go unseen during the war, as he was often rumoured to have done. Surviving four years on the front lines was a rare feat indeed. Francis himself claimed he was able to sneak across enemy lines and virtually rub shoulders with opposing forces. His success in the field was often attributed to an unusual ability to escape the notice of others.

Many Indian soldiers came to Francis for guidance before serving their terms overseas. As one of the first Indian soldiers to cross the ocean and return safely, he was well regarded by others who wished to do the same. This story is about one such soldier who came to see Francis and the advice he was given about how to remain safe in times of danger.

> *Nshke gwa iihow.*
> Now take note of this.
>
> *Ga-wiindmoon maanda bezhig.*
> I will tell you about one more thing.
>
> *Mii iw aabdeg ji-debwewendman Nishnaabe-bmaadziwin giishpin debwewendziwan kaa daa-nakiimgasinoon.*
> You have to really believe in the Nishnaabe way of life, for if you don't have faith then this will not work.
>
> *Mii-sh gaa-zhiwebzid maabam yahaa maabam ndedem gii-o-miigaazod odi gchi-gaamiing.*
> This is about what happened to my father when he went to fight overseas.
>
> *Gii-bskaabii.*
> He returned home safely.

Chi-zhimaagnish aawi mii gnimaa gii-goojninid niw yahaan biiwaabkoon gaa-bkinaaged—zhoon'yaa-waabkoon gaa-bkinaagejig.

He was a great soldier and was decorated with those medals he won—those silver medals that soldiers earned for their deeds in war.

Mii dash maabam bezhig Nishnaabe aazhgo gewiin gii-nendaagzi ji-zhimaagnishiiwid aansh gaa-shkwaa-miigaadiing go naa mii-sh miinwaa wedi bezhig gii-miigaadiing iihow.

There was this one Nishnaabe man who was now expected to go and fight in the war, for another war was now taking place.

Mii dash maabam gii-zhaad odi gii-zhimaagnishiiwid.

Francis had gone overseas and served as a soldier during the first one.

Miish go maaba besho aazhgo wii-takamiid zegzi wii-zhaad odi wenji-miigaading.

It was now getting close to the time when this man would have to go overseas, but he was afraid to go to war.

Mii-sh pii gii-mkwenmaagwen niw ya'aan Francis Pegahmagabow. "Aa nga-wi-waabmaa ow," kidowidag sa.

He remembered meeting Francis Pegahmagabow. "I will go and see him," he must have said.

"Manj gaa-zhichgegwen iihow gii-bipskaabiid?"

"What must he have done in order to have come back home safely?"

Mii-sh gii-waabmaagwen miish giiwenh egod iihow.

And so he went to see Francis to hear about this.

Gii-wiindmawaadgenan sa iw, "Mii aazhgo wii-maajaayaan."

He told Francis, "It is now time for me to leave."

Odinaadagenan iw, "Ingotaaj dash gnimaa odi ngoji indaa-aabsikooz."
And he also said to him, "I am so afraid, for I will likely be shot and killed somewhere there."

"Aansh giin gaa-zhichgeyin iihow gii-bipskaabiiyin?"
"What was it that you did in order to make it back safely?"

Mii-sh giiwenh egod iihow, "Ahaaw," digoon sa giiwenh, "giishpine aazhgo enendman iihow gegoo wii-zhiwebziyin."
So this is what he must have been told, "Well, then, if you are already thinking this way, then something will surely happen to you."

"Gnimaa ge gegoo aazhgo gtaajiyin aazhgo wii-nsigooyin baatiinwag gow zhimaagnishag engotaajiyin wii-nsigooyin."
"If you are already afraid of being killed when you are among all of those soldiers, then your fear will just get you killed."

"Mii ge-zhi-ayaayin, bookwaakbidoon yaa tkwaans ebaateg ow tkwaans mii-sh ji-zhaashaagwandaman iihow."
"So when you are there, break apart a branch, a dry dead branch, and then chew on it a while."

"Kaa-sh ga-gondaziin iw egonendman iihow."
"You are not to swallow this, but keep it in your mouth."

"Mii go ji-zhaabwiiyin."
"You will then be able to pass through the lines."

Mii sa giiwenh gaa-zhichged iihow aazhgo zegzid aazhgo gii-waabndang go naa.
So this is what he did, this man who had been so afraid, now that he had seen what to do.

"Gnabaj e-nsigoowaambaanen ninamdab," gii-mikwenmaad niw gaa-igwad iihow ji-bookbidood iw tkwaans ebaatenig.
"I'm likely going to get killed sitting here," he thought one day during the war, and he remembered Francis telling him to break apart a dry dead branch.

Gii-zhaashaagndang giiwenh gii-gonendang iw mii giiwenh go gii-zhaabwiid.
He chewed on this and was able to pass through the enemy lines unseen.

Kaa gii-baashksigaazii gii-zhaabwiid gwa.
He did not get shot and passed right through.

Mii-sh gegoo gii-zhaabwiid iihow gii-bipskaabiid.
He was able to pass through those enemy lines and made it back safely.

Mii dash giiwenh enenimawzid gesnaa gchi-nenmaadag.
He was blessed in this way and was truly grateful for Francis.

"Mii sa enenmag maabam Nishnaabe," kidod, "maabam Francis."
"It was because I thought of this man," he said, "this one known as Francis."

"Kaa ngii-nsastazii iihow manj gaa-nji-zhigwen iihow," mii giiwenh enaad niw.
"I didn't fully understand all you said to me," he must have later said to Francis.

"Aaniish gaa-nji-zhiiyin iihow geniin ngii-bipskaabii."
"What the meaning behind those words was, but I too was able to return safely."

"Aanii dash gaa-nji-zhiiyin iihow ji-agonemag ow e-baasod ow mtigoons?"
"So what was the exact meaning behind the dried branch you told me to keep in my mouth?"

"Kaa go niinaa ga-waabandaziin iihow gaa-nibomgak," wdigoon giiwenh.

"You cannot see a dead thing," he said to him.

Mii maanda Nishnaabewaadziwin.

This is the Nishnaabe way of life and spirituality.

He took its state, his body did, and the soldiers could not see him.

Miinwaa ge ow wii-daapnaman iiyoo mshkiki, aabdeg gdebwewendaan iihow—giishpine debwewendziwan kaa daa-nokiimgasinoon.

You have to believe in this—for if you do not believe, then this would not work.

An Indian at War

Mii sa wenji-zhawendaagwak bmaadziwin.
It is because life is sacred.

—Francis Pegahmagabow on his reason for going to war[1]

Stories of War

Stories of war remained strong among the Ojibwe of Georgian Bay. Francis Pegahmagabow grew up hearing tales of the fierce battles that had taken place in the lands and waters he knew so well. Although generations of his ancestors had not directly fought in battles, Francis had intimate knowledge of many of these encounters from the stories and place names that filled his childhood. He took pride in the warrior tradition that ran through his lineage, and like Ojibwe youth for generations before him he prepared himself with the vital skills to survive should such hardship ever again come to the people.

His children shared his love of war stories. They experienced exhilaration while listening to tales of epic battles on the bay. The war parties that once patrolled the lands and waters left a rich legacy for generations of storytellers. Francis would most often share such stories when the family travelled by places where historic battles had occurred. They reminded his children that even in these lands peace had been hard won and that they needed to respect the generations of warriors who had given their lives to ensure a future for the people. Francis always spoke with great respect for the opposing forces in such historic battles. This was the same way he talked about those he himself had encountered in war. Never once did he ridicule or belittle the efforts of enemy lines, simply and singularly remarking "*gii-ntaa-miigaazwag*" ("they fought well").

Becoming a Soldier

The ceremonies that prepared young people for times of change, great journey, or battle continued to be practised—albeit in modified ways—throughout Francis's youth. Francis shared details with Jenness about how both fasting and the sweat lodge or vapour bath lodge were part of historical Nishnaabe preparation for war:

> In the middle of a large wigwam, completely enclosed, the warriors erected a sweat-house covered with deer-skins, and placed inside it buckets of water and hot stones. They remained in the wigwam outside while their leader, seated within, poured the water on the stones and filled the space with vapour. The door of the sweat-house was closed, and only a tiny round opening in the wall permitted communication with the wigwam without. Each warrior called up his medicine-power with a song and entered through this hole, when the vapour in the sweat-house purified his soul and body. Those whose medicine-powers were too weak to give them entrance were rejected from the war party.[2]

Such ceremonies were increasingly difficult to perform because of Indian Act restrictions and worries about the interference of outsiders. The *madoodooswan,* crudely called the "sweat lodge" in contemporary times, continued to be practised at both Shawanaga and Wasauksing when Francis was a boy. The lodges were often immediately dismantled after use because of fear of discovery by clergy or, more worrisome, Indian agents who always seemed to be questioning the people's activities. Francis shared with his children that participating in these ceremonies later helped him to overcome the challenges the Great War presented.

One might assume a life spent navigating the difficult Georgian Bay terrain had taught Francis about surviving the extremities of war. The varied geography of rock, sand, mud, and swamp was not easy to traverse, and the temperature extremes of the four seasons brought their own challenges. Francis was accomplished at surviving life on the land—often spending days alone hunting or trapping in many kinds of weather—even as a boy. "While it is easy to fall prey to the noble savage ideal, the archival record does indicate that Indians excelled as snipers and scouts. This should be viewed as a result of their livelihood as hunters and trappers; it also bears witness to the fact that, given their realities of life during this time period, they possessed a greater skill at arms, by tradition or by necessity, than the average Canadian."[3] The

Georgian Bay terrain was a world for which Francis was fully prepared and in which there was safety even in its rugged unpredictability. Humans lived in mutual respect with their surroundings, and while the landscape could be harsh at times it could also be endured with some know-how. This was not the same as the world of war, where a harsh and foreign terrain filled with enemy soldiers made for an endlessly dangerous place that offered no sense of safety or mastery.

A natural ability with a rifle, and a life spent hunting for his immediate and extended family, made Francis a stalwart soldier and sniper who seldom missed a mark. His boyhood skills with a slingshot were well regarded by his peers and transferred nicely to a rifle when he came of age. Knowledge of plant medicine was similarly advantageous for survival: "Pegahmagabow's deer medicine is the root of the *shingoakwansiwan* ('pine-shaped herb,' probably the mugwort, *Artemisia dracunuloides*). He must find the plant to his right, for if it lies on his left it has no virtue. He buries its stem in the ground with a little tobacco, chews the root, and rubs the mingled juice and saliva over his eyes. Then he can approach a deer close enough to kill it with a tomahawk."[4] His legendary ability to disappear, or to evade notice, was enhanced by the use of plant medicines he learned from his foster mother, Louise Kewaquado. Although Francis would seldom if ever speak on the subject, his unique talents were likely the products of spiritual blessings he had received during boyhood fasts. Based upon the way he thought his own life was strengthened by the practice, he strongly encouraged all of his children to fast. His physical preparation from a life lived on the land and the blessings he received through ceremonial rites were each important to his success and survival overseas.

Leaving for War

One of the defining characteristics of Francis Pegahmagabow was his unfaltering ambition and will to make life better for himself and his people. The experience of growing up as an orphan with very few resources made him that much more determined to leave a mark on the world. He challenged himself as a young man by enrolling in high school to learn how to better speak, read, and write the English language. His efforts earned the commendations of the local Indian agent's office and the Euro-Canadian population of Parry Sound. While Francis resisted the control of Indian Affairs over his Nishnaabe people, he did not hold a grudge against non-Native peoples. He was well known by both local townspeople and his fellow soldiers for his bright smile and pleasant disposition. Duncan thought his father was always looking for a better way for all peoples to live and work together. His Nishnaabe people should not, he would say, "have to give up everything" for this to work.

Francis viewed participation in the war as an opportunity to both fight alongside his fellow countrymen and make a distinct accomplishment for his own Nishnaabe people. Native people were not initially recruited or conscripted for war service;[5] it was feared their presence might somehow deny the "privileges of civilized warfare" to the battalions to which they belonged.[6] Francis somehow managed to pass through any such restrictions and became one of the first Aboriginal soldiers to enlist for service in the Great War. While always proud of his Ojibwe heritage, he struggled with the lower expectations he thought others had for him. The war presented a rare opportunity for Native soldiers to be perceived as equals with their non-Native countrymen for perhaps the first time in their lives.[7] It was a fleeting equality, however, that so many paid for with their lives. Francis was determined not to become an Indian casualty no matter how dangerous the situations he was placed in.

Life in a military battalion inspired mutual respect and camaraderie. Francis never claimed to have any special Indian powers, but his fellow soldiers recognized him in a unique way. He had exceptional courage and instinct for avoiding danger that the men trusted. His skill with a rifle was also admired. These special abilities would earn him roles of both scout and sniper. Francis told his children it was often his responsibility to lead his fellow soldiers on the field. Helping to ensure a clear path was a responsibility he took seriously. To avoid confusion and not compromise their position, Francis devised a set of hand signals to communicate when it was safe to advance, retreat, or take cover. There was no room for error with so many lives in the balance.

Francis suffered numerous injuries in the war. None was as traumatizing as the loss of a friend and fellow soldier killed by enemy fire. Francis was leading a sniper expedition early in his military service when they were suddenly ambushed by the enemy. The men attempted to drop to the ground as the shots hit the overhead earth ridge. Francis recalled the terrifying sound of the bullets hitting the ground and the feeling of dirt falling on his back. However, it was a dull thud that most captured his attention. He looked back to see that his friend had been decapitated by enemy fire. He remembered hearing his name called out but only after hearing the sound of his friend hitting the earth. It was a memory that would haunt Francis long after the war, and it was no surprise he preferred to work alone after this incident.

The early loss of a friend and fellow soldier prompted the solitary work missions for which Francis became famous. As a scout, he was able to travel far ahead and always returned with valuable information about enemy positions, resources, and strategies. The detailed correspondence puzzled his superior officers since it appeared he had actually been inside enemy encampments on occasions. Francis carried out his work with a unique confidence that his fellow soldiers struggled to find; not only did he want to work alone, but also few others seemed to be willing to accompany him on his missions. Hayes has commented on the "invincibility" that Francis seemed to believe he had throughout the war, a fact corroborated by the stories he told his family and community.[8] The protections he had received from his boyhood fasts and Nishnaabe medicine people seemed to sustain him through even the most harrowing and dangerous situations. He attributed the injuries he sustained in war to lost faith—however momentary—in the protections he had been given. He regretted these occasions but admitted it was hard to always maintain belief in conditions that so devalued life and often obscured the presence of any higher power.

As an Ojibwe who grew up in the spirit-rich world of Georgian Bay, Francis found the world overseas foreign in many regards. He explained to his children that it felt "old" but also "forgotten" in a way he could not quite understand. It was certainly not a Godless place, even in the culture of death and destruction that pervaded it. Although he was not a smoker, Francis took advantage of the abundance of tobacco that flowed through the ranks. He was true to the Nishnaabe use of tobacco for sacred prayer and tried to offer a little each day. He would always place tobacco on the earth before dangerous missions and told his daughter Marie that had he not done so these operations surely would have failed. The presence of the Spirit seemed to be similar, particularly in the skies, trees, and earth. Francis struggled to make plant medicine work since everything felt different. Although he did not understand why then, he thought his Ojibwe language was recognized and understood whenever he used it in prayer. It wasn't until much later in his study of Latin in the Roman Catholic Church that Francis came to understand that spiritual languages would always be understood wherever and whenever they were spoken. Even in the midst of a war that defied everything good in the world, it was still possible to reach the Spirit.

One curious occurrence Francis shared with both his children and Jenness involved seeing an unusual dog during a war mission. He was fortunately with another soldier who verified the unusual observation: "During one period of the war in France I was a runner, and had as my fellow runner a Norwegian named Oscar Lund. One evening we saw a black dog with a luminous mouth carrying what appeared to be a paper tied to its neck. Believing it to be a scout for the Germans Lund reported it to the adjutant, who took me with him in a motorcycle to look for it. However, we did not see it again."[9] The dog behaved strangely and displayed unusual interest in the men. The luminous mouth was something Francis had observed only as a young boy in a rare class of individuals able to change themselves into animal form. He told his children this story after they encountered a similar creature close to their home on Parry Island. Francis was never sure why he saw that dog during the war or what its purpose actually was.

While he engaged in some playful jesting with battalion mates about his "Indian powers," he was modest and generally concealed his actual spiritual practice. He enjoyed much of the discourse and never minded being called "chief" around camp or on the field. Francis even decorated his bell tent with Indian symbols that lightened the mood for his compatriots. He told his children not all of the symbols he had drawn were for fun; some were actually protective images he had learned from medicine people before the war. During one particularly difficult mission, when the men found themselves immobilized by rain and mud, a fellow officer gave him tobacco and asked him if he could do anything about the conditions. Francis took the tobacco, quietly invoked the sky spirits for pity, and within moments the rain seemed to pass, and the sky brightened. After a short period to allow things to dry a little, the men were again able to journey safely back to their base camp.

A quiet notoriety about the Indian who could make the weather change grew after this episode. Francis seldom volunteered anything about how the Ojibwe people thought about the spiritual world, and he was surprised by the interest of the men. He shared with Duncan that, though he never taught any of the men to pray with tobacco, he was confident he saw some of them mumble a few words after lighting up during worrisome moments. Francis had been born into a world with a complex spiritual order the Ojibwe had observed for thousands of years: "the ruler of the east, *Wabenokkwe*, '*Wabeno* woman' or the moon, sister of the sun over whom she has charge; the ruler of the south, *Shauwanigizik*, 'southern sky'; the ruler of the west, *Nanibush*, and the ruler of the north, *Giyuedin*, 'wind blows home' (because the winds have their home in the north)."[10] "Tobacco" (*semaa*), a plant indigenous to the Americas, had been used in prayer by the Ojibwe since their beginning. As a young boy, Francis never observed tobacco being used recreationally by any of his Nishnaabe people. He himself tried to reserve its use for spiritual practice only. He told Marie some of his fellow soldiers would even pass tobacco to him during the war when they faced harrowing situations they were unsure they would survive.

One such episode in which Francis used knowledge of Indian medicine and prayer to help his company escape certain death involved a mustard gas attack. This was perhaps the most nefarious and feared of all the assaults a battalion might experience since there was often no possibility of escape or defence.[11] Francis shared this experience with his children in such detail they thought they could see the growing terror and anger on the faces of the men as the gas advanced. Duncan and Marie could hear the concern in their father's voice and recognized that the foreboding gas cloud in his stories was one of the few things in the world Francis feared. It was when the fate of the men was all but sealed that a most unexpected event occurred. Francis was approached by a general with a cigarette in hand asking if he could do anything to shift the odds in their favour. Francis lit the cigarette, stood facing the east, and petitioned the wind spirits of that direction to hold back the cloud from advancing any farther. He then turned to the west and asked the wind guardian of that direction to overtake the menacing gas. He stood there quietly smoking that cigarette as his grandfathers would have done—careful to never fully inhale—but imparting that tobacco with his thoughts and prayers as it passed from his being into the spirit realm.

For the Ojibwe of Georgian Bay, learning to communicate with the spirits of the world was a necessary part of life. A person unable to talk with the spirit realm was at the mercy of the elements. Francis was a different kind of windtalker, as were all of his kin who had grown up along the waters of the Great Lakes. There was no guarantee one's tobacco would effect a response, but the "old Indians" (the *Gete-nishnaabeg*, as Francis would call them) knew their tobacco was always accepted and heard.

So it was that this descendant of the Georgian Bay *Gete-nishnaabeg*, the lone hope of his battalion against the oncoming cloud of death, found within himself the strength, will, and blessing of his people to shift the direction of the wind before the gas sickened and killed his battalion: "Thirty-five years ago we suffered under the fumes of gas used in war of 1915 by Germans. I never want to see the agony of men in mass formation again. General [Sir Edwin] Alderson said Peg what can you do about this matter. I said try to change wind. He said alright go ahead. Yes the wind changes from east to west wind before the sun rise. Germans suffered just as heavy as we did. They were not prepared to take their own medicine."[12] The text is hard to follow since it was written in Francis's broken English. From a Euro-Canadian perspective, this event might seem very strange. But the unique experiences of Native soldiers in the world brought a different viewpoint and understanding.

This story is a testament to the continued strength of Aboriginal spirituality and belief. While Francis did suffer in later years from what we now identify as post-traumatic stress disorder, no evidence of any such affliction is found in this letter. We do see, however, how deeply grateful Francis was for the blessing and intervention of the Spirit in a most unexpected place. It also demonstrates how he found a position of respect as an Indian in a mixed battalion of men who might never have given his beliefs a second thought had they been at home safe, far away from the war and clouds of poison air.

After the War

Like many who return from battle, Francis found the world he had left quite different upon his return. He recognized that his experience overseas was an important source of this transformed perspective and that coming to a community that did not understand what he had experienced would be both a blessing and a curse. He soon noticed the changes that had been occurring among his own Nishnaabe people. A greater focus on individualism was perhaps the most apparent transformation, but so was a lack of interest in the traditions that seemed to him to be at the heart of what it meant to be Nishnaabe. Although there was considerable interest in stories of the war itself, they were not easily forthcoming from Francis. His lengthy career as a sniper, dedicated to the extinguishment of human life, was contrary to the day-to-day life and philosophy of a traditional Ojibwe man. It was one thing to engage in such a practice during war, but it was an entirely different thing to return home afterward and talk about it as an accomplishment.

Perhaps the greatest changes noted by Francis in the postwar experience were those he observed in himself. He no longer doubted his value in the world, feeling as if he had accomplished feats few others—Indian or otherwise—could have. He had proven to himself he could achieve whatever he set his mind to do and win the acceptance of others who might be reluctant to give it. But like all who return from such atrocity, Francis was forever changed by the extreme violence of his experience overseas. As he once poignantly remarked to Duncan, "*Kaa eta go ngii-gnawaabndaziimin*" ("We did not simply just look upon all of that"). War stories, and especially stories of death, were generally forbidden in the home unless a visiting serviceman was there. Francis would let little details slip now and again but only to make a point about the importance of having respect for life. His war narratives were carefully guarded and measured in their deployment. It was as if he did not want his children to be influenced in any way by the terrible scenes in his memory, and his unwillingness to speak openly or often about his direct experience was his way of protecting them.

In turn, his family was deeply protective of Francis. It was an unspoken rule among his children that they did not ask him directly about his time overseas. Revelations made to any one of them were intimate and private and were rarely shared among siblings. Francis is remembered as being the likeable and enthusiastic young recruit he was upon his immediate return from the war. It was only much later that his mounting frustrations with the deteriorating conditions of his people's lives made him susceptible to the trauma of his war experience. None of the accolades Francis earned after the war could ever restore what he had lost. Although he never spoke regretfully with his children of his time in the service, or the accomplishments made for the greater human good, his family sometimes wondered if he would have been happier never having gone to war.

In the years both preceding and during the war, traditional ceremonial culture in Georgian Bay experienced devastating loss. Although Jenness reported the extinction of the major ceremonial societies many years prior, Francis's wife, Eva, might have been put through an Ojibwe medicine lodge to help her recover from polio. By the end of the war, many of those who had once helped to lead such outlawed ceremonies were no longer able or willing to do so. The ceremonial rites that helped returning warriors to reintegrate into their communities would have been helpful to Francis and other returning Native soldiers. The pipe ceremony, sweat lodge, shaking tent, or entry into one of the medicine lodges had all offered healing and restoration to a wounded warrior's body, mind, or spirit. By the time Francis found his way back to Georgian Bay, however, all such rites seemed to have been extinguished, silenced, or hidden away.

The Disillusioned Hero

The legacy of Francis Pegahmagabow as both a returned hero and a disillusioned veteran is well summarized throughout Hayes.[13] His world seemed to be increasingly distributed between these two extremes as the years progressed, and he would be the worse for it. These roles were not in continuum but in dynamic relationship with each other from the moment he returned from the war. Francis would be both rewarded and punished, loved and scorned, venerated and slandered. Finding a middle ground in the dichotomy of public perception would not be easy. It was not only the Indian agents he would find adversarial but also many of his own people in this new world to which he returned. Rather than enjoying widespread welcome and appreciation, Francis was questioned by Native and non-Native sceptics alike about the scope and significance of his wartime deeds,[14] whether to silence him or to elevate their own standing by denigrating his, yet he endured these betrayals with a quiet dignity few else could.[15] He knew the truth of his work as a soldier. While others would try to paint him as either a tyrant or mentally incompetent, he endeavoured to remain who he had always been. He would always be a hero, no matter what shadow was cast on his record by the jealousy or scepticism of others.

Francis would join his many forefathers in serving a first term as chief of the Wasauksing community from 1921 to 1925. Although he would run against the old chief, Peter Megis (who died shortly thereafter), Francis did so only with his encouragement and blessing. As Duncan once said to me about these two Wasauksing leaders,

> *Gdinawendaagan gwa ow, Peter Megis. Odinawemaan maaba indedem niw. Mii giw gegaa go naa gii-wiijkiiwendwag go.*
> He was your relative, Peter Megis. He was my father's relation. They were almost like brothers.

Francis would attempt to wrest back power from Indian Affairs and help to restore a more traditional mindset among the people during his first term as chief. Both efforts were valiant but futile given the circumstances of both control and change that dominated. Indian Affairs would not relinquish any of its control and disregarded his leadership entirely. His efforts to restore the community's traditions by having elders speak in the council hall were not met with support in the long term, and Francis was painted as being backward in his thinking. As Hayes rightly suggested, the family compact that had long challenged Megis—whom Francis succeeded—now turned its attention to removing the returned war hero himself from power.[16]

His leadership style resembled traditional Nishnaabe understandings of governance and interrelationship more closely than that of his contemporaries. Francis remained proud of his family clan all of his life and suggested that historical systems of clan leadership be reincorporated into local governance. He also believed that a major responsibility of the chief himself was to help look after all members of the community. Francis dutifully fulfilled this responsibility by visiting with constituents in their homes and inquiring about their needs and interests. He also made a commitment to ensuring that the rights of individual community members were addressed at meetings of the chief and council and forwarded to Indian Affairs if necessary. When families failed to receive adequate support, he often helped them by using his own resources. This was a hard lesson for his children, who had learned to value and care for the things they had. "It seemed there were always others who needed things more than us," Marie remembered. "It was hard to give up our possessions such as articles of clothing or food even, ... but our father always came through and eventually replaced these with something else. He always wanted to make sure the people were looked after first." This was what it meant to Francis to serve as chief.

Duncan and Marie shared with me that the residual stress of war did not generally affect their father's day-to-day family or work life. His frustration with Indian Affairs, however, was legendary.[17] Writing was difficult for Francis, but that did not deter him from spending many hours composing letters to various Indian agents and other government officials over the years. He was continually advocating for change and increased independence of the Nishnaabe people. The answers he received, if any at all, were deeply discouraging. These were the moments he seemed to be most susceptible to the post-traumatic effects of the war. His children would call them "aftershocks" in which he needed both time and space to reintegrate himself emotionally into the present. This was not well understood by the community: few others from Wasauksing had gone to war, and no one else had spent the time in the field Francis had. He was truly alone in many respects after the war.

Despite the lack of authentic support or recognition from the Canadian government, Francis never lost sight of how important his work overseas had been. He placed great meaning in his military uniform and the medals he had earned. They were his foremost symbols of bravery and accomplishment. He would sometimes put on those medals in the years following the war as a means of finding strength and inspiration to face the new battles ever emerging on different fronts.

Life was hard for the people in postwar times. Poverty and discrimination became widespread. Even the traditions that had sustained the Ojibwe for thousands of years disappeared at an unprecedented pace. Furthermore, control over the lives of the Nishnaabe people was exercised with greater vigour by government agencies.[18] These were all things Francis would resist and fight against until the day he died.

As a war hero, he would receive some recognition for his service. The Wasauksing band was proud of their returned son and helped Francis and his new bride to travel to Toronto for his medal presentation. There would be similar tributes throughout the years, though fewer as time went on and his war service seemed but a distant memory. There would never be much distance for Francis, however. The incredible love of his family would help to ease the burdens of postwar trauma as the years passed by. The physical, emotional, and perhaps even spiritual injuries incurred during the war only seemed to get worse over time. His children recalled that in later years Francis would have to sleep sitting in a chair, so great was the damage to his lungs from war-induced pleurisy. Other physical injuries also ailed him, but perhaps most disconcerting were the nightmares that would frequently wake him. Even his beloved thunder would one day remind him all too much of the sound of an approaching enemy battalion.

The medals and other commendations Francis received throughout his life helped him to cope with the horror of war and the deeds he had done in service to his country. It was tragic enough that his community did not understand or accept his personal struggles after the war, but the animosity the family experienced when he was recognized for his accomplishments was misplaced. Although he would again make attempts to help the local Wasauksing tribal government, serving on council and then again as chief from 1942 to 1945, he realized his best efforts to help establish meaningful change for the Nishnaabe people would be at the national level.

Postwar involvement in the 23rd North Pioneers militia regiment provided a connection for Francis to the better parts of the war experience. He had enjoyed the camaraderie of his fellow soldiers, and the opportunity to continue such a relationship beyond the war proved to be important to him. He continued to show his dedication by serving as company sergeant-major, a rank confirmed by the Canadian Forces in 2015.[19] Maintaining contact with those who knew the reality of war, and helping to guide others who would one day go into battle, provided Francis with both a community of support and an opportunity to mentor others. Remembering the greater good that his military service had been dedicated to—and helping that work to continue into the future through the efforts of others—seemed to be a great source of healing and revitalization in the context of the various injuries he had sustained.

Marie always remembered how important the Remembrance Day ceremony was to her father. November was always a special time of pause and reflection for the Nishnaabe. Francis called this month *Niibinaasge-giizis* in Ojibwe ("Moon that shines like the summer sun") based upon the special brightness of this time and how far one could see in the dark. It was a time when even lost shadows could be seen. Remembrance Day for Francis was about more than being honoured or remembering the lives of his fallen friends and fellow soldiers; it was also a time to remember those whose lives he had taken. You had to remember them, he would say, because in your worst dreams and darkest moments you could never forget them. Remembrance Day was also thus a much-needed day of forgiveness.

It was in these moments, long outside the calendar year's day of remembrance, that Francis would sometimes wear his military uniform and medals and walk the reserve roads. It was as if he sought to fall back in step

23. Francis Pegahmagabow's war medals. Canadian War Museum, George Metcalf Archival Collection, CWM 20040035-001.

with his younger, more hopeful self who may be better able to help bring an end to the war. During those short walks, he would again find the meaning of his war actions and a reaffirmation of the need to keep fighting against the things that continued to threaten the well-being of his people. If these walks incited fear or misunderstanding or amusement among others, it was not intended. All of his children would attest to this. It was his statement to the world of his personal reclamation from the horrors he had experienced and a sign of his continued commitment to serve both his people and his country. Contemporary criticism of his action—especially by those who do not know his rationale or that which serves no purpose other than defamation—simply has no value.

The war, for all of its misery, death, and disdain, taught Francis to be resolute, strong, and resourceful like never before. It would both enslave and free him. He was never able to shake his memories of the brutal things he saw and did, but the war was the one time in his life when he was emancipated from the legal limitations of being an Indian and allowed to show his quality to the world. The war also provided Francis with a sense of belonging. He had always been the orphaned Indian boy who struggled to achieve an authentic sense of welcome anywhere. He found, perhaps for the first time in his life, a sense of belonging and accomplishment in the muddy trenches and on the blood-stained battlefields of those foreign lands. Although his involvement would cost him dearly, becoming a great soldier gave him the courage and fortitude for all of the battles awaiting him in postwar life.

Enendaagwak Bmaadziwin— What Is Expected of Life

This short excerpt was taken from a long series of reflective comments made by Duncan one late-summer evening. We had been talking about some hunting violations that had recently occurred in the area, and Duncan was adamant people would not behave in such a way if they had heard the kinds of teachings his father had given him. Not only was life sacred in the Nishnaabe world view, but also there were expectations for how they conducted themselves in the world. Duncan said this was a common code of life for all Nishnaabe people in his father's time and when he himself was young. He was concerned people were forgetting to live as expected, and it was important for people to hear and live by these teachings again.

Kidoban ndedem.
This is what my father had said.

Mii-sh maa Nishnaabe go naa gewiin geget gwa naa enishnaabewendang da-kendaan iihow ndawenjiged.
The Nishnaabe person, in the cultural way that he was given to think about the world, was to know this about hunting.

Kaa go wiin iihow ezhi-n'gajtood ndawenjiged gegoo doo-nji-ntoosiin.
It is not because he is good at hunting that he is actually able to kill anything.

Gnimaa maa go naa ge-ni-nsaad niw waawaashkeshwan gaawiin gwa epiichi-ntaa-ndawenjged baashkzwaad niw ntaa-waakwii nendam.
If he kills a deer, it is not because he is a skillful hunter that he shot that deer or that he thinks himself to be a good shot.

Kaawiin, kaawiin sa.
No, not at all.

Gii-nendaagzi sa gwa ji-nsaad niw waawaashkeshwan ji-miin'gozid iihow ji-giiwewnaad ji-shamaad niw mii go naa gewiin enchid.
It was meant for him to kill that deer; he was blessed with it to take home and feed however many were in his family.

Miinwaa go naa ge-ni-shkosed maabam waawaashkesh daa-miigwewan ngoji go odi ni-miigwe iihow wiiyaas ji-wiisniwaad giw aanind Nishnaabeg.
And that which was left over of the deer he would give away—he would go around and give away that meat so that others may eat.

Kaa go wiin go eta go kina gegoo ge nenziin.
He was not to think that this was all for himself.

Miigwe.
He gives this.

Mii iw nake ge-zhi-miin'goziiyin giin iihow giishpin miigweyin.
The way that something is given to you is how you are to give.

Giishpine gegoo miigwesiwan kaa gegoo gdaa-miin'gozisii.
If you do not give anything, then there is nothing you will receive.

Aabdeg ga-miigwe neyaab dash wenzhishing da-zhiwebad maa gbmaadziwining.
You are to give back whatever good may happen in your life.

Ga-miigwe maa naa maabam Gzhe-mnidoo gaa-miin'goyin miigwe.
You are to give back in the same way that the Kind Spirit has given things to you, for the Spirit gives freely.

Mii dash iihow wenji-nendaagwak iihow.
This is why this is expected.

Weweni ji-naadzid maa naa nake ow Nishnaabe ezhi-ndawendaagzid ji-miigwed iihow gaa-miin'gozid gewiin ji-aanke-miigwed dash.
He was careful in the way that he lived, for the Nishnaabe was expected to give in the same way that he was blessed, in order to extend the act of giving itself.

Mii enendaagwak iw bmaadziwining.
That is what is expected in life.

Community Life

Mii dash giiwenh gaa-zhi-kenmaawaad iihow maa gii-taawaad go naanaawayihiing maa iihow Nishnaabe-oodenaang gaa-zhinkaademgak.
The people knew that something was there in the centre of where they were living, in the Indian town, as it was then called.

Mii maa gaa-nji-koogedewaad giw Nishnaabeg.
This was why the people lived there together as a community.

—Duncan Pegahmagabow

Community was a most important part of life for Francis Pegahmagabow. Like his ancestors who first came to Parry Island to live in permanent settlement, Francis realized the future for the Nishnaabeg would forever be different. Gone were the large territories that had once sustained their livelihoods. The small bands that had lived in peaceful overlap throughout these vast lands would never again be viable community structures. Although the reserve system was an imposed structure, the Nishnaabeg would make the most out of it. The larger aggregate of mixed bands and tribal peoples from many places would become a cohesive and strong community at Wasauksing that benefited from the various contributions of each group.

The distribution of people on Parry Island was representative of many different waves of settlement. The two major bands that first settled in the community founded what became Upper Village (Niisaaking) and Lower Village (Nishnaabe-oodenaang), respectively. All families engaged in hunting and fishing, and gathering activities were common. Gardening also became a mainstay of life in such a fixed community setting, and the Parry Island Fall Fair was a testament to the success of the people's efforts.[1]

24. Parry Island family and visiting community children. National Museum of the American Indian, Smithsonian Institution, N14407. Photo by Frederick Johnson.

One important constant in this time of great change was the continued strength of the extended family unit. The clan system remained a strong symbol of family identity, and, though it no longer seemed to function as a means of government or decision making, people continued to practise clan exogamy in accordance with tradition. The extended family into which a child was born was responsible for the comprehensive well-being of each member. Children were encouraged to closely observe the actions of their older relations (*kinoowaabiwin* or "learning by observation") and to closely listen to whatever they were told or shown. It was not uncommon for community members to be considered as extended family members. Present-day elders remember having many "grandparents," "uncles," and "aunts" in the community even though they might have only been related to a few by blood.

Francis was committed to ensuring his children grew up in a community where they would learn to unconditionally love and respect others. He chose to raise his family among his wife's relations in the small Parry Island village of Nenabozhnaang. Francis did not want his children to grow up without a strong sense of belonging and connection. Life in this small village, sometimes called "the Halfway Point" by Parry Islanders, was happy and rich for the Pegahmagabow family. Duncan once described the curious name commonly given to Nenabozhnaang by other residents of the island:

> *Mii maanda ayhii Aabtooyihiing ezhnikaademgak.*
> This place was called the Halfway Point.
>
> *Mii odi bi-maajaawaad odi Nishnaabe-oodenaang gow Nishnaabeg zhaawaad oodenaang baa-oodetoowaad go naa ganabaj.*
> The people would leave Lower Village to go to town to do their shopping.
>
> *Enwek ko ginwenzh wodi gii-yaadgenag oodenaang.*
> They would stay in town a good while to shop.
>
> *Mii-sh aazhgo pii mii naa ni-giiwewaad mii go naa aazhgo pii wii-ni-naagshi gwa naa gii-bmi-daabaadaanaawaa maa naa giishpinadoowaad niw daabaanan giiwe-daabiiwaad.*
> When it was time to leave for home, it was already close to evening as they were carting what they had bought in their wagons home.
>
> *Mii dash zaam wiikaa wii gnimaa ayhiing iihow Aabtooyihiing ezhnikaadeg ayhii Nenabozhnaang.*
> It was already quite late when they reached the Halfway Point, which was there at Nenabozhnaang.
>
> *Mii dash go naa ndawaaj go naa nsitam go naa mii-sh go naa ndawaaj maa gii-gbeshwaagwen go naa gii-nbaawaagwen maa.*
> It was for this reason, as I understand it, that they made camp and slept here for the night.
>
> *Mii dash miinwaa waabninig mii dash bijiinag eni-giiwewaad.*
> Then again in the morning they would continue on home.
>
> *Mii dash maa gaa-nji-yaamgak ayhii Nenabozhnaang ayhii Aabtooyihiing ezhnikaadeg.*
> And that was how Nenabozhnaang became known as the Halfway Point.

The small villages were well interconnected by wagon roads and water routes. Although each settlement, including Middle Village (Gamiing) and Nenabozhnaang, maintained a sense of its original identity, it steadily became part of a larger whole. The eventual integration of the Wasauksing community was viewed as a strength by Francis and became inspirational in his later political efforts to create greater unification among the various reserves.

The Parry Island Reserve became a unique amalgamation of different tribal and family groups, each with special knowledge and skills. The town of Depot Harbour, built on the island just before the turn of the twentieth century, brought hundreds of workers in pursuit of work generated by the railway and shipping industries. People of many ethnicities made their homes on the island, including Nishnaabeg from other Georgian Bay communities. Francis reflected later in life that Depot Harbour had been an early prototype of the United Nations in the harmonious way that so many different people worked together to make a better life for their community and country.

Francis had many interactions with the Depot Harbour community and became close friends with many who lived there. He once even attempted to buy a cow from a Cape Croker band member living at Depot Harbour, but this effort was blocked by the local Indian agent.[2] So too were his multiple attempts to buy a team of horses to help him establish a farm on the family homestead. The interference of Indian Affairs did not dissuade Francis from developing and maintaining positive relationships with non-Native peoples throughout his life. Yet he would never fully accept the controls and limitations that the government held over the lives of his Nishnaabe people and his own ability to improve living conditions for his family.

Sharing stories with visitors was a favourite pastime for Francis and his family. He was a talented orator and found enjoyment in the stories of other people. Learning to listen was an important skill for children, and Marie remembered her father always encouraging her to pay careful attention to the words of visitors:

> *Aapji go nishin ji-bzindawad gwaya bi-giigdod.*
> It is so very good to listen when someone is talking.
>
> *Miinwaa noondwad gwaya gegoo kidod ga-naagadawendam.*
> And when you hear someone say something you should thoughtfully consider it.
>
> *Giishpine dash kenziwan ga-ni-kendaan iihow.*
> If you don't quite know what they mean then, you will in time.
>
> *Ga-waabndagoo gwa ngoji gwa ni-bmaadziiyin mii ji-bi-dgoshni-wamgak ji-waabndaman gaa-nji-kidod maaba Nishnaabe iihow.*
> You will be shown this; at some point in your life, you will see why this person said what they did.

Francis taught his children that their words and actions had great potential impacts within the interconnected world of the Ojibwe. The Nishnaabe strove for the "good life" and tried to live as carefully as possible. Careless speech or action had consequences. Not only could one's inattentiveness affect other people, but also it could have negative outcomes for success in any number of activities, such as hunting, fishing, and gathering. Francis once shared with Jenness that "every winter I set twenty-five or thirty rabbit snares. If I find a rabbit has carried away a snare, I warn my children that they have been making too much noise in the evenings."[3]

The many roles integral to traditional Nishnaabe community life—whether in leadership, medicine, defence, or religious practice—often necessitated long periods of mentorship. Learning in the Nishnaabe tradition is perhaps best described as an extended apprenticeship in which young children with particular talents were encouraged to build relationships with individuals who could foster those talents. Eva studied for many years with her aunts as she learned to become a midwife. It was not unusual even for children to go and live with other families for long periods of time. Community was an extension of family, and teaching and learning were shared responsibilities of all members. Humility was important, and successes were considered in the context of family and community both (as noted by Duncan in the story "*Enendaagwak Bmaadziwin*—What Is Expected of Life").

Traditionalism and Change

Traditionalism remained strong among the Ojibwe during Francis's early life. The different settlements on Parry Island practised the Midewiwin religion, and each had at least one ceremonial water drum to conduct these rites. It was also said by several community elders that the water drums provided a means for the settlements to communicate with each other in an age before telephones. The pressure to convert to Christianity became too overwhelming, and the people gradually joined local congregations to avert the hostile gaze of the local clergy or Indian agents.[4] The Ojibwe seemed to find a middle ground that allowed them to remain who they were culturally while conforming to the rigid expectations set for them by the church and Indian Department. These were years when survival was difficult and the restrictions placed on the lives of the people did not afford authentic choices.[5]

Duncan believed that Francis might have attended one of the last full-lodge Midewiwin ceremonies held on Parry Island around the turn of the century. By all accounts, these were magnificent ceremonies with broad attendance from several eastern Ojibwe communities. Francis was only a young boy, but the event made a marked impression on him. He would later describe the gathering to his children as if it were some kind of community fair—but only in the sense that there were so many people, encampments rich in resources, and an overwhelming positive and happy energy. People came on wagons and brought food, lodging supplies, and of course the articles they needed for participation in ceremonial activities. Although Francis attended only some of the actual *Mide* rites that took place, the experience would leave him with respect for traditional spirituality and provide him with insight into how to talk directly to the Spirit should he ever have need. This gathering was the first grand-scale meeting of Nishnaabe people from many different places and communities Francis would witness, and it definitely influenced his later interest in gathering the people in large assemblies to share in discussion and decision making.

The great stories of the Midewiwin inspired his love of traditional narrative and his insistence on having elders share both stories and knowledge with the community when he was chief. Francis envisioned a formal role for the elders in the political decision-making process, but this was too controversial, given the imposed structures and general acceptance of the Indian Act by the community. Older forms of governance—much like the ceremonies associated with such traditional political practice—became the subjects of suspicion and subjugation. Dissolution of the Midewiwin society signalled the end of a long period of success for the Ojibwe of Georgian Bay.

Disappearance of the Midewiwin left the community without Indigenous alternatives. Christianity was the only remaining choice and offered the community a means of prayer to and connection with the Spirit. Such practice and relationship was as essential for life to the Nishnaabe as water or food. The risks of persecution for traditional practice were too great, and any ceremonies held required absolute secrecy. Many older community elders today remember the locked-door "meetings" of their parents or grandparents. Traditionalism often had to be kept secret from other family members in such times. More involved ceremonies, such as the shaking tent or sweat lodge, had to be done at night or far from the village. The community was resilient and adapted as it could to forced circumstances. Francis's neighbour Alice King describes how it was necessary sometimes to bring in healers and practitioners from other communities in this age of persecution and discontinuity:

> *Mii dash iw gii-gnoon'gowaad niw nishnaaben nebwaakaan'jin, "Ambe gegoo zhichgen, wi-ndawaabam aw sa jiiskiiwnini, odi Daawaa-mnising ga-zhaa."*

> And then a wise Indian spoke to them, "Now do something, go and look for the shaking tent shaman, you're to go there to Manitoulin Island."
>
> *Gaasmoon-jiimaan dash wgii-yaan aw nmishoomis mii-sh gii-maajiiyaashid ngo-nme-giizhig dash gii-ndendi. Gii-biinaad niw jiiskiiwninwan mii dash gaa-kidod aw, "Gaawiin waya maa kwe besho da-yaasii."*
> Well, my grandfather had a sailboat, so he started sailing and was gone for a week. He brought the shaking tent shaman, and this one said, "No woman is to be nearby."
>
> *Gaawiin dash aw nookwmis ngoji gii-zhaasii, shpimisagoong odi gii-gaazod mii dash gii-kendang iw ningsenig iw wiigwaam. Gii-giimoozaabid maa waasechganing mii gii-waabndang nsawhigan gii-wzhitood maa shkweyaang maa wiigwaaming. Mii dash epiichi-yaad odi shpimsagoong mii iw gii-ningsenig iw wiigwaam.*
> And my grandmother didn't go outside, but she hid there upstairs, and she knew when the house shook. She peeked out a window and saw that he had made a tipi there at the back of the house. And the whole time she was upstairs the house was shaking.[6]

The *Mide* rites brought to Parry Island by the immigrant Pottawatomi families helped the community to maintain connection to some of their earlier practices. Continued pressure from the church repressed the ceremonial rites of the Pottawatomi people, but their knowledge of medicine and healing was regularly sought out by almost all Wasauksing families. The particular *mide* practice they brought to the community differed from that remembered by the local Ojibwe, and this might have been a reason the society failed to re-establish itself in the community. The immigrant Odawa—the direct ancestors of Eva Pegahmagabow—also brought a version of Midewiwin rites with them, but it was only employed in special circumstances and was never taught to younger generations given the times.

Loss of the ceremonial traditions of his people affected Francis substantially. It was a further erosion of the nation's strength and one more loss the people couldn't afford. Stories of witchcraft became pervasive in the church's discrediting of traditional religious practices. Even the Midewiwin itself, devoted to healing and the greater good, would be implicated as a society of witches and sorcerers.[7] Although Francis might have even come to question the value of the Midewiwin over time, he never lost sight of how it had helped Eva as a girl. The society's use of plant medicines was well employed by the community. There was perhaps no family that did not benefit from the local practice of plant medicine preparation.

Faith

The Nishnaabe of Georgian Bay were an intensely spiritual people who knew to respect both the physical and spiritual sides of life. The world was a beautiful and active place in which mystery abounded. Francis told his children about playing with the legendary "little people" as a young boy along the rocky shores of Shawanaga. This was one of his first memories and might even have been when he was still living with his parents on Snake Island. Francis remembered their whiskered faces and deep laugher, and though he never saw them again he would find evidence of their presence at the most unexpected times and places. He shared with Jenness about one occasion when he came across evidence of their passing: "Pegahmagabow once saw their tracks, like those of a tiny baby, on a muddy road on Parry Island."[8] His children remember making offerings of tobacco with their father if ever they saw spirit lights travelling in the air or water, or if ever they should come across lost spirit beings like those he described to Jenness:

> Sometimes a little before the dawn you hear a shrill, whistling sound high in the air, or perhaps only at the level of the treetops. It is a *baggak*, the ghost of an Indian who died of starvation.... Now it blows wherever the wind carries it, or it may be travels round and round with the sun. Do not be afraid, for it will not harm you. But if you happen to be cooking when it passes over the treetops, out of charity place some grease on a bough. It will descend and feast on the odour, then proceed on its way.[9]

Connection to the spiritual side of life was important to all Nishnaabe of his generation. Although the great medicine societies of the Georgian Bay Ojibwe would fall silent during his lifetime, the Nishnaabe people found other formal means of prayer and connection.

The churches that opened their doors to the Ojibwe communities offered a means of fulfilling key rites of passage stripped away from the people with the loss of their traditional spiritual practices. The community found a safe meeting space in the church, and many of the old religious concepts and words were incorporated into prayers and songs. The Ojibwe-language hymns

25. Parry Island Catholic Church. Photo by Brian McInnes.

were distinct in both tune and tempo. It was a hopeful yet sorrowful sound that reflected the soul of the people during that age. I remember attending such services as a young boy and being enraptured by the rows of white-haired people who knew every word and note by heart. There was a gentle and quiet passion in their singing that made for an expression of prayer and thanks unique to the Nishnaabe Christian faith tradition. This might also have been one of those facets of life particular to twentieth-century Indian community experience. The people had been as instrumental as the clergy in building a community of ritual and worship that helped them through a time when the incredible losses that affected their lives might otherwise have overwhelmed them.

Francis's wartime convalescence in an overseas hospital seemed to have inspired his deep interest in the Catholic faith. His resolve was strengthened after the war when he became ill and required hospitalization for a number of weeks.[10] In these states of physical weakness, his spiritual senses became strong, and the Christian way of prayer he adopted held true to what he needed in those moments. Francis told Jenness about his transformative experience: "After I returned from the war I was ill and unable to do a hard day's work. One night I dreamed that Jesus approached me, clothed in a loin cloth and with bleeding wounds as He appears in pictures. I threw myself at His feet and asked for a blessing. Then I awoke, and told my friends that Jesus had blessed me and was restoring me to health. I recovered my health, and am now as strong as ever."[11]

Duncan remembered how his father showed great interest in the use of Latin during parts of the service. Latin reminded him of his own Native language—deep in meaning and unbroken in its connection to ancient spiritual truths and understandings of the world. To him it was invocative of the spirit and important to learn. Francis was regularly asked to recite prayers or devotions as a part of the church service, and it was important to him that his family participate in regular services. Eva supported his participation in the church since it brought him such great peace, but she maintained her traditional "pagan" beliefs, as they were then called. She was given a Bible that she kept all of her life. Marie noticed after her mother's passing four words written on the inner pages: "I am a pagan."

Marie especially enjoyed attending church with her father as a young girl. One particular episode was curious to her, but she never quite thought she should ask her father about it afterwards. She arrived at church early with Francis one Sunday and was waiting outside when the Schneiders, a local family that Francis would occasionally guide, drove by. She remembered Mr.

Schneider slowing down and calling out to her father, "What are you doing there, Peggy?" He was surprised to see them outside the church. Francis warmly greeted them and welcomed them to attend the service. "Chief, I didn't know you Indian people walked into churches," Mr. Schneider said to Francis, "show me how you pray!" Marie was not certain how her father would react. He was good natured and enjoyed conversation, but he took his religious practice seriously. Marie thought the man's comments were made in ridicule and poor taste. After a brief pause, Francis responded in his characteristic soft-spoken way. "I'll show you how we pray," he said to the family. He then rolled up his pant leg, got down on one knee, made the sign of the cross, and began to pray. "All I heard was a bang," Marie remembered, "and of course everyone jumping for cover!" The large lightning strike that hit the ground nearby seemed to startle everyone but Francis. "Well, you sure showed us how you pray, Peggy," said Mr. Schneider, who promptly drove off. Her father said nothing about the lightning strike until later that day when they were nearly home. "That's why you shouldn't tease people," he said to her, "you never know what's in store." It was a lesson Marie would remember all of her life.

No matter what a family's formal religious orientation was, certain aspects of cultural practice remained consistent from home to home. The Nishnaabe people remained true to several traditional rites that the church could not provide assistance with, such as the bestowal of Indian names, fasting, umbilical cord ceremonies, or the annual feasts to remember loved ones who had passed on. The shaking tent and sweat lodge continued to be practised—albeit in secret—throughout much of this era. It is no small wonder that these ceremonies of life were not talked about with Jenness or that he was instructed not to write about them. To share details of one's involvement in such a ceremony would be to implicate oneself in an action undesirable to the local Indian agent.

The remembrance feasts that took place every fall were perhaps the largest traditional community gatherings that continued to be held. They were held on Halloween so as to allay suspicion. The community would call it All Souls' Night as a means of continuing their customary memorial celebration. The Pegahmagabow family would participate in it every year in order to remember their many relatives who had gone on before them. The annual memorial was of deep meaning to many community members and a testament to the cultural resilience of the people in times of profound external control over their affairs. Duncan had fond memories of attending this event as a child.

All Souls' Night

Jiibyiihaa-dbikak mii pii gwa kina gegoo gii-maawndoon-gaademgak gtigaaning mziwe ngoji gii-chigaademgak.
On All Souls' Night, everything was gathered up from all the gardens and set out so nicely.

Mii aazhgo gaa-zhiwdoowaad odi Mzhakdookwe endaad aansh gii-yaadogenag gow kwewag waa-jiibaakwejig.
They would take their produce over to Mzhakdookwe's home, where the ladies would have gathered to prepare the food.

Jiibyiihaa-dbikak mii ko zhaayaang odi.
On All Souls' Night, we would go over there.

Oonh mii sa geget gtaamgwiinak miijim.
There was truly so much food there.

Chi-wiisni-waagan maanda epiitaangdeg kina gegoo miijim—wiiyaas, waawaashkesh-wiiyaas, giigoonh, waashkbang, kina gegoo gii-te miinwaa dabwaad ge giw getzijig wiintamwaa mii-sh dash nshamaamin dash.
That big kitchen table was filled with all of this food: meat, venison, fish, sweets, everything was there—those elders would sit down, and we would serve them.

Mii dash go bezhig ow getzid kina maawndoon maa eteg miijim.
There was this one old man who would gather some of the food that was there.

Mii-sh odi zhiihaaksidood odi gchi-box-stove ko gii-yaanaawaa giw ngii-mikwendaan gchi-box-stove gii-zhiihaaknang maabam Bepesh mii-sh odi gii-jiichiikzhehang shkode.
He opened up that big box stove they had—I well remember how he would open up the door to that big box stove to stir the coals.

Mii-sh odi gii-pagidang iw miijim.
He would then offer that food there.

"Gego naabkegon wodi."
"Now don't look over there," we were told.

Mii-sh ko genii aabdeg waabndamaan.
But I absolutely wanted to see.

Pii naa gaa-zhi-nda-waabmagwaa giw ji-wiisniwaad odi giw gaa-nbojig maa.
I wanted to see all those people who had passed on eating in there.

Mii gaa-zhi-debwewenmaan ji-waabmagwaa baanda-wiisniwaad.
I truly believed that I would see those ones show up to eat there.

Mii-sh ko gaa-nakamigad ensa-dgwaagig Jiibyiihaa-dbikak.
This happened every fall on All Souls' Night.

Kina go zhaa waya kaa go memkaach invitation gii-kendaa-naawaa enkamigad.
Everybody went, it was not necessary to have an invitation, everybody knew it was happening.

Kina waya odi ezhaad.
Everybody went over there for this.

Oonh geget sa gii-minkamigad.
Oh, it was truly such a good event.

Mshkiki—"Medicine"

For the Ojibwe of Georgian Bay, knowledge of plant medicine was essential for life. Francis's adopted relatives at Shawanaga were well known for their ability to find and prepare traditional remedies for everything from toothaches to various cancers. Francis shared one such application with Jenness: "My foster-mother put wild ginger in all our food to prevent any ill-effect, and she gave me wild ginger to chew."[12] Health-care facilities were few and far between and thus difficult for the Nishnaabeg to access at the best of times. Community members knew everything they needed was at hand if they paid attention to where things could be found and had knowledge of how to collect and prepare such medicines properly. Esteemed Wasauksing elder and orator Fred Wheatley fondly remembered how much effort his aunts put into the collection, storage, and preparation of traditional remedies. It seemed every family had a dedicated space in their home for the preparation and storage of certain plants. Francis's children remembered their parents saying that every illness had a plant nearby that could cure it. Understanding how to access the healing power of a plant was the key to effecting a cure.

Francis shared the following with Jenness: "Talk to the tree or plant when you are gathering its bark, leaves, or root. Tell its soul and shadow why you are taking away part of its body. Say to it 'Help me to cure such and such a malady.' Unless you do this your medicine will not be of much avail. Moreover, if it is the root of the plant you need, take only part of it and leave the stem if possible undisturbed."[13]

Duncan shared a similar story about how to gather such medicines. He had been talking with me about the importance of tobacco as a medicine plant and how older, more traditionally minded community members such as his father would never use tobacco for idle purposes. It was a sacred plant, a necessary part of the offering made to the earth before harvesting other medicines. The following story reveals much about the nature of community life and practice. Wasauksing members relied on the resources available to them locally and helped to look after each other when possible.

> *Ngii-wiindamaag maandan ndedem nshke go maabam yahaa Nishnaabe baa-mshkikiiked.*
> This is what my father told me about how a Nishnaabe person is to go about getting and preparing medicine.
>
> *Mii go naa geniin enenmaan iihow maabam ewaabshkiiwed naadin iihow mshkiki: oonh gtaam-gwiindoon moodensan odi etegin shkweyaang mii odi gezbinang mii odi kina tenig niw mshkikiiman eyaabjitoojin.*
> For this is what I understand about how a white person gets medicine: all of those many remedies he uses are neatly arranged behind the counter there.
>
> *Maabam dash wiin Nishnaabe mii niw ntam bzindawaad niw gaa-bi-waabmigojin niw eyaakozin'jin go naa.*
> But the Nishnaabe first listens to the one who has come to be seen by him in order to determine what is needed.
>
> *Mii aazhgo kendang iihow bzindawaad gwa wiinmaagwad iihow nake enaapinenid niw mii aazha gii-kendang wodi eyaanig iihow waa-aabjitood.*
> He knows from listening to what he is told about the sick person's condition about where and what medicine he will have to use.

Mii sa odi zhaad odi kendang gii-yaa gii-mnjimendang odi gii-waabndang iihow mii odi ezhaad mii-sh pii gii-waabndang iihow maa bdaksinig.
Once he knows the medicine he needs, and remembers where he last saw it, he then goes over to that place where he saw it growing.

Bmaadziwin gwehow mii-sh wenji-gnoonaad niw mii pii jibwaa daapnang iihow.
It is life that he is seeking, and this is why he addresses the plant before he takes it.

Mii kawe dbaajmotawaad niw maajiigininig iw mshkiki.
He first tells that medicine that is growing there the story behind the person's sickness.

Mii wiinmawaad iihow, "Mii sa gegii maa gaa-nji-sigooyin iihow ji-naadamaageyin maanda bmaadziwin ngii-kenmaa dash maaba Nishnaaḅe maanaazhiyaa."
He then tells this plant, "You were put here for a purpose, to help with this life, and I know this Nishnaabe who is not well."

"Mii dash gaa-bi-nji-zhaayaan maa gii-kenmin maa yaayin ji-wiidookwad maabam Nishnaabe eyaakozid."
"This is why I have come, because I know you are here to help this Nishnaabe who is sick."

Mii-sh dash aazhgo daapnang kaa go wewiip gwa daa-pkwa-jibidoosiin iihow; negaaj gwa daa-waankaadaan iihow mii-sh daapnang iihow.
He then takes this medicine, but he does not just simply rip it out; he gently digs it out as he takes it.

Mii dash ge maa epiichi-miigwechwendang mii maa semaan maa gii-saad niw.
To show the extent of his thanks, he offers some tobacco for what he has been given.

Mii-sh giiwewdood iihow daa-aangwaamnaan ni-giiwewdood iihow daa-ni dbaajmotaan ge gwa ow mii dash ozhitood iihow mshkiki.
He then takes it home, being so careful in the way he takes it back there—talking to that plant as he goes—and then making the medicine that is needed.

Mii-sh maabam Nishnaabe naadmaagwad iihow.
The sick person can then receive the help that is needed.

Dbishkoo go naa eni-dgwaagik bngising niw niibiishan—bngising niw niibiishan mii gwa ni-bgashknak mii go maa eni-zhaamgak maa kiing ji-maajiigid miinwaa bezhig ow mtigoons.
This is like the way it is when fall approaches and the leaves fall—those leaves fall and rot and go back to the earth so that another tree can again grow.

Mii go naasaab enendaagwak iihow ji-maajiigiwaad giw mtigoog waya ji-nji-bngising niw niibiishan aabdeg gwa gegoo ji-nbomgak ji-maajiimgak dash wii-de-bkaanak.
In the same way that the trees grow is it for a person—and that is why they lose their leaves—something must die so that another may grow.

Witchcraft

Witchcraft is a troublesome subject that seems to uniquely characterize that era. Jenness appeared to be fascinated with the stories of witchcraft among the Parry Island people and devoted much of his work to documenting beliefs about such practices: "It is pathetic to observe how universal is this fear of witchcraft among the present inhabitants of Parry Island. Every man suspects his neighbour of practising the nefarious art to avenge some fancied grievance, and the older and more conservative the Indian, the more he is held in suspicion. Probably there is not a single adult on the island who has not been accused of sorcery at some time or other, and who has not himself suffered some misfortune which he attributes to the same cause."[14] Duncan recalled that his father's only negative comment about the work of Jenness was how fixated he had been on the subject of witchcraft and its implications for community life. Some of Jenness's informants might have found his overzealous questioning style deserving of creative answers. There seems to be little doubt among community members today that the discourse on witchcraft originated primarily from clergy and Indian agents dedicated to dissuading the people from any kind of traditional practice.

The culture of fear that originated during the witchcraft years was damaging to the long-term vitality of the community. Members began to make false accusations against each other in most cases, and traditionalists were assumed to be practitioners of dark arts. It was a dangerous time in that traditional ways were forbidden under the Indian Act and provided the Indian

Department with considerable power over individuals accused of paganism. Indian agents no longer had to be watchdogs in communities: they had successfully turned the people against each other in many instances. The division this created among the people in life was even more demarcated in death, as Duncan recalled:

> *Mii giiwenh gaa-namhaajig biinjiyihiing giiwenh maa iihow mjikanaakoong mii maa gii-n'gohgaazowaad go yahaag Gaa-namhaajig giw dash gaa-namhaasigook gwajiing wodi iihow mjikanaak gwajiing wodi gii-n'gohgaazowag go giw go naa gaa-nishnaabewaadzijig Nishnaabeg.*
> Those who were Christian were buried inside of the cemetery fence, but those who did not follow Christianity and were true to their traditional way as Indian people were buried outside of the fence.

Francis's children believed their father positively balanced Nishnaabe and Christian spiritual traditions. They also suspected he was unduly influenced by the witchcraft propaganda of the Catholic Church as reflected in some of his comments to Jenness. Francis always told them the misuse of power of any kind was against the traditional way of the Nishnaabe people and should be avoided at all costs.

It would be easy—in the changed circumstances of the present—to simply dismiss all of the witchcraft and sorcery dialogue of that era as rumours, lies, or scary stories. It is almost inconceivable that the life-giving and healing power of the Ojibwe medicine lodges could ever be used for anything negative. Everything in the Nishnaabe world was bound to this order. Duncan once told me a story similar to the one featured in the Jenness text about how the spirits of the world, the *mnidoog* themselves, were also held to this standard of character and action: "Some Georgian Bay Ojibwa once heard two *manidos* conversing in Henvey inlet, near French river. One was scolding the other for doing wrong, and reminding it that the Great Spirit had instructed them to do no evil, but to remain in their appointed places as long as the earth lasted and to take care of his Indian children."[15] Life was often a balance of extremes. The above story illustrates that even the protective spirits of the world had their moments of indecision and error. Nishnaabe people were supposed to learn from these stories, so perhaps there was a need for such reminders in life.

Survival was difficult in an era of religious disconnection and hand-to-mouth existence. Although it would be easy to categorically deny that people would try to gain advantage over others using available means, this might also seem to be naive given the changed system of values that came with colonized life. It was this "bad medicine" that Francis found the most insidious and harmful of all. Witchcraft, however understood or practised, would have a short duration in the history of the people; however, the resultant culture of fear and distrust created in this era would have significant and long-term consequences. Behaviours that had once been taboo suddenly became possible. They included the drinking of alcohol and the recreational use of tobacco. The changes introduced in this era of externally driven disempowerment and manipulation would take deep root and lead to many of the social maladies that continue to plague Indigenous communities today.

A Greater Good

Perhaps most absent in the historical description of the era that Francis lived in is all of the good that remained. The community remained a safe place where the people felt more at home than in any other place. The Nishnaabeg—"the good beings" of creation—endeavoured to remain true to their traditional ways despite external pressures to do otherwise. What existing historical renditions do not advance is that those often seen as witches or sorcerers were the same people the community often relied on for life-giving medicine and healing. And the Midewiwin—so often cited as an evil or nefarious society of practice[16]—was the original religious practice of the people that guided them for thousands of years of positive, productive, and good life. The general dismissal of the tremendous good that traditionalism and its practitioners brought to the community remains a serious historical error.

Every Wasauksing elder I have met spoke of this as a special time during which the people worked hard and—as much as possible—treated each other well. Things were changing quickly, but the Nishnaabeg held to certain absolutes. Maintaining their language and the capacity to make a life for themselves remained at the core of their efforts. They were broadly successful in both regards. Even if cultural practice had to be set aside, the potential for its return was contained in these two facets of life.

The Parry Island community that Francis came to as a young man seeking connection and belonging became his lifelong home. Through hard work and determination, he renewed his family's legacy that had nearly been extinguished by historical circumstances. Francis brought great pride to the Wasauksing people from his accomplishments as both a soldier and a political leader. He was troubled by the handling of the community by Indian Affairs and at times by the treatment he received from his fellow Nishnaabeg. The

26. Parry Island reserve road, community hall, and middle village. National Museum of the American Indian, Smithsonian Institution, N14426. Photo by Frederick Johnson.

strength of his character and the love of his family allowed him to endure such hardships. Francis refused to be discouraged by the circumstances facing the people. No matter how his faith was tested, it would be within the community structure that he would ultimately place his hope for the collective future of the people and their continued identity as Nishnaabeg.

Ndedem Gaa-Giiwed—When My Father Went Home

This story was recorded one summer at Duncan's Wasauksing home. It was a beautiful July evening, and the sunset seemed to last well into the night. We had been reminiscing about historical community life practices when Duncan suddenly became quiet and contemplative. After a long pause, he told the following story about when his father passed away. It is a remarkable and touching account about his final walk home. Duncan's story, in the true spirit of Ojibwe life and storytelling, has a strong connection to both community life and the spirit world. It is a beautiful affirmation of the continuity of the journey after one's physical life has ended and that the spirit walk home was unimpeded by the challenges Francis had faced during his life.

Ga-dbaajmotoon gegoo ndedem miinwaa gaa-zhiwebziyaan.
I will tell you about my father and what happened to me.

Maaba ndedem gii-bmi-wiijiiyaawag ngii-gchi-piitenimaa maaba Nishnaabe.
During the time I lived with my father, I so admired this man.

N-dedem gchi-zhimaaganish ge gii-aawi.
My father was a great soldier.

Aapji go geget go ngii-zaaghaa ngii-gchi-piitenimaa.
I so truly loved and respected him.

Mii go geget gii-bi-gwiiwzenswiyaan gwa naa mii ow geget gaa-nenmaan iihow gaa wiikaa ji-ni-nbosig.
When I was a young boy, I was certain he would never die.

Mii gaa-piitenmag iihow gwnimaa go naa gegaa mnidoong ngii-nenmaadag gaa-gchi-piitenmag maaba ndedem.
I admired him to the point that I almost thought of him as some kind of god, that is how much I admired and respected my father.

Mii go maa naaniibwid naaniibwiyaan genii aapji go ngii-mshkozii.

When he stood there, and I stood beside him, I was so strong.

Weweni ngii-zhiyaa wewiijiiwag weweni ngii-nendam bmi-wiijiiwag.

I was very good when I was with him—this was how much I thought of being with him.

Mii-sh go nendmaan iihow kaa wiikaa daa-nbosii ndedem ngii-nendam.

I was certain that my father would never die, this is what I thought then.

Pii dash gegoo ezhiwebzid kaa ngii-daapnaziin maanda.

And then when something happened to him, I couldn't accept this.

"Gaawiin," ngii-kid. "Gaawiin maaba gii-nbosii."

"No," I said. "He did not die."

Gaa-gchi-gwaansigendmaan mii go gaa-zhiyaayaan gaa-zhi-giikmanziiyaan.

I felt so terrible about this that I was almost numb.

Gaa gegoo ngii-moozhtoosiin gaa-piichi-gwaansigendmaan.

I wasn't able to feel anything, that was the extent of my sorrow.

Gaa go gegoo ngii-moozhtoosiin.

I didn't feel anything.

Kaa maanda ngii-daapnazii maaba iihow ganawaabmag odi bmaakshing mkakoong.

I couldn't accept this even when I went to see him lying in the casket.

"Gaawiin," ndikid. "Gaawiin."

"No," I said. "No."

Mii dash ngoding enaagshig gii-niibebiwag maa naa gbe-dbik gii-temgad wodi namhew-gamgoong.
And then one evening the people held an all-night wake over there at the church.

Aapji go naa gii-gchi-nendaan iihow namhew-gamig iihow niisaaki noongo etemgak.
He thought so highly of the church, which is now over there down the hill.

Mii dash wodi gii-bid gii-bi-giigdowag gegoo waasa wenjibaajig wii-bizhaawaad.
That was where he was, and people came from many faraway places to speak at his funeral.

Mii dash gbeyiing gaa-nji-ganawenjgaazod wii-bi-waabmaawaan maa naa go gaa-kenmaajig gwa naa.
He was kept there a long time so that all of those he had known would be able to see him.

Mii dash ngoding enaagwshig go baatiinwag eyaajig gwajiing naaniibwiwag.
At one point in the evening, most people had to stand outside.

Kaa maa kina debshkinesiiwag biindig gaasin maa naa namhew-gamgoons.
They couldn't all fit inside—that little church was just too small.

Naaniibwiwag wodi gwajiing aanind.
So some of them had to stand outside.

Mii-sh ezhid maaba nmamaa, "Aazhgo giiwen," ndig.
And then my mother said to me, "Now go home," she said.

"Naajbatwaadin iihow ayhii ziisbaakwad ngii-jaagsemin kaa geyaabi gegoo ziisbaakwad."
"Run home and fetch some sugar, we have run out, and there is no more sugar here."

Mii-sh gii-maajiiptooyaan shkode-daabaan miiknaang maa ngii-ni-batoo.

So then I started out running on the train tracks, I ran straight away from there.

Mii dash noongo wodi iihiing wodi GK endaad chi-ktigaan go maa gii-yaamgad gii-gtige maa Nishnaabe.

And where GK's house is now, there was a big garden there where this one Nishnaabe man farmed.

Mii-sh maa gaa-ni-zhaayaan nakeying gtigaaning tkambatooyaan maa gtigaaning mii-sh gii-ni-zhaayaan odi gaa-daayaang.

I went over toward where that garden was and ran right through it as I made my way over there to where we lived.

Kaa maa naa kwa gchi-miikan maa gii-namsinoon wodi gaa-daayaang.

There was no big road then that led to where we lived.

Mii go naa eta miikaans wodi gaa-ni-namog mii-sh ni-bgambatooyaan wodi—jibwaa ni-bgambatooyaan wodi endaayaang mii gii-waabmag ow gchi-dbik-giizis.

There was only a path that led toward there, and just as I was running up to it, before I ran up to our house, I saw this huge moon.

Gtaamgwaadkamig sa naa enginad orange-naaza.

Of such magnitude was its size, and it was an orange colour.

Bijiinag go gii-bi-mookam gaa-zhi-noogbatooyaan gii-waabmag ow.

It had just started to rise, and I stopped running when I saw it.

Miinwaa nganawaabndaan iw endaayaang kaa go gegoo waaskonesinoon.

And then I looked at our home, and there was no light on there.

Megwaa gii-bmaadzid ow noos mii go pane gaa-zhi-waaskoneg wiigwaam.

When my father was living, there was always light in that house.

Pane maa naa gii-yaa.

It was always there.

Bboong gbe-dbik gii-boodwe wii-gzhizyaang miinwaa naa niibiing mii go pane waa-zhi-waaskoneg endaayaang.

Throughout the winter nights, he would make a fire so that we were warm, and then in the summer he kept our home well lit.

Pii waabndamaan iihow kaa gegoo waaskonesinoon.

But when I saw it that night, there was no light.

Mii sa bijiinag gii-daapnamaan.

It was at that moment I accepted it.

Geget gii-maajaad maabam noos.

My father was truly gone.

Gtaamgwaadkamig gaa-piichi-gwaansigendmaan mii sa bijiinag gii-daapnamaan.

The extent of my sorrow in that moment of acceptance was something terrible.

Kaa maa naa waaskonesinoon maanda wiigwaam.

There was no more light in this house.

Mii sa bijiinag geget gii-daapnamaan aapji go geget ngii-gwaansigendam.

So right then I had to accept it, and I was so very sad.

Mii go dbishkoo go naa gaa-zhiyaayaan gii-bngishnaan maa gaa-piichi-gwaansigendmaan.

It was just like I had collapsed there, that is how sad I was about losing him.

Mii dash gaa-waabmag maabam gchi-giizis, dbik-giizis, bijiinag gii-bi-mookam.
And then I saw this great moon, this night moon, that had just emerged.

Mii go gaa-bi-zhi-niisaakiyaaskoned ow yahaa dbik-giizis.
A ray of light came down from that moon.

Mii maa gii-waabmag ow nimsed.
And then I saw him walking away.

Mii ge gwa gii-nsidwinawag.
I recognized him then.

Ndedem nimse.
It was my father walking away.

Mii odi ezhaad dbik-giiz'soong.
He was going toward that moon.

Ngii-waabmaa nimsed gaa go waya nake gii-zhi-bmosesii mii go eta go Francis Pegahmagahbow gaa-nosed iihow.
I saw him walking away, for there was no one else who walked that way, it could only be Francis Pegahmagabow walking away there.

Mii sa gii-nsidwinawag.
I recognized him then.

Mii sa gii-kenmaan bijiinag gii-giiwe.
And just then I knew that he had gone home.

Gii-giiwe—gaa gii-nbosii.
He had gone home—he did not die.

Gii-giiwe—wewiip gii-maajiiptooyaan gii-biingeptooyaan wodi endaayaang.
He had gone home—so I hurried up and started running and ran right inside the house.

Ngii-kendaan ge kaa memkaaj ngii-waaskonechigesii.
I knew that it was not necessary for me to turn on the lamp.

Kaa maa go naa gegoo electric yaasinoon mii eta go waaskonenjigaansan.
There was no electricity there then, only the lamps.

Kaa-sh memkaaj gegoo waaskonenjigan ngii-kendaan maa naa odi temgak ziisbaakwad.
But I didn't need the lamp as I knew where the sugar was.

Gii-naadiyaan iihow gii-maajiiptooyaan yaapiichi-batooyaan neyaap odi shkode-daabaan-miiknaang bgambatooyaan namhew-gamgoong.
I went and got it, and I started running—I ran back down the railway tracks all the way until I made it back to the church.

Gaa-ni-biindgeyaan namhew-gamgoong wodi gii-ni-tooyaan iihow iihii ziisbaakwad wodi jiibaakwewaad giw jaabaakwejig gii-ni-zhaayaan wodi niigaan temgak iw ayhii mkak.
I entered the church and put that sugar down where those cooks were preparing the food, then went over to the front of the church where the casket was.

Mii sa bijiinag gii-daapnamaan iihow gaa-zhiwebzid maabam ndedem.
For in that moment I accepted what had happened to my father.

Gaawiin gii-nbosii iihow gaa-waabndahigowaan Mnidoo maa ngii-waabndahig
He did not die, this was what was shown to me by the Spirit.

Ngii-waabmaa gii-ni-giiwed Francis ndedem.
I was shown that I could see my father Francis going home.

Mii dash maa gii-ganawaabmag maa bmaakshing.
And then I looked at him lying there.

Ngii-zhoomiingwen ngii-baap.
I had a smile on my face, and I laughed a little.

Mii sa gii-gchi-nendmaan gii-ni-giiwed.
I was so happy that he had gone home.

Mii gaa-naadzid maaba Nishnaabe iw aapji gii-nishnaabewaadzi.
This was how he had lived his life as a Nishnaabe man, he was Nishnaabe right to the core of his being.

Ngii-waabmaa dash gii-ni-giiwed.
I saw him go home.

Mii sa iw weweni gii-nendmaan.
And I could again think in a good way.

Mashkowendaagwad sa nii iihow mii go eta nendawendaagwak ji-debwewendmang.
This was a very powerful occurrence, and all that is needed is for us to believe.

Mii sa genii gaa-zhiwebziyaambaan.
This is what happened to me.

Gdakowaabmigonaan sha go ow Mnidoo gdakowaabmigonaan.
We are always being watched over by the Spirit, he is watching us.

Gzaagigonaan maa naa.
He loves us, he truly loves all of us.

Kina go wegwenshidog go eyaagwen gzaagigonaan.
No matter who or what, he loves us all.

Gnoonad kaa wiikaa "ndoonmitaa" gdaa-gwasii.
If you speak to him, he will never say to you, "I am too busy."

Ga-bzindaag gwa gnoonad.
He will listen to you when you speak to him.

Gaa wiikaa "Baamaa pii maa bi-zhaakan" gdaa-gosii.
He will never say to you, "Come back here another time."

"Biindgen," ga-ig.
"Come on in," he will say to you.

Haa, miigwech.
Thank you.

CHAPTER 9

The Fourth Day

Mii go gaa-bi-zhi-niisaakiyaaskoned ow yahaa dbik-giizis.
A ray of light came down from that moon.

Mii maa gii-waabmag ow nimsed.
I saw someone walking away there.

Mii ge gwa gii-nsidwinawag.
I recognized him then.

Ndedem nimse.
It was my father walking away.

Mii odi ezhaad dbik-giiz'soong.
He was going toward that moon.

Mii sa gii-kenmaan bijiinag gii-giiwe.
And just then I knew that he had gone home.

Gii-giiwe—gaawiin gii-nbosii.
He had gone home—he did not die.

—Duncan Pegahmagabow, from "*Ndedem Gaa-Giiwed*"

The story of Francis Pegahmagabow was a tragic tale nearly from the outset. The survivor of a curse that took almost every member of his family, Francis was a fighter from the beginning. He endured numerous harsh realities throughout his life: the loss of his parents, a childhood beset with sickness, four years on the front lines of the greatest war the world had known, the deaths of innumerable friends and relatives, and the systematic failure of his government to help him in times of true need. A sense of loss and abandonment ran deep within him. Racist treatment by non-Indian society and government further limited his ability to succeed. Efforts by the Indian Department to control his influence by portraying him as unstable only added insult to already great injury. Survival remained a constant theme in his life.

Through sheer will, Francis survived all presented challenges and rose to a place of accomplishment and leadership that continues to inspire people. An army sergeant twice elected chief of the Wasauksing band forged deep connections in Indian country that would win the respect of people far and near. He supported foundational initiatives to unite First Nations people everywhere. Francis would be among the first to help other Native people understand that they had real and meaningful rights and needed to stand together in solidarity.

The independent and widespread political organizing Francis and his contemporaries advanced was not without cost or challenge. Such action was almost impossible in an age when communication across distance depended largely on handwritten English-language letters many Native people were unable to read. Meetings required great expense and travel over long distances. There was no support from Indian Affairs for these initiatives. Moreover, there is significant evidence that Indian agents actively worked to prevent many of these meetings from ever taking place.[1] Aboriginal organizations emerged in this era from the sheer determination of leaders such as Francis Pegahmagabow willing to put the needs of the people before their own. We owe much to the brave men and women who dared to stand up in defence of their people when it was not safe or even advisable to do so.

One of the political groups that Francis was instrumental in forming was the Native Independent Government (NIG). This organization would advocate for the autonomy of First Nations from the Indian Act and the tyrannical Indian agents who enforced it. Francis encouraged resistance against the external structures and dispositions that proved to be not only ineffective but also antithetical to Indigenous values and political systems. The Native Independent Government, like the League of Indians in Canada, became a true forerunner in the fight for Native rights. Such grassroots political organization indisputably led to the many subsequent gains in the protection of Aboriginal rights and sovereignty.

The years Francis spent working on national initiatives represented a unique time of political richness and First Nations unity that—like the individuals who led these foundational efforts—has not been given the recognition deserved. Many contemporary political structures evolved out of these early efforts, such as the Union of Ontario Indians and the Assembly of First Nations. Yet, at least at the community level, the political arena continues to be defined or heavily influenced by structures created by the Indian Act. Such oppressive and often ineffectual structures of government were recognized as problematic then by leaders such as Francis Pegahmagabow, Frederick Loft, John Tootoosis, Jim Horton, and Jules Sioui. Perhaps now is the time to seriously consider their vision and ask if complacency with the official political structures of the present will truly lead Indigenous communities to a better future.

Niigaanziwin—"To Be a Leader"

Francis Pegahmagabow would serve in positions of leadership throughout much of his life. It was not a responsibility he took lightly or used to gain advantage over his fellow Nishnaabe. Quite the opposite. He saw how the Indian Department had manipulated the people and often set them against each other. It was this hegemony that he vigorously resisted even when he was not serving as a councillor or chief: "A highly determined man who seemed to enjoy controversy, he engaged in active campaigns against Indian agents, the Indian department, and both the federal and provincial governments.... He attempted in various ways to address long-standing treaty grievances and disenchantment with the department's handling of the band's natural resources. He believed that the chief and council should have considerably more power than the Indian agent system allotted to them."[2] Francis would always be a leader, no matter what office he held. He was fiercely loyal to his Nishnaabe people no matter the cost to himself. The target of vicious smear campaigns on behalf of non-Indian governments and co-opted members of the Native community, he staunchly and consistently held true to his beliefs about First Nations autonomy and inherent rights no matter what scorn befell him.

Francis's work as a leader locally and nationally was always for his people first. His consistency over time healed many rifts created through jealousy or conflict promoted by Indian agents. Leadership for the Nishnaabeg was never about securing advantage over others; rather, it was dedicated to helping others improve their conditions. This often meant survival in those times, and Francis's children remembered their father sharing their family's food with neighbours or families who struggled. As described by Duncan,

> *Mii gaa-zhichgewaad iihow giishpine gwaya kendaagzid aakzid mii go nda-waabnjigaazod.*

> They would do this if it was known that a person was sick, he would be sought out.
>
> *"Wenesh nandawenman?"*
> "What is it you are wanting?"
>
> *"Ga-biidmaagoo."*
> "We will bring it to you."
>
> *Mno-bmaadziwaad giw.*
> They lived a good life.
>
> *Gii-onishin.*
> It was good.
>
> *Gii-naadmaadwag giw Nishnaabeg.*
> Those people helped each other.

Ojibwe leadership in the day of Francis Pegahmagabow meant being steadfast to one's values and showing concern for the community first. It was about being true to one's word and faith. Leadership was never about power but absolutely about the way one carried oneself and how much one was willing to give up for the people.

Being a leader has perhaps always required making tough decisions. One of the hardest is to challenge the ineffectiveness of the very system in which a leader participates. The Indian Act–elected governments in which Francis served multiple times as either a chief or a council member were not authentic or effective structures. Significant change or reform seemed to be impossible given the short terms of office and the ability of Indian Affairs to ignore decisions made by the chief and council. Francis's work at the political level was often criticized by the local Indian agent and even several community members who sided with, or were coerced by, Indian Affairs staff.[3] Hayes cites Indian agent Daly, ultimately successful in his quest to have Francis leave the office of band chief in 1925: "The general conversation was that Francis Pegahmagabow, the whole time that he was chief[,] was causing trouble and going to lawyers and defying the Department and causing the band to be dissatisfied with their lot and the Indian Department's method of running of the reserves. The band doesn't want their chief to be going to other bands trying to cause trouble about treaties, which they think the Department is capable of looking after."[4]

It was nearly impossible in that era to oppose the will of the department, and Hayes provides valuable additional commentary about the questionable means by which Daly gained signatures to discredit Francis in the eyes of the community. It was a tenuous time in young Francis's life. His popular status as a war hero drew the envy of more established families who did not recognize his war efforts as service to the Indian community. Francis also had the disadvantage of not having grown up on Parry Island and was viewed by many as an outsider despite his band membership there. He was not defeated by his loss of office; he spent the next several years building community relationships necessary for him to lead in the future, and he continued to refine his ideas about what it meant for Nishnaabe people to be free of the external controls that so dominated their lives.

Many of the matters Francis thought unsettled in his tenure as chief remain that way for the Wasauksing community today. Matters of ownership of several Georgian Bay islands and mainland locations, and property matters pertaining to Salt Point and railway holdings, continue to occupy space on council meeting agendas. Francis's concern for the continuity of cultural practices seems to be even more critical today because the permanent loss of cultural and linguistic traditions is now entirely possible. The language, Francis thought, was key to the people's Nishnaabe identity no matter what changes occurred in the surrounding world. All of these issues were part of a bigger struggle for Native rights at a national level to secure the existence of the Nishnaabe people into the future. His great-grandfather had been one of the signatories to the 1850 Robinson-Huron Treaty that negotiated political and economic relationships between the government and the First Nations. It was in the spirit of protecting this nation-to-nation relationship that Francis fought so passionately.

A commitment to ensuring that historical wrongs were redressed so the people could move unimpeded into the future was what Francis would call, according to Duncan, his "last war." Much of his political career is described in the following way by Hayes: "Although appearing to always be revisiting old grievances, Pegahmagabow could also be progressive."[5] His advocacy for the "spirit of the treaties" was before his time politically and laid an important foundation for the work of the present, particularly as the Robinson-Huron Treaty itself is scrutinized now for historical shortcomings by its First Nations signatories. Although the term "self-government" had not yet been coined, it is clear that Francis and his contemporaries were already working toward that goal in the emerging sovereignty movements of the early to mid-twentieth century.

Honour

Desire to succeed, courage, and talent earned Francis many accolades. His documented accomplishments are impressive, especially having served throughout almost all of the Great War and suffered significant injuries while doing so. Francis was awarded the Military Medal with two bars for his associated acts of heroism throughout the war; this was the equivalent to earning the Military Medal three distinct times. Whether it was through carrying vital messages, rescuing his fellow infantrymen, or retrieving essential supplies during heavy fire, Francis proved to be a soldier worthy of distinction. He did not receive any military commendation for his duration of service or his work as a sniper. His record states that he made 378 kills and captured 300 enemy soldiers. That record would make him the most accomplished sniper in Canadian or American military history.

The culture of disbelief that surrounded his accomplishments as a sniper was a lifelong source of irritation for Francis. The presence of a witness to document one's kills seemed to be an unnecessary and strange risk; furthermore, having to coordinate an emergent strategy with another person in such harrowing circumstances was not worth the compromise. He believed the work of a sniper was necessarily and best done alone. It was a dangerous job, and Francis did not emerge unscathed. Duncan even possessed one of his father's military journals that had been grazed by a bullet in the Great War. Francis knew he was not invincible but believed in the protective blessings he had received. The taking of life, even in war, was not something about which the Ojibwe should ever brag. It would be an even greater dishonour to lie about such action. The number of 378 that Francis and others reported at the end of the war was not out of line with his demonstrated military prowess. There also does not exist any counter-evidence to unsubstantiate the report. Yet the claim continued to be met with scepticism, as noted by Hayes: "Boasting, or perhaps being truthful, Pegahmagabow told reporters that he had done in 378 of the enemy with his rifle."[6] The cynicism was deeply injurious to Francis, who had to live every day with the memories of war and the 378 lives he had taken.

Whether Francis should have been given greater acclamation for his many achievements lingers as a question. The recent recognition of his sergeant rank, long advocated for by Duncan, has begun to find expression in the written record.[7] Soldiers with lesser accomplishments have been awarded the Victoria Cross, something author Joseph Boyden has asserted might have been denied to Francis because he was an Indian.[8] It is true that his identification as a Native soldier was disregarded by many during the war. He often felt the bias of fellow officers or military commanders. But clearly there were many of higher rank who admired his accomplishments in the field and might have recommended him for a Victoria Cross the same way he was recommended for a Distinguished Conduct Medal. Hayes notes many of the positive sentiments expressed by military personnel.[9] War-time records were inconsistent and often missing. Just as documentation concerning Francis's recommendation for a Distinguished Conduct medal has only recently been discovered, perhaps record of a Victoria Cross recommendation might also soon emerge. With respect to criticism that Francis may have made up the Victoria Cross recommendation, Duncan thought it unlikely Francis would have known about the Victoria Cross had he not been presented with the idea he should be awarded one.

Much of the recognition of Francis has occurred long after his death. His induction into the Indian Hall of Fame, his name being given to a headquarters building at Canadian Forces Base Borden, and a commemoration plaque that now stands in Parry Sound are all testaments to his service and accomplishments. The descendants of his children gathered in early 2015 through an initiative of the Wasauksing First Nation and Ontario Heritage to create a historical plaque that now stands in the community. This plaque is especially significant in that it shares some key details about Francis's life and work in both English and Ojibwe. A bronze statue designed by sculptor Tyler Fauvelle will be erected in Parry Sound in 2016; the portrayal of Francis as a young soldier, along with the spirit guides he depended on throughout his life, will stand as a permanent reminder of the historical and continued presence and contributions of Indigenous peoples. Advocacy continues for both a highway bridge and a navy ship to bear his name. All of these efforts further the work of both Duncan and Marie in seeing their father recognized as a political leader and military hero.

Hayes notes that a petition to have Francis recognized as a Canadian of national historical importance by the Historic Sites and Monuments Board of Canada remains outstanding.[10] This would surely be a distinction of significance to Francis, who fought hard for his country, believed in the greater good that came from unity among peoples, and hoped there might one day be a respectful means of First Nations inclusion and participation. Francis would not live to see this wish fulfilled, but through his life's work he helped to sow the seeds for this vision to be realized. He would also never be recognized as a Canadian citizen in his lifetime. Legislation that made status Indians citizens would not be passed until 1956, four years after his death.

27. Family of Francis Pegahmagabow at the 2015 provincial plaque unveiling. Photo © Ontario Heritage Trust 2015. Used by permission.

A Royal Affair

Francis was the second in his family to be commended by royalty for contributions to the development and safety of the country. His great-grandfather James Pegahmagabow Sr. was presented with an Indian Treaty Medal by the Prince of Wales, the future Edward VII, in 1860. The day in 1919 Francis was presented by the Prince of Wales, the future King Edward VIII, with his war medals was one of his proudest. Francis had always thought there was a special relationship between the First Nations and the Crown, and the direct recognition by a future monarch was of great meaning to him. Francis also served in the honour guard that welcomed King George VI to Canada in 1939. As a politician, Francis later encouraged unified Indian bands to appeal directly to King George VI for intervention following the Canadian government's general treatment of Indian peoples and demonstrated unwillingness to follow the terms of the treaties made in the name of the Crown. As Francis once shared with a news reporter, "the Indian Act must go. It has been changed and distorted so that now everything lies in the hands of one minister. There must be restitution for the timberlands which have been destroyed in spite of our stated rights to them. The Imperial treaty must be restored. It must be made with the King, because the [Canadian]

28. Theresa Pegahmagabow presenting flowers to Queen Elizabeth II. Courtesy of Parry Sound *North Star*.

government has shown that it cannot be trusted."[11] Francis would certainly have been proud of his granddaughter Theresa Pegahmagabow (current Wasauksing First Nation chief councillor), who welcomed King George VI's daughter Queen Elizabeth II to the traditional territory of the Ojibwe in Parry Sound in 1959.

The Fourth Day

The night Francis died was a difficult one for him. The simple act of breathing had become almost impossible—a latent effect of poison gases he had been exposed to during the war. His last years were spent sleeping upright in a chair; it was the only way any significant rest was possible. Francis did not fear death. A life of hard work and integrity, and a deep connection to the Spirit, left him confident in the road ahead. It was the inability to further provide for his family that proved most troubling to him. He had always found a way around a lack of money in the past, but a complete loss of his ability to work was lamentful. His youngest daughter was only twelve and his youngest son not quite a man. He also worried about his beloved wife, Eva, to whom he had made a commitment to always look after and protect. Her leg had never fully healed, and walking became difficult as she grew older. Although Eva had developed considerable renown for her black ash baskets and quillwork, it was hard to support a household on craft sales alone. His oldest children had all married into strong local families and were now having children of their own. It was in them that he would rightly place his faith. Francis did not believe that Veterans Affairs would provide any lasting or substantial help to his family, and he was correct.

In the end, it was also the community Francis had worked so hard to find a place of belonging within that would help him home. All of the years he had helped others were at last reciprocated. It was a freeing moment of vindication for a man who was at times as scorned as he was celebrated in life. Marie remembered people bringing food, water, and wood to the house when he found himself too weak to procure any himself. Eva's family brought over herbal medicines that helped to alleviate any pain and made his breathing easier. Many other families helped by preparing the church, hosting visiting attendees, and providing food for the family and visitors when Francis finally passed on. Even the thunders seemed to gently rumble far off in the distance the night he left. It was a wonderful final tribute from all of those he had found as family throughout his lifetime.

Like all Nishnaabeg before him, Francis believed the "spiritual part of his being" (*ojichaagwan*) would pass into a different realm free from the troubles of life he had experienced in the physical world. He was not sure it would be exactly like the way described by the church, but he knew it would be a peaceful and happy place where even his "pagan" relatives were welcome. The old Indians trusted there were many ways home. Francis also believed part of his spirit would remain in the earth realm. This part of his being—*ojiibiiyiman* (his "shadow" or "ghost spirit")—would allow him to help his descendants in their moments of need on this physical earth.

Death would be marked by a long and beautiful spirit journey home. Francis knew it would be filled with all of the challenges and triumphs that defined his life. But as a man of integrity, he did not fear the journey. He knew the old stories would guide him home. From time to time, he would tell his children about the final road, including what to be wary of and which way to go should they encounter a fork in the road. They were to use their Nishnaabe names and remember their clan. Tobacco should also be taken for any offerings needed along the way. It was well known to the people that there would be three long and sometimes trying days as they made it closer to the final crossing place. They were to walk with respect and caution and, as much as possible, without regret. On the fourth day, they would make it home. And all of the struggles they had known would be left behind forever. It was a special and beautiful place where their spirits were reunited with all of those they had known and loved in life. It was this road Francis hoped his children, and all his descendants in time, would one day also find when their time came to return home.

Gchi-Mishoomisaatig—Grandfather Tree

The world of the Georgian Bay Nishnaabeg remains one of legendary beauty. The interactions of rock, earth, water, and wind have produced one of the most remarkable ecosystems in the world. This special quality was not lost on the Nishnaabeg, who regarded their existence in the territory as one of great privilege and responsibility. Part of their duty was to remember the stories of the land, which included those spirit entities placed on the earth to look after and protect it. The sacred places were well known to the historical Nishnaabeg, and many such locations continue to be carefully regarded. As did each Ojibwe band, the plant and animal worlds had their own leaders or chiefs. Each had a part to play in the shared responsibility for the world. When a leader fell, a new leader necessarily rose up. A moment of reverence was shared by the membership whenever such a loss was experienced. This was attested to by Jonas King in Jenness: "Before the white man reached Georgian Bay a certain Indian gathered many beaver, otter, and other skins, which he kept in his wigwam in the woods. One still night he heard the crashing of a tree, and then a wailing of many voices 'Our king has gone.' When morning came he found that a giant white oak had fallen, being rotten at the base; the white oaks around it had bewailed its fall."[12]

The following story was told to me in the late spring. Duncan related his father's teachings about how plants and animals have both a spiritual nature and a physical nature. This story is similar to one that Francis shared with Jenness: "Sometimes a tree will fall when there is not a breath of wind. Its soul dies, just as the soul of a man dies and goes to the land of the west. But where the tree's soul goes no one knows."[13] The kind of tree Duncan refers to in this story was one of those special "chief" trees to which humans also had special connections. Duncan remembered his father making special offerings of tobacco and food to such trees, particularly in the spring and fall.

Mii wedi gchi-mishoomisaatig.
Over there is that great grandfather tree.

Mii ow kina gegoo debendang gnoonag naan'godnong, "debendgeyin," ndinaa.
This is the one within whom you can see the Creator, and sometimes when I speak to him I address him as the one who owns everything.

Mii ow.
That is the one.

Mii go kina odi enamog niw miikanan.
The place where all roads lead.

Ndedem ko dbaajmaabaniin niw.
My father used to talk about those ones.

Giw go naa ewaabmangid go naa gchi-mishoomisaatig.
Those ones that we could see, like that grandfather tree.

Mii go naan'godnong ge-ni-kidad—kidoban kwa.
From time to time, he would say this—this is what he said.

Gnimaa gwa naa iihow go naa pii wendaajmod maanda gii-zhiwebak gii-bzaanyaawag maa giw Nishnaabeg.
He must have been speaking about how life was for the people then, how peacefully and quietly they lived in the world.

Naan'godnong gwa naa ni-naagshig gwajiing gii-naanaamdabwag gnimaa ge gii-boodwewag odi gwajiing bkwenezgewag giw yaawag maa naa zgimeg ezhi-pkwenezgewaad zagswaawag zhaashaagmikwewag ge aanind semaan.
In the evenings, they would sometimes sit outside making a fire and a smudge to help with all of the mosquitoes that were around—some would even smoke or chew a little tobacco.

Mii dash iw mii kidoban kwa, "Naan'godnong kwa gchi-nawaating," kida.
This was what he said, "Sometimes it would get perfectly still out," he said.

"Mii ji-noondwad gchi-gtaamgwewesiing gegoo odi megeyaakwaa," kida.
"And you would hear something crash very loudly over there in the woods," he said.

"Gnimaa go ngoding zhaayin odi mii ji-waabmad ow chi-mtig—chi-mtig," kida.

"If you should happen to go that way sometime, you would see this big tree—this great tree," he said.

Weweni go bgashknini mii gwa nshike gwa gaa-zhi-bngishing.

It had rotted all the way through and then suddenly fell all on its own.

"Mii iw pii bngishing mii aazhgo gii-bgidendang," kida.

"That moment he fell was the moment he had given up," my father said.

Maaba mtig mii iw bngishing.

This tree would then fall.

"Mii aazhgo gii-wnitood iihow wii-gzhiibendang ji-bmaadzid," kida.

"For he had lost all will to live," he said.

Mii ow bngishing.

And so he fell.

Kidoban ko ndedem.

This is what my father used to say.

Aapji geget gii-nendam ow ndedem iw nake.

This really was the way that my father thought.

Aapji go gii-mshkawendam iihow.

He was such a strong believer in this.

EPILOGUE

> *Mii go pane ezhi-biimskoshkaag maanda mii go naa bmaadziwin.*
> Life always comes around full circle.
>
> —Duncan Pegahmagabow

Full Circle

The legacy of betrayal and frustration that marred much of Francis's experience is perhaps finally shifting to a place of enduring honour and reconciliation. As for many soldiers who return home from war, the world Francis found was fundamentally different from the one he left. A series of profound social and cultural changes in the Native community was an important factor in his displacement. Francis had also both seen and done things during his time overseas that made returning to his relatively cheerful and carefree pre-war self somewhat impossible. The old ceremonies for helping returned warriors were long gone by this time. His fellow community members, or even the local townspeople he knew, seemed to be unable to understand his new perspective on the world. It was for this reason that he especially valued his connections to other veterans. The local Northern Pioneers militia unit provided an invaluable source of support and camaraderie for Francis and others who returned home from the Great War. Later absorbed into the Algonquin Regiment in 1936, Francis served in this unit with distinction. One cannot help but wonder if the unit's Ojibwe-language slogan, *Ne-Kah-Ne-Tah* ("We Lead, Others Follow"), was a contribution from Francis himself. It was certainly an expression he said with pride.

His foundational efforts to improve the plight of Aboriginal peoples would find expression in numerous initiatives that continue in the present. Francis helped to found the first major Indian political organization and lobby group with the incorporation of the Brotherhood of Canadian Indians in 1943. It was imperative to him that First Nations peoples have a national voice to express their rights and concerns to the country and the world. Formation of the National Indian Government in 1945 represented a significant political accomplishment in this regard. Francis demonstrated his capacity for such leadership in becoming elected the supreme chief of the National Indian Government in 1949. The accomplishments of the National Indian Government and other early Indigenous political organizations, such as the Union of Ontario Indians, set an important example and precedent for future action and organization. Many contemporary Aboriginal organizations and lobby groups, such as the Assembly of First Nations, have their roots in the efforts of early grassroots political organizers and leaders like Francis Pegahmagabow.

Recognition of his military and political accomplishments has come in significant measure since his death. His military medals and chieftainship headdress—truly symbols of national pride and heritage—were entrusted to the Canadian War Museum for permanent display in 2003. In this great selfless act by his family, some of his greatest symbols of achievement are forever shared with the world. It is my wish that the long-overdue tributes to Francis Pegahmagabow continue into the future. This book itself will help to ensure that his story, or perhaps more accurately his stories, find lasting expression and remembrance. Perhaps every Canadian should have to read a book such as this in the spirit of understanding the unique and significant contributions of Native peoples. The opportunity to present some of his stories in their original Ojibwe language is important given the near extinguishment of Indigenous languages today. Having these stories again told to young people in Ojibwe helps to bring the true legacy of Francis Pegahmagabow full circle.

Perhaps as important to completing and closing the circle in his story is the standing place of respect that should be given to all war veterans for their service. This Aboriginal tradition was nearly lost during the shift to agrarian and reserve life, but veterans again have a lasting place of recognition and appreciation in Indigenous ceremonial and community celebrations, feasts, and everyday life. Blessing ceremonies for new soldiers, and healing ceremonies for those who return, are experiencing revivals. Even the old warrior societies are again finding expression in modern acts of courage and proactivity such as Idle No More. As young Native people become modern-day warriors for languages and cultures nearly extinguished by colonial policies, the circle moves beyond closure to a critical and just new beginning.

Finding a place of reconciliation for past wrongs and building respect for the lasting rights of Indigenous peoples comprise a mission of Francis Pegahmagabow's that remains unfulfilled. Strides have been made to better protect Native land rights and political sovereignty, but there remains much ground to cover. Francis would have been proud of the opportunities that his efforts helped to create for Indigenous communities in the present. More than ever before are Native peoples aware of their rights and how to advocate for them. Critical gains continue to be made in the area of land claims and treaty rights, but it has been a tedious and painful process. Although continued effort and dedication are required in the resolution of these matters, equally important parts of Aboriginal life, such as the preservation of language and culture, surely deserve the same focus, attention, and long-term commitment.

Francis had a deep belief in the Ojibwe language as a vessel of the heart and soul of the people. I once asked Duncan about the most important thing his father would have wanted to see restored today. He replied, without hesitation, the Native language. Duncan said this would be the only true source of justice for First Nations peoples who had been stripped of their lands, dignity, and, through the experience of colonization, language and culture. Apologies for the treatment of Aboriginal students in residential schools have been important but largely meaningless in the sense of making true amends for what was lost in those institutions. Empowering Indigenous peoples to sustainably give voice to their spirits through their own languages might be the only just recompense.

The Story Behind the Name

The many tributes made to Francis Pegahmagabow after his death ensure that his name lives on. This book has been an attempt to make certain that some of his stories help to fill that name with meaning. Francis had many roles in life: soldier, guide, politician, fisherman, father, and storyteller. He was a kind and gentle man at the core, and, contrary to whatever conclusion about him might be drawn from his military record alone, he walked on this earth in a good and peaceful way. Yet he was a descendant of Begamigaabaw, the great "standing storm" that could approach from the horizon in an instant. For a time, Francis would even sign his letters with "Approaching Tornado." It was not so much the destructive power of the storm he wielded as the capacity to speak to the storm and ensure the safety of others as it passed.

Francis once told Duncan—when he was explaining to his son about the importance of tobacco—that he would regularly borrow a pinch of tobacco from his fellow soldiers during the war. He would ask for the protection of his battalion mates and the well-being of their families. It was his way of finding peace amid the chaos and disorder of war. At the end of each day, he would wish for the safe spirit journey of all those who had perished on those cold and haunted fields. This was especially so for those who had found themselves in the sights of the sniper rifle Peggy so expertly wielded. Although he did not tell his son he ever asked for their forgiveness, it seemed clear to Duncan that the tobacco offering was his way of making that request.

For all of the trauma he knew in life, Chief Francis Pegahmagabow stayed true to the good being—the Nishnaabe—at his core. He knew he was flawed and in some ways irreparably damaged by the war, but he aspired to never extend his suffering to those he loved. He rightly directed his anger at and dissatisfaction with the continued oppression of his people toward the Indian agents who exercised such undeserved and sweeping powers. This notwithstanding, Francis remained an individual who would always look first for the greater good in others. He always reminded his children to say "*boozhoo*" to even the most contemptible person in the hope of connecting with the good that must be there—however hard it might be to see in moments.

Francis remained proud of his military and political service to the last. His accomplishments allowed him to prove he was equal in measure to any other man despite his humble beginnings as a poor orphaned Indian boy. His feelings about the role of Aboriginal participation in the wars of foreign countries would change over time as he realized there was a greater fight for freedom on behalf of his own people. Francis joined the call to end conscription for young Native men. This seems to be inconsistent with his having been one of the first to voluntarily enlist in the First World War and the most decorated Aboriginal serviceman for bravery of all time. But he could not, in the end, stand to see his people go off to fight for a country that would not recognize Indigenous peoples as equals or help them should they survive and return home wounded in body, mind, or spirit.

Circle of Family

It was within his family that Francis finally found the sense of belonging he had searched for his entire life. He was proud of all his children and took great interest in their endeavours. They all spoke of him in the kindest of ways. As the toll of war began to catch up with him in later years, and his body began to systematically break down, he resigned from direct political action and devoted his attention to his wife and grandchildren. Francis was remembered in the end as the kind grandfather in the garden. If he was not writing a letter advocating for the well-being of his people, he could always

29. Wasauksing Traditional Gathering and Powwow. Courtesy of Cody Storm Cooper Photography.

be found walking around the family property with one of his grandsons on his shoulders.

What Francis could not have known was that those little boys he spent so much time with during his last days would do much to help the Nishnaabe community as adults. Two of his oldest grandsons would play special roles in helping to revitalize language and culture locally. The late Merle and Earl Michael Pegahmagabow, sons of Joe and Mike, respectively, were at the forefront of the restoration of the Midewiwin lodge in the community. Their children, nieces, and nephews have followed their example of how to live a good life free from drugs and alcohol and rich with traditional ceremonial practice and participation, the kind of future Francis would certainly have wanted for his descendants. Duncan and Marie believed he would have been equally proud of the efforts of his many grandchildren and great-grandchildren who have taken political offices and helped to advance the front of Native rights and self-governance. Warriors are needed on all fronts.

Proudly leading the grand entry at the last Wasauksing Traditional Gathering and Powwow were the eagle staffs carried in by community and area veterans. They were followed by dancers of many different styles and tribal affiliations. One of the new dancers was Francis's great-great-granddaughter Eva. A gentle Ojibwe-language blessing filled the dance arena during the opening ceremony, and kind words of thanks were offered for all of those veterans who continued to stand for the freedom of the people and for all of those who had fallen in service. A calm and constant breeze kept the heat and insects at bay, and gentle low thunder rumbled far off on the horizon that evening. It was peaceful and calming—a rhythmic voice affirming that someone is indeed watching and encouraging us on. It was the same thunder that Francis found connection to through his great-great-grandfather—a man whose only name was Pegahmagabow (Bebamigaabaw). Gentle "offerings of thanks" (*ziskamwaajgewinan*) were made at the sacred fire, and the circle was again renewed and strengthened.

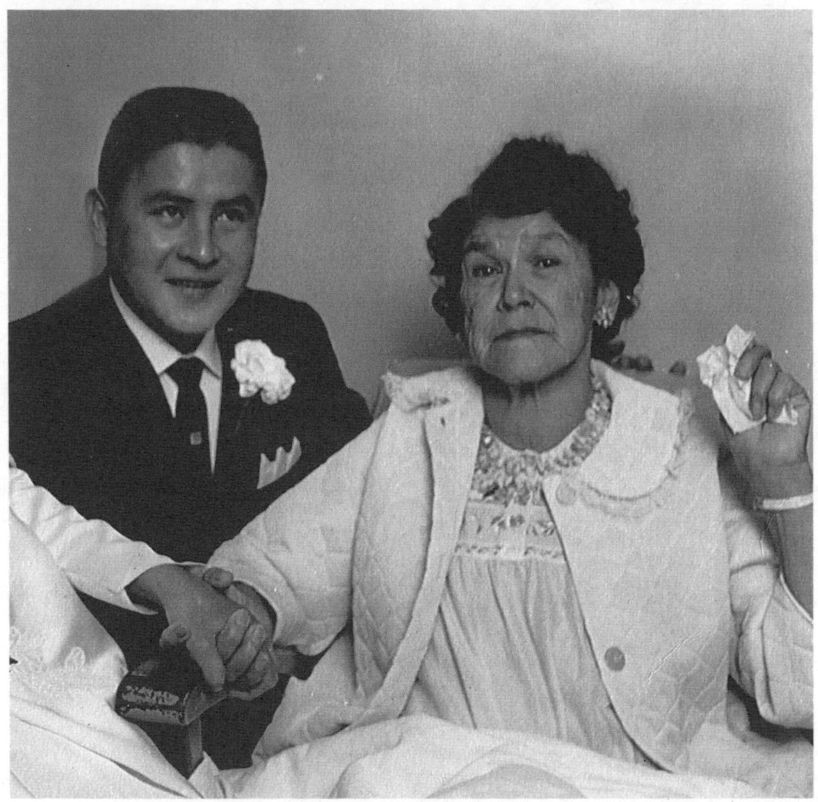

30. Duncan and Eva Pegahmagabow, 1969. Courtesy of Dora Tabobondung.

Mnidoo—The Spirit

All of the children of Francis Pegahmagabow struggled terribly with his death. The ensuing years would be difficult for the family without their beloved patriarch. The unexpected and tragic loss of a number of his children and grandchildren added to their collective sadness. Duncan shared that one of the hardest parts of Nishnaabe life was the ever-present grief that came from the constant loss of life and dignity as a people. On one occasion, he struggled with whether he should continue his membership in the Catholic Church, fearing that God would abandon him if he failed to attend services. His mother, Eva, gave him the following counsel, which brought Duncan and the family much peace knowing that the Spirit was always present, in all things and in all people, and that he would never be without such a connection.

> *Mii ko nmamaa gaa-zhid iihow.*
> This is what my mother said to me.
>
> *"Kaa memkaaj gdaa-zhaasii iihow gchi-namhew-gamig ji-waabmad Mnidoo," kida.*
> "It is not necessary for you to go over to that big church in order to see the Spirit," she said.
>
> *"Dbiyiidog sa nii go ge-naabiwinen mii ji-waabmad Mnidoo."*
> "Wherever it is that you look you will see the Spirit."
>
> *"Waawaaskones be-bimaajiiging—mii go ow," kida.*
> "In the way that a flower grows there in front of you—that is the one," she said.
>
> *"Miinwaa gegoo mtigoons niw niibiishensan bmaasingin."*
> "And again in the way the leaves of trees flutter in the wind."
>
> *"Mii go ow."*
> "That is the one."

"Gego memkaaj zhaaken namhew-gamgoong."
"You don't have to go to church."

"Mii go kina maa enaabiyin eyaamgak."
"It is in everything that you look at."

"Miinwaa gegoo giiji-bmaadiz."
"And also in your fellow human being."

"Mii go ow."
"This is the one."

"Mnidoo."
"The Spirit."

31. A bronze statue designed by sculptor Tyler Fauvelle was erected in Parry Sound in 2016; the portrayal of Francis Pegahmagabow as a young soldier, along with the spirit guides that he depended upon throughout his life, stands as a permanent reminder of the historical and continued presence and contributions of Indigenous peoples. Courtesy of Tyler Fauvelle.

ACKNOWLEDGEMENTS

The greatest of thanks I extend to Duncan Pegahmagabow and Marie Anderson, who shared their father's stories with such generosity and love. May their words live on in both our actions and the stories we continue to tell. I am particularly grateful for the gentle affirmations and corrections of history and language by my grandmother Priscilla (King) Pegahmagabow, who had a special relationship with both Francis and Eva. A special note of appreciation must also be made to my parents, Don and Theresa, for their encouragement to compile and make sense of many disconnected facts and stories and for helping me to track down the most obscure of leads and photos. *Chi-miigwech.*

Many Wasauksing and Shawanaga elders and community members shared their stories and perspectives with me over the years. Although several of these wonderful people have now left us, their thoughts and words find expression and continuity in these pages. Thank you, Edward Eagle, Roger Jones, Deanna Jones-Keeshig, Stewart King, Sam Kewaquado, Fred Nanibush, Irene Pawis, Earl (Mike) Pegahmagabow, Merle Pegahmagabow, John Rice, Flora Tabobondung, and Dan Wheatley. A special thank you to the late Hubert Tabobandung, best friend of Francis's son Chief Michael Pegahmagabow, who helped to map so many of the locations and place names found in this book.

I am indebted to my advisors at York University, who oversaw much of the original research used in the production of this book. Thank you,

Shirley Williams, Mary Bernard, and Joe Sheridan. Many friends and content experts helped with research and production work: Tara Chadwick, Brock Pitawanakwat, Mike Linn, and Gerry Weaver (text reviewers); Alan Corbiere (Ojibwe-language specialist); and Adrian Hayes and the late Franz Koennecke (historians). Photographers Thom Morrissey and Cody Storm Cooper provided many of the beautiful landscape images featured in this book. A special note of appreciation to Eddie Benton-Banai and Jim Dumont for their leadership and encouragement to restore traditional Nishnaabe lifeways and languages and to help the people learn stories they might not even know they have. Thank you also to Blaine and Bruce Olson for their support throughout the writing process.

A final thank you to Francis Pegahmagabow (Bnaaswi) for leaving the legacy he did. It is an honour to offer these extensions of his greater story and to encourage further exploration of his life. Perhaps one day his full story might yet be told.

NOTES

Chapter 1: Stories as a Means of Understanding Life

1 Jenness, *Ojibwa Indians*, v.
2 Ibid., 53.

Chapter 2: Indigenous Life and Community in Georgian Bay

1 Benton-Banai, *Mishomis Book*, 89.
2 Warren, *History of the Ojibway People*, 78.
3 Benton-Banai, *Mishomis Book*, 4.
4 Cary, *A new map of Upper and Lower Canada*, 1807.
5 Koennecke, "Wasoksing," 5.
6 Johnston, *The Manitous*, xx.
7 Benton-Banai, *Mishomis Book*, 100.
8 Schmalz, *Ojibwa of Southern Ontario*, 33.
9 Koennecke, "Wasoksing," 43.
10 Benton-Banai, *Mishomis Book*, 100.
11 Schmalz, *Ojibwa of Southern Ontario*, 17.
12 Napier in Koennecke, "Wasoksing," 6.
13 Johnston, *Ojibway Ceremonies*, 44.
14 Koennecke, "Wasoksing," 4.
15 Wright in Rogers and Smith, *Aboriginal Ontario*, 30.
16 Koennecke, "Wasoksing," 113.
17 Ibid., 7.
18 Ibid., 125.
19 Rogers and Tabobondung, "A Period of Change," 125–27.
20 Koennecke, "Wasoksing," 175.
21 Jenness, *Ojibwa Indians*, vi.
22 Koennecke, "Wasoksing," 5.
23 Rogers and Tabobondung, "A Period of Change," 281.
24 Schmalz, *Ojibwa of Southern Ontario*, 6.
25 Koennecke, "Wasoksing," 222.
26 Rogers and Tabobondung, "A Period of Change," 280–82.
27 Jenness, *Ojibwa Indians*, 8.
28 Rogers and Tabobondung, "A Period of Change," 102.
29 Koennecke, "Wasoksing," 192.
30 Rogers and Tabobondung, "A Period of Change," 76.

31 Francis Pegahmagabow, in Jenness, *Ojibwa Indians*, 104.
32 Ibid., 37.

Chapter 3: Wind, Rock, and Water: Maps and Names at Wasauksing and Shawanaga

1 Rogers and Tabobondung, "A Period of Change," 307–08.
2 McInnes, "Waasaaksing," 44.
3 Rayburn, *Place Names of Ontario*, xvi.
4 Basso, *Wisdom Sits in Places*, 73.
5 John Manatuwaba in Jenness, *Ojibwa Indians*, 42.
6 Koennecke, "Wasoksing," 16.
7 Brunton, *Notes and Sketches*; LACAC, *Parry Sound Directory*.
8 See, e.g., Jenness, *Ojibwa Indians*; Koennecke, "Wasoksing."
9 Magee, Douglas E., Land Surveyor Affidavit, 27 October 1992.
10 Koennecke, "Wasoksing," 16.
11 Ibid.

Chapter 4: Language, Culture, and Story

1 Koennecke, "Wasoksing," 195.
2 Schmalz, *Ojibwa of Southern Ontario*, 161.
3 Saville-Troike, *Ethnography of Communication*, 33.
4 Johnston, *Ojibway Ceremonies*, 110.
5 Spielmann, *You're So Fat!*, 46.
6 Jenness, *Ojibwa Indians*, 19.
7 Carroll, *Language, Thought, and Reality*, 33–41.
8 Whorf, *Language, Thought, and Reality*, 272.
9 Jenness, *Ojibwa Indians*, v.

Chapter 5: Learning from Stories

1 Jenness, *Ojibwa Indians*, iv.
2 Rogers and Smith, *Aboriginal Ontario*, 122.
3 Valentine, *Making It Their Own*, 190.
4 Jenness, *Ojibwa Indians*, 42.
5 Valentine, *Making It Their Own*, 201.
6 Veterans Affairs Canada, *Native Soldiers*.

Chapter 6: Family

1 Francis Pegahmagabow in Jenness, *Ojibwa Indians*, 8.
2 Benton-Banai, *Mishomis Book*, 74.
3 Francis Pegahmagabow in Jenness, *Ojibwa Indians*, 92.
4 Rogers and Tabobondung, "A Period of Change," 280–82.
5 Koennecke, "Wasoksing," 19.
6 Francis Pegahmagabow in Jenness, *Ojibwa Indians*, 68.

7 Hayes, *Pegahmagabow*, 21.
8 Ibid., 57.
9 Francis Pegahmagabow in Jenness, *Ojibwa Indians*, 20.
10 Brownlie, *Fatherly Eye*, 17.
11 Hayes, *Pegahmagabow*.
12 Francis Pegahmagabow in Jenness, *Ojibwa Indians*, 93.
13 Hayes, *Pegahmagabow*, 84.
14 Jenness, *Ojibwa Indians*, 87.
15 Hayes, *Pegahmagabow*, 85.
16 Francis Pegahmagabow in Jenness, *Ojibwa Indians*, 107.
17 Jenness, *Ojibwa Indians*, 16.
18 Schmalz, *Ojibwa of Southern Ontario*, 233.
19 Brownlie, *Fatherly Eye*, 107.
20 Hayes, *Pegahmagabow*, 60.
21 Quoted in Brownlie, *Fatherly Eye*, 33.
22 Ibid., 33.
23 Hayes, *Pegahmagabow*, 88.
24 Ibid., 88.

Chapter 7: An Indian at War

1 Duncan Pegahmagabow heard his father say this to a visiting serviceman before the Second World War.
2 Jonas King and Francis Pegahmagabow in Jenness, *Ojibwa Indians*, 102.
3 Winegard, *For King and Kanata*, 117.
4 Jenness, *Ojibwa Indians*, 83.
5 Winegard, *For King and Kanata*, 77.
6 Ibid., 43.
7 Ibid., 6.
8 Hayes, Pegahmagabow, 38.
9 Francis Pegahmagabow in Jenness, *Ojibwa Indians*, 87.
10 Jim Nanibush in ibid., 30.
11 Winegard, *For King and Kanata*, 2.
12 Francis Pegahmagabow in Hayes, *Pegahmagabow*, 129–30.
13 Hayes, *Pegahmagabow*, 53–97.
14 Winegard, *For King and Kanata*, 115.
15 Brownlie, *Fatherly Eye*, 102–04.
16 Hayes, *Pegahmagabow*, 76–78.
17 Brownlie, *Fatherly Eye*, 104.
18 Ibid., 38.
19 Patrick Bryden, letter from Canadian Army, 29 April 2015.

Chapter 8: Community Life

1 Koennecke, "Wasoksing," 195.
2 Veterans Affairs Canada, *Native Soldiers*.
3 Jenness, *Ojibwa Indians*, 94.
4 Koennecke, "Wasoksing," 149. Koennecke notes the influence of missionaries on the lived expression of traditional spirituality. No outside writer seems to have captured the sense of fear and religious oppression that permeated the community.
5 Brownlie, *Fatherly Eye*, 18.
6 Nichols, *Ojibway Text Anthology*, 74–75.
7 Jenness, *Ojibwa Indians*, 78.
8 Ibid., 43.
9 Ibid., 79.
10 Hayes, *Pegahmagabow*, 57.
11 Francis Pegahmagabow in Jenness, *Ojibwa Indians*, 48.
12 Ibid, 97.
13 Ibid., 76.
14 Jenness, *Ojibwa Indians*, 87.
15 Ibid., 45.
16 Ibid., 40.

Chapter 9: The Fourth Day

1 Hayes, *Pegahmagabow*, 73; Winegard, 2012, 162.
2 Brownlie, *A Fatherly Eye*, 63.
3 Ibid., 67.
4 Hayes, *Pegahmagabow*, 77.
5 Ibid., 67.
6 Ibid., 54.
7 Weaver, "Courage Under Fire."
8 Joseph Boyden in Wyile, 226.
9 Hayes, *Pegahmagabow*, 81-83.
10 Ibid., 42.
11 Francis Pegahmagabow in ibid., 119.
12 Jenness, *Ojibwa Indians*, 23.
13 Francis Pegahmagabow in ibid., 21.

REFERENCES

Basso, Keith H. *Wisdom Sits in Places: Landscape and Language among the Western Apache.* Albuquerque: University of New Mexico Press, 1996.

Benton-Banai, Edward. *The Mishomis Book: The Voice of the Ojibway.* 2nd ed. St. Paul: University of Minnesota Press, 2010.

Brownlie, Robin J. *A Fatherly Eye: Indian Agents, Government Power, and Aboriginal Resistance in Ontario, 1918–1939.* Toronto: Oxford University Press, 2003.

Brunton, Sam. *Notes and Sketches on the History of Parry Sound.* Parry Sound, ON: Parry Sound Historical Society, 1969.

Canada. *Indian Treaties and Surrenders, from 1680 to 1890.* Vol. 1. Ottawa: Brown Chamberlin (Queen's Printer), 1891.

Carroll, John B. "Introduction." In *Language, Thought, and Reality: Selected Writings of Benjamin Lee Whorf,* 2nd ed., edited by J.B. Carroll, S.C. Levinson, and P. Lee, 1–43. Cambridge: MIT Press, 2012.

Cary, John. *A new map of Upper and Lower Canada.* London: Strand, 1807.

Hayes, Adrian. *Pegahmagabow: Life-Long Warrior.* Toronto: Blue Butterfly Books Publishing, 2009.

Jenness, Diamond. *The Ojibwa Indians of Parry Island: Their Social and Religious Life.* Ottawa: Patenaude, 1935.

Johnston, Basil. *The Manitous: The Spiritual World of the Ojibway.* New York: HarperCollins, 1995.

———. *Ojibway Ceremonies.* Toronto: McClelland and Stewart, 1982.

Koennecke, Franz. "Wasoksing: The History of Parry Island, an Anishnabwe Community in the Georgian Bay, 1850 to 1920." MA thesis, University of Waterloo, 1984.

Local Architectural Conservation Advisory Committee (LACAC). *Parry Sound Directory, 1898–1899.* Parry Sound, ON: Ireland and Bundy, 1899.

Magee, Douglas E. Land Surveyor Affidavit. 27 October 1992.

McInnes, Brian D. "Waasaaksing: Stories, Land, and Language." Master of Environmental Studies Major Paper, York University, 1999.

Nichols, John D., ed. *Ojibway Text Anthology.* London, ON: Centre for Research and Teaching of Canadian Native Languages, 1988.

Rayburn, Alan. *Place Names of Ontario.* Toronto: University of Toronto Press, 1997.

Rhodes, Richard A. *Eastern Ojibwa-Chippewa-Ottawa Dictionary.* New York: Mouton de Gruyter, 1993.

Rogers, Edward S., and Donald B. Smith. *Aboriginal Ontario: Historical Perspectives of the First Nations.* Toronto: Dundurn Press, 1994.

Rogers, Edward, and Flora Tabobondung. "A Period of Change in the Way of Life of the Algonkians of Southern Ontario: Parry Island Farmers." National Museum of Man, Mercury Series, Canadian Ethnology Service Paper 31. In *Contributions to Canadian Ethnology,* edited by D.B. Carlisle, 247–359. Ottawa: National Museum of Man, 1975.

Saville-Troike, M. *The Ethnography of Communication: An Introduction.* 2nd ed. New York: Blackwell Publishing, 1989.

Schmalz, P.S. *The Ojibwa of Southern Ontario.* Toronto: University of Toronto Press, 1991.

Spielmann, Roger. *You're So Fat! Exploring Ojibwe Discourse.* Toronto: University of Toronto Press, 1998.

Valentine, Lisa Phillips. *Making It Their Own: Severn Ojibwe Communicative Practices.* Toronto: University of Toronto Press, 1995.

Veterans Affairs Canada. *Native Soldiers—Foreign Battlefields—A Peaceful Man.* Ottawa: Veterans Affairs Canada, 2010.

Warren, William W. *History of the Ojibway People.* 2nd ed. St. Paul: Minnesota Historical Society Press, 1984.

Weaver, Gerry. "Courage under Fire: First Nations War Hero a Fighter on Two Fronts." *WindSpeaker*, 1 June 2015.

Whorf, Benjamin L. *Language, Thought, and Reality: Selected Writings of Benjamin Lee Whorf.* 2nd ed., edited by J.B. Carroll, S.C. Levinson, & P. Lee. Cambridge: MIT Press, 2012.

Winegard, Timothy C. *For King and Kanata: Canadian Indians and the First World War.* Winnipeg: University of Manitoba Press, 2012.

Wyile, Herb. *Speaking in the Past Tense: Canadian Novelists on Writing Historical Fiction.* Waterloo, ON: Wilfrid Laurier University Press, 2007.

INDEX

Bold numbers indicate photos.

Q